MAINE'S MUSEUMS:

ART, ODDITIES & ARTIFACTS

MAINE'S MUSEUMS:

ART, ODDITIES & ARTIFACTS

JANET MENDELSOHN

Portions of the text are adapted from articles by the author published previously in the *Boston Sunday Globe* and *Maine Boats, Homes & Harbors,* the magazine of the coast. Used by permission.

CIP data have been applied for.
Maine's Museums: Art, Oddities & Artifacts
978-0-88150-915-1

Map by Mapping Specialists, © The Countryman Press
Book design and composition by Melanie Jolicoeur
Chapter-opening-page photographs by Janet Mendelsohn, except as noted.

Page 17: *(top)* Elizabeth Perkins House, Museums of Old York. **Page 42:** *(top)* Winslow Homer (United States, 1836–1910), "Weatherbeaten," 1894, oil on canvas, 28 ½ x 48 ⅜ inches. Portland Museum of Art, Maine. Bequest of Charles Shipman Payson. Photo: by Melville D. McLean, courtesy of the Portland Museum of Art; *(bottom, left)* Casco Bay from Portland Observatory; *(bottom, center)* Courtesy of Museum of African Culture. **Page 68:** *(left)* Courtesy of Fifth Maine Regiment Museum Collection, Peaks Island, Maine. **Page 74:** *(top)* Friendship Sloop Regatta, Rockland Harbor. **Page 104:** *(left)* Courtesy of Penobscot Marine Museum; *(right)* Center for Maine Contemporary Art. **Page 123:** *(bottom, left)* Bar Harbor Whale Museum; *(bottom, center)* Eastport fisherman's statue; *(bottom, right)* Life-size barn owl carving by Wendell Gilley. Photo: Jack Ledbetter, courtesy of Wendell Gilley Museum. **Page 147:** *(top)* Scottish Highland cattle, Sabbathday Lake Shaker Village; *(bottom, left)* Bates College Museum of Art; *(bottom, right)* Nowetah's American Indian Museum. **Page 174:** *(top)* Skowhegan State Fair prizewinners; *(bottom)* Old Fort Western. **Page 187:** *(left)* Colby Museum of Art; *(right)* Washburn mansion, Washburn-Norlands Living History Center. Page **199:** *(top)* loon, Moosehead Lake; *(bottom, left)* Katahdin wheelhouse, courtesy of Moosehead Marine Museum; *(bottom, right)* Aroostook County. **Page 220:** *(left)* Courtesy University of Maine Museum of Art; *(right)* Ways of the Woods mobile museum in Concord, NH. Northern Forestry Center photo.

Published by The Countryman Press, P.O. Box 748, Woodstock, VT 05091
Distributed by W. W. Norton & Company, Inc.,
500 Fifth Avenue, New York, NY 10110
Printed in the United States of America

10 9 8 7 6 5 4 3 2 1

For
Bob Mendelsohn,
my husband and travel companion
in life's many adventures
and
Gail O'Donnell,
our friend always

THANK YOU

to Perry Lowe, whose enthusiastic phone calls from the coast of Maine while I worked indoors in Massachusetts led to my being here in the first place;

to Delphine Lowe, Phil Knutel, and Jen Knutel for our community on Chauncey Creek, and especially to Pat and Charle Tobey, whose stories about Maine are the best part of countless shared breakfasts, along with Phil and Jen's waffles;

to Rosemary Herbert, who triggered this project when we met over coffee to discuss the Maine Folk Art Trail; Charles Burden, M.D., who generously shared his expertise on museums and collecting; Keith LaFerriere and Steve Pereira; and Gretchen Piston Ogden and Peter H. Spectre at *Maine Boats, Homes & Harbors* magazine;

to the staff at Maine Archives and Museums, the Maine Arts Commission, and reference services at the Maine State Library, and the many collectors, curators, volunteers, directors, and museum personnel who answered my questions and shared their knowledge in conversations that were great fun and resulted in my writing a more informed book;

to MPBN, the Maine Public Broadcasting Network, which made the many miles fly by;

Bob, David, Josh and Jamie Mendelsohn for their love and encouragement; to my sister, Tama Borer, for her daily e-mails that are my virtual coffee breaks; and my fellow writers Hilary Bennett ; the Chicks Who Write, especially Lynette Benton, Maria Judge, Betsy Lawson, Jane Whitehead, Jeri Zeder, and Tracy Palmer; and the Parlor Girls—Ginny Reiser, Kitty Forbes, and Natasha Bauman—who know what it takes to find the right words;

to the talented crew at The Countryman Press: Kermit Hummel, Lisa Sacks, Tom Haushalter, Lucia Huntington, Melanie Jolicoeur, Caitlin Martin, Fred Lee, and Jessica Stevens, who made this project a pleasure from start to finish;

and to my parents, Nat and Sonia Kern, who always believed I could accomplish whatever I set out to do.

Janet Mendelsohn

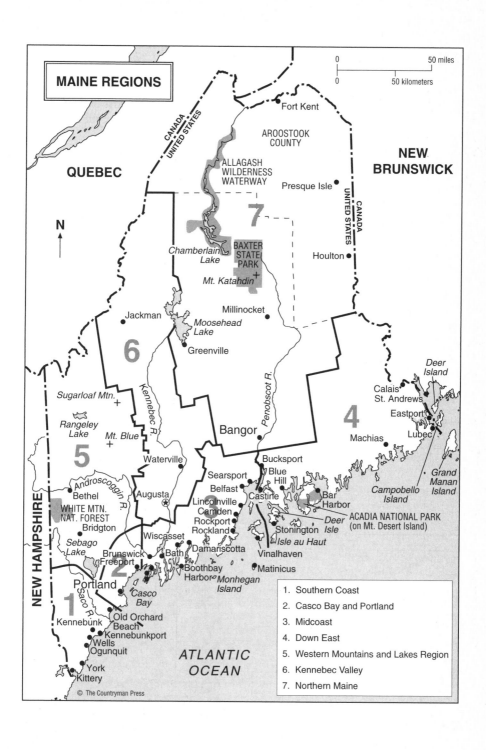

MAINE REGIONS

QUEBEC

NEW BRUNSWICK

N

CANADA
UNITED STATES

CANADA
UNITED STATES

Fort Kent

AROOSTOOK COUNTY

ALLAGASH WILDERNESS WATERWAY

Presque Isle

7

Chamberlain Lake

BAXTER STATE PARK

Houlton

+ Mt. Katahdin

Jackman

Millinocket

Moosehead Lake

Greenville

Deer Island

Calais
St. Andrews

Sugarloaf Mtn. +

Eastport

Rangeley Lake

Mt. Blue +

6

Kennebec R.

Penobscot R.

Bangor

4

Machias

Lubec

Waterville

Bucksport

Grand Manan Island

5

Searsport

Blue Hill

Campobello Island

Androscoggin R.

Belfast

Castine

Bethel

Augusta

Lincolnville
Camden

3

Bar Harbor

WHITE MTN. NAT. FOREST

Rockport

Deer Isle

ACADIA NATIONAL PARK
(on Mt. Desert Island)

Bridgton

Rockland

Stonington

Sebago Lake

Wiscasset

Damariscotta

Isle au Haut

Brunswick
Freeport

Bath

Vinalhaven

2

Boothbay Harbor

Matinicus

Portland

Monhegan Island

Casco Bay

Saco R.

Old Orchard Beach

1

Kennebunkport

Kennebunk

Wells

Ogunquit

ATLANTIC OCEAN

York
Kittery

© The Countryman Press

NEW HAMPSHIRE

1. Southern Coast
2. Casco Bay and Portland
3. Midcoast
4. Down East
5. Western Mountains and Lakes Region
6. Kennebec Valley
7. Northern Maine

0 ___ 50 miles
0 ___ 50 kilometers

CONTENTS

Janet Mendelsohn

Janet Mendelsohn

INTRODUCTION

Midway through our conversation, the director of a small museum in the lakes region paused and looked at me. "If you tell them everything about our museum, they won't need to come," she said. I saw in her eyes that this was no jest or fleeting concern. I was well aware of the dilemma faced by museums nationwide. At some, there has been both a drop in attendance figures for various reasons and a decline in vital financial support from federal, state, and local agencies, philanthropies, and private donors. Before and while researching this project, I feared that by the time the book was published, some museums I wanted to see might be forced to make drastic cuts in staff or exhibits, or even shut their doors. Some have. But things are better than they first appeared. Many museums are adapting with fewer, longer shows and more reliance on volunteers. The recession has inspired the best museums, of every size, to take stock of what they do best and experiment with themes, new media and programming. As the Maine Arts Commission's Donna McNeil told me, "Museums are rethinking how they connect with communities," and people are searching for ways to enjoy themselves close to home.

I thought long and hard about that director's fear but I've never wavered from my reply: The more you know about museums in Maine, the more you'll want to see what they offer and hear their stories yourself.

Taken together, these museums paint a portrait of Maine. They frame the state's beauty and its character. They honor people, from the past and present, who are creative, innovative, and industrious in commerce and the arts. They celebrate the mundane. They educate and inspire children through play. They teach us about everything from the art of shipbuilding to the business of carving decoys and about Mainers who fought in the Civil War. Each is different from the rest.

Two lessons I've learned while writing this book:

• Ask lots of questions and you'll turn a pleasant hour into a memorable visit. Volunteers and staff are almost always well-informed and excited about the stories behind what you see. They might be working artists themselves or may have retired from an industry showcased by the museum, or maybe they grew up riding the trolleys or working on antique cars—whatever it may be, their knowledge can add a lot to the experience. Only a few of those folks are there strictly as security guards. Speak to these people, who have a special interest in the collection, and you'll hear details not printed on any sign. I repeat: Ask lots of questions.

• Maine is a very big place. When you have a mission—like visiting every museum in your special area of interest—your quest will take you to parts of the state you might not otherwise see. I didn't know how beautiful the mountains, lakes, and farms of Aroostook County are until my trip north to the Acadian Village. Until I went to the Wilhelm Reich Museum, I'd never been to Rangeley, where "Moose Danger" signs on the roads are intimidating and the vistas equal our great national parks. Maine will surprise you, too.

A few notes:

• Information is current as of August 2010.

• When admission is free, donations are extremely welcome. Please be generous.

• A museum's absence from the book may not reflect its merit. A huge effort was made to include a wide variety in all parts of the state. If all the worthy local history museums and historic homes were included, you might need one of those old steam-powered Lombard log haulers to carry the book around.

• I visited each museum described and personally interviewed everyone quoted. Any opinions expressed are my own.

• Facilities are handicapped accessible except when indicated, but access may be affected by renovations. It's best to call ahead to be sure or if special arrangements are needed.

• Pets are almost never permitted.

And especially this:

• Phone ahead. It's the only way to be sure a place will be open when you plan to go. Don't rely on websites, which too often are not up-to-date. Many museums in Maine are seasonal, with dates and hours that vary year to year. Many are run by volunteers; if no one is available, or foul weather is forecast, the place may be closed. But if they know you are coming, often they'll make a special effort to be there for you.

Working on this book has been a terrific experience. I met an amazing number of good people who are passionate about what they do. I hope you meet them, too.

Janet Mendelsohn

A Conversation with Donna McNeil, Director, Maine Arts Commission

Is the arts community more vibrant here in Maine, or does it just seem that way?

It often feels like there are more painters, poets, photographers, musicians, sculptors, weavers, writers—creative artists of all stripes—per square mile in Maine than any other place I've lived. But I could be wrong. So when I sat down to talk with Donna McNeil over coffee in Portland, I went straight to that question. Without hesitation, the director of the Maine Arts Commission replied, "Yes. It's true. I believe it comes from the beauty of the place."

Boothbay Harbor.

In 2006, a survey* was conducted by the Creative Capital Foundation, a national nonprofit organization that provides integrated financial and advisory support to artists. Its goal was to identify infrastructure support for contemporary art in Maine and Arizona, the only two states chosen for study. CCF also wondered whether the state's arts community is as healthy as it seems, said McNeil. The researchers found that as a whole, people in Maine recognize and embrace the artist's role as crucial to building dynamic communities, and that many state agencies and arts groups count visual, literary, and performing artists among the state's many "natural resources." McNeil said that in addition to the landscape, artists are attracted by the general quality of life, including such practical matters as artist-driven development of studio spaces where they have ownership and can live and work, and Maine's low-cost healthcare options. A rich variety of cultural offerings, not the least of which are a plethora of summer residency programs in the arts paired with what she described as "unparalleled opportunities for interaction with the environment, clean air and water, good education, and benevolent politics," are among reasons local artists stay here, and why for more than a century others have come to study, spend a summer, or make this their permanent home.

"We have a deep, long, and rich artistic legacy in Maine," said McNeil. "It may have begun in the mid-1800s when Thomas Cole traveled Down East to paint the Acadia region. Through his paintings, he relayed what the landscape looked like before the national park was founded, before it was captured in photography. Combined with that extraordinary beauty, Maine is affordable. There is an unpretentiousness here, a live-and-let-live, do-it-yourself attitude, 'pull yourself up by the bootstraps' Yankee sensibility that is the kind of person artists tend to be. Artists are resourceful and self-reliant. They are all sole proprietors of businesses as themselves, which takes a lot of moxie. Nothing exists in a vacuum, however, and in Maine there exists support from all sectors for the diverse benefits artists bring to the community.

"Maine is a wonderful place. The myriad of museums reflects a diversity of interests and serious collectors and collections," she said. "Everything from lumbering to music boxes and Native Arts through the more expected contemporary and historical museums is represented. Almost every community has a history museum. Maine possesses the oldest housing stock in America and house museums are in abundance. The church in Solon houses amazing frescoes by a contemporary artist. The Nathan Clifford Elementary School in Portland houses Works Progress Administration [WPA] paintings. These examples cause one to rethink what a museum is."

The Maine Arts Commission was established 30 years ago. It is an independent state agency, funded by the state legislature, dedicated to increasing exposure to the arts statewide. Its focus is on helping arts organizations and individual artists through grants, workshops, programs and arts education, primarily pre-kindergarten through grade 12. But community support for the arts is far from new here. Since the mid-1800s, civic leaders have understood that art and culture are part of civic engagement, said McNeil. "As a collection, one could consider our Grange halls and opera houses as examples of civic commitment to performance. When most of the small towns in the state built their city hall, a fine arts center was part of it. That's what these opera houses are—Camden Opera House, Merrill Auditorium, the theater at Monmouth is Monmouth City Hall. Then when there was money in the 1990s, they refurbished those buildings for reuse."

She also points to the legacy of the summer art colonies, long flourishing on Monhegan Island and even earlier in Ogunquit and Bar Harbor, as a genesis of the cultural vibe. "The summer colonies started here because people were attached to the landscape," said McNeil. "They gave rise to places like the Skowhegan School of Painting and Sculpture, Haystack Mountain School of Crafts, and music residencies. Did you know Maine has one of the most prominent summer residency schools for conductors in the United States, the Pierre Monteux School? Even now, we have more summer residencies in the arts than any other state."

Size matters. That's a factor, too, said McNeil. "Maine is manageable. We're big enough that we don't know everybody but we're small enough to know everybody, if that makes sense. It's a big community. Boston probably has more people than the State of Maine but, in terms of the Arts Commission, because we support the individual artists, we have a grassroots connection. Many states have a lot more money than this one does. The commission gets about $700,000 from the state legislature every year, about 52 cents per person, to support arts and culture, and about that much again from our funding partner, the National Endowment for the Arts. In many states, the NEA money is a drop in the bucket because their legislative allocation is much more. It is everything to us. Without the NEA, we wouldn't be able to give grants."

How important are museums to the state economy? "In Portland, Rockland, Ogunquit, and Bar Harbor, they are major economic drivers," she said. "They bring in cultural tourism and a recent economic impact study conducted by [the national nonprofit] Americans for the Arts indicated that for every dollar spent on an admission ticket, $1.72 is spent [by tourists] on hotels, restaurants, transportation, recreation, and in boutiques. They even buy art! Moreover, they are typically highly educated, have more discretionary funds than other folks, and come to make a day or weekend of it. They spend money here. I think people in the economic development field and town officials are starting to get a handle on that. We've been talking about it for 10 years and our [former] governor, John Baldacci, recognized the economic benefits of culture and created the Governor's Creative Economy Council.

"It's tough to quantify what it's like to have a poet as a neighbor and how that kind of over-the-fence parlance enriches both of you. And that's another cool thing about Maine—the poet lives next door to the fisherman, who lives next door to the construction guy, who lives next door to the university professor and the doctor. There are people tucked in pockets throughout the state with tremendous expertise as guitar makers or antique map collectors, and you meet them casually. They're completely accessible. Our communities aren't as stratified as other places, certainly in the smaller towns. You can meet anybody from any walk of life and although we don't have a lot of ethnic diversity, we do have a lot of economic diversity which enriches everybody.

"The museums try to be welcoming to everyone," she noted. "When I first started working in museums, I remember thinking that I didn't know enough or have on the right clothes, that my shoes made too much noise on the floor. I felt completely intimidated. So I tried to make people understand that there's joy to be had in looking at any level, and I know other museum directors try to do that as well."

Nationwide, reports are mixed on whether museum attendance has been affected by the recent recession. Some indicate they've benefitted from more visitors looking for things to do close to home. Others have struggled with shrinking budgets and fewer grants for exhibitions, renovations, staffing, or programming. In Maine, especially at less well-known museums, during 2009 hours and staff were cut; others closed all or part of a building, planned fewer costly new exhibits than in the past, or even considered merging their collections with larger, more solid institutions. But the larger museums are "going great guns," said McNeil, noting that the Farnsworth, for example, launched a capital campaign, which requires confidence in a strong economic future. The Portland Museum of Art is moving ahead with plans for a contemporary wing and restoring Winslow Homer's studio.

"I know there have been some layoffs. Maine never loosened its belt, we're already frugal folks, so belt-tightening wasn't as drastic as other places that are singing the blues," she said. "We in Maine state government have to produce balanced budgets every year, which puts us in better shape to handle economic ups and downs. The recession meant people had to find creative solutions to cutbacks and institute economies of scale. Museums are rethinking how they connect with communities. Instead of repeating expensive Impressionist blockbuster shows, a lot of curators said let's look at local artists, let's see how they intersect with the masters, what are interesting curatorial pairings."

Emerging technology has an interesting role in all this, expanding opportunities at the same time that some would argue it makes brick-and-mortar museums less relevant. Archiving collections in easily searchable databases that take advantage of the Internet makes collections accessible to those who can't easily travel to a particular place. It's great for students, genealogists, and historians, and delivers art to the public in a much broader way. Moreover, noted McNeil, technology has changed art-making, introducing new media and multidimensional exhibitions. Museums are trying to accommodate this, and video rooms are only the beginning. "There was an early fear that we'd put ourselves out of business by putting collections online, but that hasn't been the case."

Courtesy of Brick Store Museum

Ship Nathaniel Thompson, artist unknown (probably Chinese in origin), c. 1859, reverse painting on glass, 23"x 30". Brick Store Museum Collection, 1999.79. Gift of Thomas E. Green, 1999.

I asked her: If there is one thing the public can do for museums, what would it be? Without hesitation, she said even if you take advantage of free admission days or subsidized tickets from your local library, "Go. Numbers count. If the Board of Directors and the people writing checks see visitorship is up, they're going to keep supporting that place. And those that are doing smart educational programming are really on the top of the curve. A lot of organizations that don't fund arts and culture, per se, will fund education. That's how they can also add to their funding base, which will help them survive. Museums also need to leverage the importance of their place in the larger concept of community.

"I can't emphasize enough how important audience is. Artists make work that we then become the decoders of. We complete the circle. Our appreciation of that art is the completion of that work. The public is enormously important. Museums are not just storage sites. They hold the legacy of what societies are remembered for. They hold our treasures and are meant to be interactive places. I love museums. To engage with them is a great gift, a huge education. Being around things that are historically meaningful or beautifully designed, wrought, and displayed, changes you."

In 2005, the Creative Capital Foundation commissioned research to explore the interest in and feasibility of adapting its national grant-making and services to artists as a pilot program in specific states. The national nonprofit issued a call for proposals in the summer of 2005, and 17 applicants responded. From this pool of interested states, CCF decided to conduct research in Maine and Arizona. Research on the State of Maine was conducted in 2006 by Kathie deNobriga and Barbara Schaffer Bacon. Donna McNeil of the Maine Arts Commission helped facilitate focus groups and interviews.

Among other things, the "Creative Capital Foundation State Research Initiative Findings for Maine"* concluded:

• Maine is a state of and for the arts. Maine has a rich heritage as a place where creativity and art are appreciated as part of everyday life. Its craft traditions are world-renowned, from Native American basketry to fiber and wood-working. Maine's musical gifts include traditional Franco fiddling, the root of Cajun music; vaudeville was reborn in Maine through the work of master clowns and mimes.

• Maine's landscapes have long attracted artists and writers who have summered, studied, or settled in communities throughout the state, alongside artists "from here," to create a legacy as a place where creativity is valued. Among them: John James Audubon, Thomas Cole, Andrew Wyeth, and Robert Indiana.

• Maine is also known for its writers, from Henry Wadsworth Longfellow to Nathaniel Hawthorne, who studied in Maine and spent summers here in his youth. Their contemporary, Henry David Thoreau, focused on Maine's natural wonders as an outsider in his travel narratives. Researchers cited Edna St. Vincent Millay among Maine-born poets, and temporary residents included Willa Cather, Sinclair Lewis, Mary McCarthy, Robert Lowell, Rachel Carson, and E.B. White, a frequent summer visitor who moved here in 1938 and has been adopted as a native son. Contemporary writers are abundant and prolific. Maine has the highest number of writers per capita in the country.

• Residency programs like those at Skowhegan School of Painting and Sculpture, Haystack Mountain School of Crafts, Bates Dance Foundation, and numerous others also cultivate new ideas, bring in outside voices, and encourage innovation. Arts exploration is fueled by strong college and university programs including the Masters of Fine Art at Maine College of Art and the New Media Program at the University of Maine/Orono. Student artists often choose to stay in Maine after graduation, and artists from other areas come to the state because of familial ties, the slower pace and lower cost of living in the more rural areas, and the perceived quality of life.

• Maine has been proactive in protecting and expanding its cultural resources. Its nationally recognized Creative Economy Initiatives are now producing results in communities and have buy-in from leaders in government and business. Maine's strong foundation in the creative economy lays the groundwork for public and private investment in creative assets—including artists. The drive for a creative economy accentuates the value of creativity generally and of artists specifically. Business leaders and elected officials at state and local levels are pre-disposed to developing cultural assets as a strategy to economic growth.

* Excerpted with permission of the Creative Capital Foundation

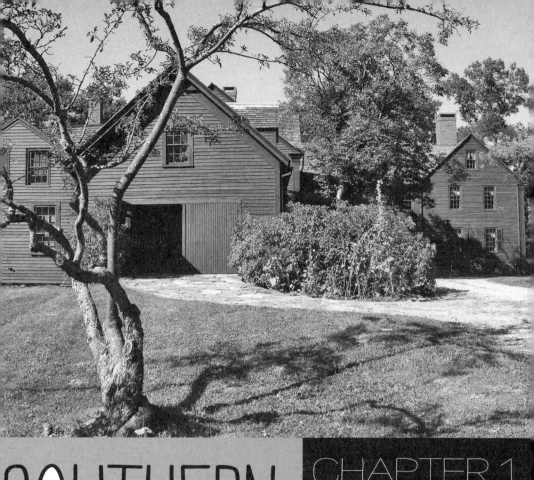

SOUTHERN MAINE

CHAPTER 1

Alfred Shaker Museum
118 Shaker Hill Road, Alfred
www.alfredshakermuseum.com
207-324-9630

WHAT YOU'LL FIND HERE: Photos, crafts, and history of the Shakers' 138-year settlement in Alfred. Original building containing Shaker store, exhibits, and new barn-like room for workshops and events.

Courtesy of Alfred Shaker Museum

WHY GO: In 1793, a small group of Shakers settled in Alfred, where they established the first and, eventually, the largest Shaker community in Maine, with 60 buildings and a cemetery spread out over 300 acres that included agricultural land worked by the Shakers themselves. It was also one of the longest-surviving active Shaker communities anywhere. In 1931, the last Alfred member, Sister Mildred Barker (1897–1990), moved to the Shaker community at Sabbathday Lake in New Gloucester, Maine, and the Alfred property was sold to the Brothers of Christian Instruction of Notre Dame. Shakers follow the teachings of the New Testament and are pacifists. They have always welcomed orphans and children of the poor, caring for and educating them until they reach adulthood. As young adults, each person can choose to go out into the world or remain within the community of faith, an option that requires a vow of celibacy. Their story is told here through exhibits and examples of their crafts.

Sister Mildred entered Shaker life at age seven, when her mother left her with the Shakers. Her brother was already with the community. Nine years later, their mother returned but Mildred, then 16, refused to leave, reportedly saying, "No, this is my home." She became a covenant member in 1918 and became renowned for her lovely singing voice and efforts to keep Shaker songs and hymns alive, including those she learned from the Alfred Believers in her youth. Sister Mildred was awarded a Heritage Fellowship from the National Endowment for the Arts in 1983.

The original wood, lumber storage, and carriage house has been converted to a small nonprofit museum operated by volunteers who have fully restored the structure for preservation of the Shaker legacy through education, craft workshops, and special events. Authentic Shaker-made items in the small historical exhibit range from sturdy wood furniture, spinning wheels, and oval wooden baskets to historic photographs, apparel, and other handcrafted items. Items for sale in the gift shop area are typical of those made by the Shakers who sold "fancy goods," herbs, and practical handmade items to tourists and locals to help support the community.

Curator Linda Aaskov said the Alfred Shakers felt it was their moral obligation to pay taxes. The same is true of the Brothers of Christian Instruction, who now use the remaining buildings as a retirement home for their order and to run the York County homeless shelter and food pantry. The Shakers supported themselves by growing and shipping blueberries as well as by making items for the tourist trade. They were a resourceful group, said Aaskov. "Although most people considered the wood from poplar trees to be junk, the Shakers figured out how to strip and weave the wood into baskets and boxes they edged with white kid leather for their customers."

USEFUL INFORMATION:

• Late spring through fall, one-day workshops for adults teach traditional rug hooking, tatting, felting, chair caning, stenciling, basket making, rug braiding, and other arts for which the Shakers earned a wide-reaching reputation for quality construction and simple, elegant design.

• Applefest in early October welcomes visitors to pick apples on Shaker Hill, enjoy fresh-pressed cider, and witness Shaker craft demonstrations, including broom making, spinning, and weaving.

• For more information on the Shakers, see the description of Sabbathday Lake Shaker Village, pages 152–155.

Time to allow: 15 minutes
Admission: Free
When it's open: Mid-May to early fall
     Wed. and Sat., 1–4 pm
Directions: From US I-95, Exit 19 (ME 9/ME 109), take ME 9 North. At the traffic circle, take the first exit to ME4/Alfred Street. Turn right at Anthony Road and take the second left to Shaker Hill Road.

FUN FACT: The Shakers at New Lebanon, New York, were the first to sell seeds in bulk as a business. Several other Shaker communities, including the group in Alfred, soon followed suit, selling packaged seeds that they referred to as papers. Early varieties were beets, several kinds of beans, sage, turnip, peas, spinach, carrots, parsnips, and onions, to name a few. Most sold for six cents per package. Today, Sabbathday Lake Shaker Village has a thriving mail-order and retail herb business. The herbs, often sold in tins, are available at the Alfred Shaker Museum.

The Brick Store Museum
117 Main Street, Kennebunk
www.brickstoremuseum.org
207-985-4802

WHAT YOU'LL FIND HERE: Vintage postcards, quilts, clothing, furniture, photographs, toys, maritime and folk art from a collection of 70,000 artifacts, and archival materials related to the Kennebunks. Early American fine and decorative arts (circa 1830–1920). Civil War artifacts. Eighteenth- and 19th-century portraits of local residents. Small book store. Research library.

WHY GO: Should a historical museum ignore the present while honoring the past? This one doesn't. When George Herbert Walker Bush turned 85 in 2009, the Brick Store Museum marked the occasion with "Happy Birthday '41," an exhibit about the 41st president's relationship with Kennebunk communities. From Walker's Point, the Bush family vacation retreat and one-time Summer White House, there were news clippings, memorabilia from his rise to the presidency, and photographs of "41" relaxing with neighbors and famous friends on area golf courses, his boat, or with rod and reel. Sure, it was a tribute to the town's biggest celebrity, but at the same time, there was a message: History isn't decades old or something for the classroom. It is happening all around us, all the time.

The Brick Store Museum fills five 19th-century mercantile buildings at the southern entrance to town. William Lord built his dry goods store in 1825, making the unusual choice to use locally made bricks rather than less expensive, abundant timber. Wise move. The brick exterior remains almost unchanged. On the second floor, look up to see the windlass, or pulley system, that Lord installed to hoist heavy items into his store. Adjacent buildings had previous lives as a tobacconist shop, library, market, restaurant, and auto supply store before they were combined to house the museum. Renovations in 2008–2009 uncovered the usual array of old medicine bottles and crispy yellow newspapers, but also centuries-old wooden pegs used as nails and evidence of what powderpost beetles and other pests do to wood. There's an ongoing exhibit of these construction artifacts.

The Brick Store feels like a cross between art gallery and history museum. From the collection of more than 40 handmade quilts, you might see a gallery of inspirational handwork, such as the patriotic quilt made in 1864 by the Ladies Aid Society of Portland, whose members stitched cannons, flags, swords, an eagle, anchor, bible, and drums on a field of golden brown, bordered in bright red. There might be several log cabin quilts, a popular 19th-century pattern, or asymmetrical, luxurious silk and velvet "crazy quilts." Upstairs, the Salon is a permanent exhibit of fine art in ornate gilded frames from the 1830s to the 1920s. The 32 still life, seascape, and landscape paintings complement a portrait gallery of early citizenry who lived in the Kennebunks when this was a shipbuilding center. Summer and fall walking tours of Kennebunk's National Register Historic District include an October walk through

Portrait of Captain James Fairfield (1784–1820), artist unknown, oil on canvas, circa 1810. Brick Store Museum Collection, 75.13.

Courtesy of Brick Store Museum

the nearby cemetery, where many of those same citizens are buried.

"We try to do at least one art-themed exhibit during the year when local residents are able to come," said Tracy Baetz, former executive director, referring to the months when the summer crowd is gone. Past shows invited local artists to interpret an archival piece from the collections and featured juried work by international artists. But you might also be treated to collections of photography, folk art, painted canoe paddles, or rustic camp furniture.

Genealogy researchers can make appointments to use an extensive library and archive of diaries, family papers, commercial records, photographs, indexes of Kennebunk-built ships, and periodicals.

USEFUL INFORMATION

• The museum is partially handicapped accessible. First-floor galleries and the rest room are wheelchair accessible, but the second-floor galleries can be reached only by the central staircase.

• Kennebunk was the first town in Maine to create a Historic District, in 1963. Walking tours (60–90 minutes and covering about one mile) depart from the museum seasonally.

Time to allow: 45 minutes
Admission: Free
When it's open: Tues.–Fri., 10 am–4:30 pm
  Sat., 10 am–1 pm
  Closed on national holidays, on the day after Thanksgiving and between Christmas and New Year's Day.
Directions: From I-95, Exit 25, turn left to go east on ME Route 35. At the traffic light at the intersection of Route 35 and US Route 1, the museum is across the street.

Janet Mendelsohn

Kittery Historical & Naval Museum
200 Rogers Road Extension at Route 1, Kittery
www.kitterymuseum.com
207-439-3080

WHAT YOU'LL FIND HERE: Pre-revolutionary and naval history. Portsmouth Naval Ship Yard memorabilia. Models of ships built in Kittery including a large-scale, ship-rigged, wooden model of John Paul Jones's USS *Ranger*. Reconstructed garrison house (circa 1600). Bellamy eagles; a Fresnel lens and a history of Boon Island lighthouse; scrimshaw, uniforms, and diving gear; guns and furniture owned by native son Sir William Pepperrell. Kittery history video (25 minutes). Gift shop.

WHY GO: The state's first incorporated town, established in 1623, Kittery has provided some of the most illustrious chapters in Maine's story. This comprehensive small museum contains exactly what its name indicates. Beyond whaling harpoons and guns, scrimshaw, Colonial-era tools, paintings, old photos, and milliner's dolls (circa 1830) with leather bodies, papier-mâché heads, and wooden feet, there is an actual garrison house that until recently still stood on the other side of town. During the Indian Wars (1675–1763), the house with walls thick enough to withstand arrows was one of 40 dwellings in a network of neighborhood defense. But above all you'll find a wealth of information and artifacts that relate the town's ongoing naval connections.

Kittery is the southernmost town in Maine, lying abreast of Portsmouth (New Hampshire) Harbor. On the swift-flowing Piscataqua River, within the town limits, is Seavey Island, home to the Portsmouth Naval Shipyard, founded in 1800, when John Adams was president. Despite the name, the shipyard is in Kittery. During the American Revolution, the PNSY-built USS *Ranger* was launched at Badger Island, Kittery, on May 10, 1777, under the command of John Paul Jones, and set sail for France with the message of General John Burgoyne's surrender. The ship arrived at its destination in December that year with two captured British ships. A 12-foot-5-inch-by-12-foot-2-inch wooden model of the *Ranger*, with a 2-foot-8-inch beam, is surrounded by a chronology of the ship's role in the final British attack on Charleston in 1780, when the *Ranger* was captured. During her three years in the Continental Navy, the ship's crew captured or assisted in the capture of 30 vessels. Among other ship models is the steam frigate USS *Wabash*, the flagship of the Union Naval Fleet blockade during the Civil War.

Everyone in town knows about Sir William Pepperrell (1696–1759). His gracious home looking out on the harbor sits near others from its era. Pepperrell is widely recognized for organizing, financing, and leading the 1745 expedition that captured the French garrison at Fortress Louisburg during King George's War, an event commemorated by Louisburg Square in Boston's Beacon Hill. Along with his solid, 8-foot-high mahogany desk, you'll find the sailing orders he wrote in 1741, maps of British and French settlements, and a mid-1800s collection of pistols, rifles, and revolvers.

Early navigation equipment, ceramic and glass souvenir plates, and a detailed exhibit about Boon Island Lighthouse are among the finds that are well described.

Kittery is particularly proud of another native son, John Haley Bellamy (1836–1914), an eminent American master carver whose wooden eagles are prized by collectors of folk art. One powerful eagle has a wing span of 48 inches. Patriotic in spirit and known for their simplicity of design and expression of movement, his eagles are distinctive examples of Americana. An elegant clock is among other examples of Bellamy's fine work.

In 1937, the USS *Squalus* was launched at PNSY, commencing sea trials in May 1939. The submarine completed 18 successful dives before failing to recover while operating off the Isles of Shoals, 7 miles offshore Kittery, on May 23 that year. The *Squalus* sank 240 feet to the bottom of the sea, trapping the crew and making headlines nationwide. The next day, the newly developed "diving bell" chamber was lowered and contact established with the crew. Twenty-six men died but 33 were rescued in four trips by the diving bell. Salvage teams raised the sub after 113 days. The *Squalus* was decommissioned, overhauled and returned to service as the USS *Sailfish*, earning nine Battle Stars in the Asian-Pacific Theater during World War II. Photos and accounts of the tragedy are deeply moving.

Time to allow: 30 minutes
Admission: $5 Adults
    $3 Ages 7–15
    $4 AAA, seniors and families of three or more with children under 10
When it's open: June–Columbus Day
    Tues.–Sat., 10 am–4 pm or by appointment
    Mid-Oct. to Thanksgiving
    Wed.–Fri.
    Open House, second full week in Dec.
Directions: Take I-95, Exit 2 to ME Route 236 South. At the traffic circle, take the fourth exit (US Route 1 North). The museum is on the right, just off the traffic circle.

Museums of Old York
207 York Street, York
www.oldyork.org
207-363-4974

WHAT YOU'LL FIND HERE: Nine historic sites covering 350 years of community life. Guided tours of two furnished, historic homes. Self-guided tours of the Old Gaol (jail), a National Historic Landmark; a one-room schoolhouse (1754); Jefferds' Tavern; John Hancock's wharf and warehouse; and the George Marshall Store, now a contemporary art gallery. Historical and art exhibits in Remick Barn. Ongoing preservation project at the Ramsdell House shows how archeologists and curators are studying everyday life of a working-class 19th-century York family.

WHY GO: This is history from a personal point of view. "The things you see in the Museums of Old York were owned by real people who lived in this community. You can go into the local cemeteries and find their graves," says Mary Harding, curator of the museum's George Marshall Store Gallery of contemporary art. In the riverside Elizabeth Perkins House, the dining room table is set for a formal dinner actually held here in 1905 for dignitaries involved in the signing of the Treaty of Portsmouth, which ended the Russo-Japanese War. The home's bookshelves hold souvenirs Perkins and her mother collected on their travels around the world, and its rooms are decorated in the Colonial Revival style that Perkins championed around town, adding much to York's current charm. Thanks to her efforts, the schoolhouse, tavern, and other properties were protected. In the museum's main building, Remick Barn, are exhibits that draw from a rich collection of handsome furniture, decorative art and textiles, antique toys and decoys, portraits, signs, scrimshaw, and other folk art pieces, many of which have stories of their own.

"This was once a thriving seaport and these were the family possessions of people who lived in the Yorks (York Harbor, Cape Neddick, York Beach and York Village)," said Scott Stevens, the museum's executive director. "Many families still here go back to the 17th century. The local historical society began collecting these pieces in the 1800s. It evolved into this museum. We became the town's attic or repository as they gave us things, like the Bulman bed hangings, that large national museums covet."

Kids and adults may get a charge from exploring a warehouse on the wharf owned by American patriot John Hancock from 1787 to 1793 when goods passed back and forth to the holds of schooners running trade between Maine and the West Indies. A modest exhibit on the second floor describes the era's local lobstering, milling, shipping, farming, and wood industries, but it's more fun to imagine using the pulley to haul those big wooden barrels of china or coal through the opening in the second floor where they were stored. When the last oceangoing coal schooners sailed down the York River in 1916, the adjacent George Marshall Store shifted its focus from coal to finished goods and building supplies. Today it is an outstanding contemporary art gallery featuring works by many of New England's finest visual artists.

At the Old Gaol, you'll see the stone dungeon and cells where prisoners were held until 1860. Most often, they were locked up for "moral crimes," including lying, swearing, not attending church, fornication, and blasphemy, but there were also thieves and murderers. The gaoler's family lived in the same building. You'll see the children's bedroom, the parlor, and the kitchen where the gaoler's wife and her servant prepared meals for prisoners and family alike. Signs throughout include questions especially for youngsters, who are asked such things as "Do you think the gaoler's children spoke to the prisoners in their cells?" There's even a vocabulary list for the "Flash Language" invented by prisoners in the 18th century so they could communicate without tipping off the sheriff or gaolkeeper. Among the terms they used were "grub" for food, "chiv" for knife, and "pops" for pistols.

The museum's library and archives welcome those conducting research on genealogy or local history.

USEFUL INFORMATION

• Visit the Remick Barn Visitor Center for information on tours and special programs, or to obtain foreign-language brochures.

• Guided tours are the only way to see two historic homes, the Emerson-Wilcox House, featuring early furnishings and decorative arts, and the Elizabeth Perkins House and gardens. Reservations can be made at the Remick Barn or in advance by calling 207-363-4974. Custom and group tours are available by advance reservation.

• Buildings have limited wheelchair and stroller accessibility.

• Restrooms are available at Remick Barn, George Marshall Store Gallery, Elizabeth Perkins House, and the Administration Building.

• Parking is adjacent to the Remick Barn and Jefferds' Tavern, and at the Hancock Wharf and George Marshall Store Gallery.

• With advance reservations, groups and families can meet costumed interpreters such as the jailer's family, or participate in Colonial era activities like baking journey cakes on a hearth, or carding and spinning wool for blankets and clothing.

Time to allow: Half a day or less
Admission: Tickets are available for one building/or the entire museum and valid for two consecutive days.
    $6/$12 Adults
    $5/$10 Seniors
    $3/$5 Ages 4–15
    Free Children younger than 4
    $15/$25 Families
When it's open: June–Columbus Day weekend
    Mon.–Sat., 10 am–5 pm
    Closed Sun.
    George Marshall Store Gallery and the John Hancock Warehouse,
    140 Lindsay Road
    April–Dec. (call for dates)
    Tues.–Fri., 10 am–5 pm

Sun., noon–4 pm

Closed Mon.

Directions: From I-95, Exit 7 to US Route 1 South. Follow Route 1 for 0.25 mile to the traffic light. At the light, turn left onto York Street (Route 1A) and go 0.25 mile. Turn right onto Lindsay Road. The Visitor Center is on the right.

FUN FACTS:

• Documentary producer and director Ken Burns, whose work includes the landmark series *The Civil War,* used materials from the Museum of Old York's library when he conducted research for his film *Mark Twain.*

• At the peak of his career, Twain, whose real name was Samuel Langhorne Clemens, spent summers in a rented house across the river from Elizabeth Perkins's house. The author of *Adventures of Tom Sawyer* and *Adventures of Huckleberry Finn* told his neighbors it was an exceptionally good place for writing because it rained so often and his house had no phone. But when his wife suddenly took ill and needed immediate attention, he was grateful his neighbors, the Perkinses, owned the second phone in York.

• The Bulman bed hangings in the Emerson-Wilcox House make up the only complete set of 18th-century crewel embroidered bed hangings known to exist. The beautiful needlework was completed nearly 300 years ago by Mary Bulman (1754–1792) of York, who embroidered a love poem that is visible inside the canopy. During the 1920s, the bed hangings arrived at the museum door, folded in two cardboard cases, carried by women who found them while cleaning out a relative's home. The richly decorated bed hangings—canopy, skirt, quilt, and drapery—helped keep sleepers warm and were valued for their decorative appeal.

SPOTLIGHT

When errors led to enduring style: Elizabeth Perkins House in York

In the Elizabeth Perkins House, the dining room is perfectly appointed for a formal dinner held in 1905. Places are set with bone china, delicately etched wine glasses, amber fruit cups and water goblets, and sterling flatware. Two crystal decanters rest in a silver-trimmed basket. A tall, slender vase of old-fashioned flowers from the garden is surrounded by three creamy white plates, each painted with a heraldic eagle in burgundy rimmed by Cyrillic lettering in royal blue. Surrounding the table are antique sideboards laden with *de rigueur* formal candlesticks, platters, and teacups, grouped by brass or pewter or glass. The elegant preparations contrast markedly with the heft of the room's Jacobean dark-paneled walls, heavy beams, and large stone fireplace, in which cast iron kettles and tools hang. It's all typical of the Colonial era. Or is it?

The house on the banks of the York River is perhaps the region's finest representation of Colonial Revival design, a movement that swept the nation in the late 19th and early 20th centuries. While professing to preserve early American style, the Colonial

Elizabeth Perkins House as seen from the garden.

Revival was based on misinformation fed by the fertile imaginations of men and women enthralled with their own vision of the past.

Here in York, no one was more captivated by the period than Elizabeth Perkins (1869–1952). More than half a century after her death, her home still feels as if Perkins might be in the next room, focused on her favorite pursuits—preparing for guests, conjuring up a story to intrigue them, and organizing efforts to preserve the history of her adopted town.

Now one of nine properties owned by the Museums of Old York, the Elizabeth Perkins House and gardens are open to the public mid-June through September for guided tours on request.

"This is one of the best examples of capturing the character and mentality of the person who lived in what became a historic home," said Scott Stevens, executive director of the Museums of Old York. "Miss Perkins left us her whole collection. We have photos and documentation so that we know what we present is totally accurate. This is not a generic house but rather an expression of the Colonial Revival and the way Elizabeth Perkins and her mother lived."

Elizabeth's mother, Mary Sowles Perkins, was a wealthy, well-educated native of Vermont whose stepgrandfather was a Vermont Supreme Court justice. She traveled extensively; attended the coronation of Nicholas II, Russia's last czar; and supported numerous social causes, including that of the Italian national hero Giuseppe Garibaldi. Her family did not approve of her marriage to the Reverend Joshua Newton Perkins, whom they considered a man of lower means (although reportedly his parents later lost today's equivalent of $10 million during the Panic of 1873). Assigned to a parish in New York, the Reverend Mr. Perkins devoted himself to his congregants and was an early supporter of New York City's Fresh Air Fund, which still sends underprivileged inner city children to the country each summer. His wife preferred her social circle and seeing the world. As was common at the time, they led fairly separate lives. Elizabeth was their only child.

Mother and daughter developed an enduring bond, nourished by their passion for travel and a fondness for acquiring fine china, silks, and antiques. In 1898, while visiting the summer colony in posh York Harbor, Mary Perkins was enchanted by a dilapidated seven-room house, circa 1720, that she thought was built in 1680. She bought the Piggin House for $1,300, placing the property in her daughter's name. Thereafter, the two women spent summers in York, where the reverend rarely visited them. Little is known of their life in New York.

By all accounts, Elizabeth lived in her imposing mother's shadow until Mary Perkins's death in 1929. But she visited five of the seven continents and with her mother shared a love of history that led to the tradition of historic preservation and civic pride that lives in York today.

Both women were founding members of the still-active Piscataqua Garden Club and the town's Old Gaol Museum. In 1939, Elizabeth Perkins founded the York Historical Society, predecessor to the Museums of Old York, to which she later donated the house in memory of her mother. The following year, she was a prime mover in transforming the old Jefferds' Tavern into a museum. But the Perkinses' greatest influence grew out of Elizabeth's enthusiasm for the Colonial Revival.

"Miss Perkins went on a campaign to get people to paint their houses white with black and green shutters and to refrain from picking wildflowers," said Cindi Young-Gomes, the museum's registrar and acting curator, who has worked here since 1991. "She thought that's how houses looked in the Colonial era, whereas actually white wasn't in vogue until the Federal period in the 1820s. Interestingly, she painted her own house a more authentic 'cottage red,' but it's one of the reasons we have so many white buildings around here."

The Colonial Revival in America began around 1876, when an appreciation for our national heritage was sparked by the Centennial Exhibition in Philadelphia, coinciding with the 100th anniversary of the signing of the Declaration of Independence. It was the first official World's Fair in the United States. Early into the 20th century, America was permeated by a desire to recapture an allegedly more manageable time before industrialization, urbanization, and mass immigration. Colonial Revivalists surrounded themselves with objects and architecture that captured their version of early American life. Spinning wheels and other objects that had been purely functional became for the first time decorative objects or screens to hide modern creature comforts such as heating systems and electricity, which people had come to enjoy during the late Victorian era.

During the 1920s, the Perkins women added a wing that doubled the size of the house, which ultimately had 32 rooms including furnished hallways. For her bedroom in the addition, Elizabeth hired tradesmen to reproduce a smaller version of the authentic Colonial fireplace that still exists at the Old Gaol. Throughout the house, she evoked different periods in different rooms, but increasingly she focused on Colonial style, with antiques and locally made furniture that she had doctored to fit her sense of how they should be. She incorporated the largest collection of Vermont-made furniture belonging to one family that still exists. The pieces had been inherited by her mother, whose bedroom is simpler than the rest of the house. Mary Perkins preferred more modern décor, four-poster twin beds and her collection of Currier and Ives prints of the presidents up to Ulysses S. Grant. The rest of the interior reflects the women's global travels, Americana, and the younger Perkins's theatrical bent.

Like actors in a play, overnight guests were instructed to select from a tray of brass candlesticks in the front hall before climbing the stairs for the night. Candles were needed because some guest rooms had only one electrical outlet—unlike their hostesses' rooms, which were amply supplied with electrical light.

In the dining room, Elizabeth had paneling installed and replaced a single horizontal summer beam that she considered too modern with five heavy non-supporting beams darkened and roughed-up to appear authentic. She staged the fireplace for pioneer cooking, but didn't equip it to function for that use, and she found straight-backed wooden chairs with mushroom finials for the table. A porcelain bust of George Washington was positioned amidst shelves brimming with collections of dishes, more typical of her own late Victorian era.

In 1905 the Perkinses hosted an historic dinner. Dignitaries from three nations were invited to celebrate the signing of the Treaty of Portsmouth, which ended the Russo-Japanese War. The dinner was the only event connected to the ceremony that was held in a private home in Maine, a mark of Mary Perkins's impressive connections. Even now, it has not been forgotten, especially in Russia. Several years ago, a group of Russian business people visiting the York Rotary Club toured the house.

"When the Russians saw the plates with their Cyrillic lettering they became very animated," said Young-Gomes. "They told us the spelling and grammar are in an old style, not used anymore, and they were determined to interpret what they read. After much argument, they concluded the words are old Russian proverbs relating to food. One translated, 'Without a piece of bread there will be sadness in the palace.' Another was, 'If the bread doesn't belong to you, don't put it in your mouth.'"

The Maple Room was Elizabeth Perkins's favorite. A Shaker-style bench and a three-legged milking stool from 1920 are tucked between a fireplace and a short closet door. "When I was growing up in York, more than once I heard that in this house there was a china closet that led to a tunnel to the river," said Young-Gomes, opening the fabled door. "The tunnel supposedly was a hiding place for local people during the Indian wars. At one point, we did archeology behind the house but there was no sign a tunnel ever existed. It was a myth invented by Miss Perkins."

She pointed out an antique desk, table, and chairs that Perkins bought in the seacoast area. She had the paint stripped, returning the chairs to what she erroneously thought was their original state. The wallpaper, a digital reproduction made during the museum's 1998 renovation of the house, is heavily illustrated with Colonial farm scenes based on an existing piece of the original pattern in the room. Perkins often boasted of her rare find, a "butterfly table" in the center of the room, but neglected to mention that she hired a carpenter to add the distinctive wings supporting its pointed ovoid top.

One reportedly true story about Perkins was that she was unable to tolerate the idea that her maid, Lizzie Grant, owned something truly colonial that she coveted. Grant was a descendant of the Sewall family, who owned an earlier house on the property that was known as Sewall's Hill. In her own home, Grant found stenciled patterns under many layers of wallpaper. Not to be outdone by her maid, Perkins had a duplicate of its maroon pineapples and leaves stenciled on her parlor's gray walls.

It seems Elizabeth Perkins said whatever was convenient or added to her possessions' prestige. But she based her stories on enough truth to make them believable. It was also her premise that children learn history through stories well-told.

She must have been delighted that Samuel Langhorne Clemens rented a house directly across the river for one year during the peak of his fame. No doubt, during social visits Clemens sat in the parlor where he perhaps browsed through shelves of leather-bound classics that Perkins treasured. They were part of her father's library. The great author might have sat on the graceful pink upholstered sofa, a Duncan Phyfe reproduction, and admired one of his hostesses' three Aubusson silk rugs. Surely he inspected souvenirs on the mantel which held T'ang Dynasty terra cotta figurines, circa 800 a.d., and "shawbti," funerary statuettes found buried in Egyptian tombs, made of blue faience (a rough glass).

Although her relationship with the truth was a curious one, with fact and fiction intertwined to suit her own preconceived notion of the past, it would be wrong to dismiss Elizabeth Perkins as foolish, said Young-Gomes. In 1914, Perkins joined the American Committee for a Devastated France, a dedicated group of women who volunteered to help the wounded during World War I. She subsequently served as a nurse but primarily as an ambulance driver for the French military. For her service, she was awarded the French Legion of Honor. In York, without fanfare, for many years she anonymously provided holiday meals to needy families. She also supported two training programs in Newfoundland and Kentucky that taught women trade skills so they could become self-sufficient. The charming small rugs the women made are scattered about her home.

In 1929, Elizabeth Perkins made an ill-timed purchase: a small theater in York called The Little Picture House. She ran it for 10 years, through the Depression, and closed it when she was in her 70s, at which time she turned her energy to rolling bandages for the Red Cross during World War II. Part of her admitted motivation for participating in the bandage-rolling effort was to use Jefferds' Tavern; the gatherings enhanced the building's profile when she sought to secure its historic status.

At her home, on many an evening guests enjoyed a popular Victorian entertainment called *tableaux vivant*. Costumed and directed by their hostess, her friends posed as vendors selling baskets of produce and maids carrying baskets of laundry, reenacting scenes from a series of framed English prints, called "Cries of London," that hang in a guest bedroom. Perkins also fancied herself a writer and had many rejection slips to prove it, said Young-Gomes. A few of her pieces were published, including a flowery script titled *Stage Struck* that was published in *Harper's Bazaar* in 1902. A copy is in her bedroom, along with her Remington typewriter, French Legion of Honor medals, and the passport on which she deducted 10 years from her age.

The museum also owns a manuscript Perkins apparently never submitted for publication. "It is the story of a woman who desired love so much that she was willing to give up her beauty and wealth for the right man," said Young-Gomes. "The main character then looks at her reflection in a mirror, imagining herself and her surroundings with her wealth gone, and realizes she couldn't separate herself from the trappings of her status. Miss Perkins never married. In her later years, she was considered a formidable woman, but perhaps the story hit too close to home."

Unlike Mary Sowles Perkins, whose correspondence was kept by her daughter, there is much we don't know about Elizabeth Perkins's inner life, said Young-Gomes. "After her death, a friend destroyed all of her friend Bessie's letters and diaries, at her request. Yet she kept receipts for everything she bought and we know she was an excellent organizer who really came into her own upon returning from France."

Two stone markers indicate graves behind a bench that overlooks the river, facing west. One bears just the initials "EBP." On the other, her mother's, is a poem composed by Elizabeth, describing the setting sun.

"There is much more to be discovered about these two women and their times," said Young-Gomes. "Museums have two ways of looking at life. One is to present things as how they were. Another is the way our museums relate to our lives today. There are many historic homes in the seacoast area. If you connect their collections and their stories, you create ties and learn so much more about our past."

Elizabeth Perkins House, historic property of the Museums of Old York
Tours of the house are available by appointment. Inquire at the MOY Visitor's Center in Remick Barn.
www.oldyork.org
207-363-4974
Open June–Columbus Day, Mon.–Sat., 10 am–5 pm by guided tour only
Closed Sun.

AMONG OTHER FINE HISTORIC HOMES . . .

Victoria Mansion
The Morse-Libby House (1858-1860)
109 Danforth Street, Portland
www.victoriamansion.org
207-772-4841
Open May–Oct. and Dec.
Opulent Italian villa with authentic Victorian interior décor.

Historic New England
The nation's oldest regional heritage organization, has preserved 36 historic properties, including six homes in Maine: **Castle Tucker** (1807), Wiscasset; **Nickels-Sortwell House** (1807), Wiscasset; **Marrett House** (1789), Standish; **Sarah Orne Jewett House** (1774), South Berwick; **Hamilton House** (circa 1785), South Berwick; and **Sayward-Wheeler House** (circa 1718), York Harbor.
617-994-5910
www.historicnewengland.org

Ogunquit Museum of American Art
543 Shore Road, Ogunquit
www.ogunquitmuseum.org
207-646-4909

WHAT YOU'LL FIND HERE: Permanent collection of 1,600 works emphasizing American Modernism and Maine artists. Sculpture garden overlooking the rocky coast. Oils, watercolors, sculpture, prints, and photographs by established and emerging artists, most with connections to Maine. American art from the 19th century to the present. Research library. Gift shop.

WHY GO: Artists have gravitated to this coastal community since at least the late 1890s. Many of their works are represented at the museum, which was founded by Henry Strater after he fell under the area's spell in 1919 while studying at one of numerous schools in the emerging Ogunquit Art Colony. In 1925, he moved here permanently, leaving his home and studio in Paris where, as a member of the "Lost Generation," Strater was friends with writers James Joyce, F. Scott Fitzgerald, and Ernest Hemingway, with whom he shared a love of deep-sea fishing. Eventually, Strater purchased this property on Shore Road, designed and had built the museum with four galleries to house his works and that of his peers. Strater issued a standing invitation to his friends who were *plein air* artists, and today, artists are still welcome to set up in the garden or by the shore after checking in at the visitors' desk inside the museum. In 1953, Strater donated the museum to the community. Although most of the art schools are gone, Ogunquit remains an active arts center with many nearby galleries.

A beautifully landscaped sculpture garden surrounds the elegantly simple, contemporary museum which overlooks a small cove where Atlantic waves crash against rocky shore.

"As the only art museum in southern Maine and as keepers of a special collection for the common trust, we have a dual responsibility and unique role in

Courtesy of the Ogunquit Museum of American Art

Marsden Hartley, Still Life with Eel, circa 1917, oil on canvas, collection Ogunquit Museum of American Art, gift of Mrs. William Carlos Williams.

the Ogunquit community," said Ron Crusan, director and curator since 2009. OMAA collects art and artifacts, papers and ephemera pertaining to the area's role as a summer arts colony. Until recently, the museum emphasized New England artists and living artists working in the region. The permanent collection includes major paintings by Marsden Hartley, many of which were acquired early in the life of the museum. OMAA is also well known for oils, watercolors, sculpture, prints, and photographs by prominent and rising artists including Dozier Bell, Charles Burchfield, Alexander Calder, Wolf Kahn, Rockwell Kent, Winslow Homer, Edward Hopper, and Reginald Marsh. Crusan's primary interest is American Modernism. Going forward, he anticipates OMAA exhibitions will become a little more *avant garde* while blending with the more traditional art of American Modernism.

Always a seasonal museum—the galleries are not heated—Crusan said OMAA is extending its role in the community, in part by reaching out to local residents and school groups in the off-season. A research library contains more than 1,000 books and museum catalogues on Maine artists and American art.

USEFUL INFORMATION

• Ogunquit is often clogged with traffic during the summer. Getting around is easiest on weekdays or via the town's trolley, which makes numerous stops. If you drive, parking at the museum is free.

• Although handicapped accessible, there are stairs connecting galleries. Wheelchair access is convoluted, requiring some exiting and re-entering the building from the garden path at several points.

Time to allow: 1 hour
Admission: $8 Adults
 $7 Seniors and students 12 and older
 Free Ages 11 and younger
When it's open: May 22–Oct. 31
 Mon.–Sat., 10 am–5 pm
 Sun., 1–5 pm
Directions: From the south, take I-95 to Exit 7 toward ME-91 (Ogunquit/US Route 1) and continue straight for 0.2 mile. Turn left on Route 1 and go 4.4 miles. Take a slight right at Pine Hill Road, follow for 2.1 miles and turn right onto Pine Hill Road South. After 0.4 mile, turn right onto Shore Road. The museum will be on the left.

From the north, take I-95 to Exit 19 (ME-9/ME-109) toward Sanford/Wells. Go 0.5 mile. Turn left at ME-109/ME-9/Sanford Road and go 0.5 mile. Turn right onto Chapel Road; follow for 1.2 miles to Route 1; follow that for 4.4 miles to Shore Road. After 0.5 mile, bear left to stay on Shore Road to the museum.

FUN FACT The view is spectacular through a wall of windows in the main lobby, at times competing with the art itself. Behind the building, winding paths in the sculpture garden lead to quiet areas where benches beneath the trees are surrounded by native and rock garden plants and offer ocean views, perfect for bird watching, reading, or simply unwinding.

Saco Museum
371 Main Street, Saco
www.dyerlibrarysacomuseum.org
207-283-3861

WHAT YOU'LL FIND HERE: Eighteenth- and 19th-century cultural and industrial history of the Saco River valley. Genealogical and historical documents related to Maine. Fine furniture, household objects, and paintings, including 13 portraits by John Brewster, Jr. Period bedchambers. Antique natural history specimens. Temporary exhibits on regional history and works by contemporary Maine artists. Colonial Revival (1926) building designed by Maine architect John Calvin Stevens. Gift shop.

WHY GO: The Saco Museum is a standout among Maine's many local historical society collections. Through the stories of those who lived and worked in the Saco River valley long ago, we hear as much about the mill girls as we do about the elite sea captains and factory owners. Exhibits are professionally designed with signage that places events in the context of their times. They draw from an eclectic collection that ranges from 19th-century taxidermy to oil paintings and tools used in local textile factories. One of the small pleasures here is to slide open "discovery drawers" that hold century-old invoices, newspapers, and ephemera that cannot be exposed to constant light; or snoop at the letter on a mill girl's desk in which she tells her family about everyday activities in her new life far from home. The past becomes personal.

The third-oldest museum in the state, it was founded as the York Institute in 1866 and merged with Saco's Dyer Library during the 1970s. With the merger, the library's Roy P. Fairfield Maine History Room collections, containing 10,000 manuscripts, historical papers, photographs and maps of York County and the areas surrounding Saco, and genealogical records, became an integral part of the museum, whose name was changed in 2000. Temporary exhibits feature diverse populations that contributed to the area before and after the affluent Federal era (1790–1830), as well as artists with connections to Maine, from works on paper by Winslow Homer to contemporary photography.

Until 1883, Saco, Biddeford, and Old Orchard Beach were all within the city of Saco. A recent exhibit explored four centuries of life in the region which, in many ways, has been defined by its geography. From the museum collections came Native American artifacts unearthed in archeological digs; handsome 19th-century, locally made furniture, portraits, and fine china from the homes of prosperous merchants and sea captains; and cotton cloth, shoes, and candles produced in riverfront factories and shipped around the world. For thousands of years before European immigrants arrived around 1630, the valley was the home of the Wabanaki nations (the Abenaki, Penobscot, Maliseet, Micmac, and Passamaquoddy people), who relied on the river for fishing and transportation. When the English began establishing settlements in Winter Harbor (Biddeford Pool), hostilities broke out between the colonists and Native Americans, leading to King Phillip's War. Many settlers abandoned the area for more established towns in Massachusetts, but others remained.

By the late 1700s, shipbuilding and seafaring trades were influential occupations. The Saco River's rapid current carried logs here from the northern woods for masts and lumber. A sawmill industry boomed, harnessing the power of the river. Timber and fish were exported to Africa, the West Indies, and Europe. Soon merchants, artisans, and craftsmen in the valley produced pewterware, silverware, and clocks; the Saco Iron Works manufactured nails; and during the Federal period, the region became known as a center for furniture-making. Newly wealthy families bought elegant cabinets, desks, and dining tables and chairs. The valley's industries dramatically altered life for people in every tier.

They also brought waves of immigrants who came here to work—Italian merchants and stonecutters, Irish sailors, Scottish weavers, and especially French-speaking Canadians, joining farm girls from throughout New England. Most arrived on their own, but not all. Slavery was not outlawed in Maine (still part of Massachusetts) until 1783. As mass production changed community life in Maine's cities and towns, the potpourri of languages, traditions, arts, craftsmanship, economic status, and aspirations enriched the communities while simultaneously creating tension throughout the 1900s.

The Scamman Jug, circa 1689-1702, Westerwald, Germany, salt-glazed stoneware, gift of Katharine Deering. Photo courtesy Colonial Williamsburg Foundation.

Courtesy of Dyer Library/Saco Museum

First-floor exhibits change periodically, but from the not-so-distant past you might find a white peaked mask worn by a local member of the Ku Klux Klan, which opposed African Americans, Jews, and Catholics, but especially French-Canadians, who were seen as competition for jobs. You might learn about the Blue Ribbon Shoe Co., which changed its name to Nike in 1978 and opened its second American plant on the Saco River to manufacture its first children's shoes until 1985.

Upstairs are two fully furnished bedrooms—one a floral Victorian bedchamber (1830–1870) with heavily carved wooden cabinetry, the other a typical mill girls' dormitory. The latter explains how family life was changed forever as daughters who previously helped produce goods at home—spinning wool or making cloth, candles, and soap that the family sold—were recruited to work in Saco's burgeoning textile industry, carding cotton, filling bobbins, and running looms. Thousands of mill girls, the first in their families to work outside the home, quickly knew how it felt to earn their own wages and live independently.

The American folk artist John Brewster, Jr. (1766–1854) is represented by 13 portraits and paintings that form the largest collection of his work. Born deaf and never learning to speak, read, or write, Brewster nonetheless had a highly successful art career, travelling throughout New England, negotiating his own fees, and communicating with individuals whose families he immortalized. Brewster's paintings are notable for the fine details of the sitters' clothing and faces that are expressive despite their formality.

The centerpiece of a planned 2012 exhibition is a real treasure, an 800-foot-long painting, *Moving Panorama of Pilgrim's Progress* (1851), that's being restored at the Williamstown Art Conservation Center in Massachusetts. The work is a religious allegory composed of painted scenes wound on giant spools that are unrolled a section at a time. In their heyday, moving panoramas were exhibited on theater stages to the accompaniment of music. Hundreds of these monumental artworks were painted during the 19th century, movable and not, but few of this type have survived. This remarkable piece was exhibited around the nation and later donated to the museum, where it was soon forgotten in storage for close to a century. It was rediscovered in 1999.

Time to allow: 1 hour
Admission: $4 Adults
 $3 Seniors
 $2 Students and ages 7–18
 Free Ages 6 and younger
 Free on Fridays from 4–8 pm
When it's open: Tues., Wed., Thurs., noon–4 pm
 Fri., noon–8 pm
 Sat., 10 am–4 pm
 Sun., noon–4 pm, June–Dec. only
Directions: From I-95, Exit 36, take ME Route 195 to Exit 2A (US Route 1 South/Main Street). After 0.8 mile, turn left into the parking lot.

FUN FACT: The annual Festival of Trees, from Thanksgiving through Christmas, features dozens of elaborately decorated holiday trees and wreaths offered in a silent auction to raise funds for the Saco Museum. The festival is a local favorite, with a tree-lighting ceremony, visits with Santa, a gingerbread village, and activities for children and adults.

Seashore Trolley Museum
195 Log Cabin Road, Kennebunkport
www.trolleymuseum.org
207-967-2712

WHAT YOU'LL FIND HERE: Reportedly the oldest and largest museum of electric streetcars in the world, founded 1939. Historic and newer mass-transit vehicles from around the globe. Horse-drawn streetcars, trolleys, and a modern subway car. Two-mile trolley rides. Birds-eye views of restoration projects. The National Collection of American Streetcars, including 10 from Maine listed in the National Historic

Janet Mendelsohn

Register. Library and gift shop. Photo exhibits of public transportation that connected Maine's communities and changed lives.

WHY GO: If you think trolleys are just fun rides for kids, relics of a bygone era, or open-air transport in vacation destinations, think again. The Museum of Mass Transit, the collection's second moniker, includes more than 250 vehicles, indoors and out, on a 350-acre site, representing many of the most popular transportation systems in the world. Imagine San Francisco without its famous cable cars. Consider life in old New York before automobiles. Since 1888, when streetcars first moved Bostonians around town, that city's transportation system has relied in part on electric buses connected to overhead lines. Today, it is still one way Boston moves people through its neighborhoods and adjacent towns. Moreover, interest in electric streetcars as a means of mass transit is on the rise.

Since the mid-1990s, major U.S. cities have been taking a fresh look at what appears to be a more efficient, "green" alternative to road-clogging, environmentally questionable cars and trucks. More than a dozen cities with large urban populations have built, expanded, or launched electric streetcar projects to reduce road congestion, parking problems, and environmental damage. Among them are Dallas; Seattle; Vancouver; Tucson; Albuquerque; Kenosha, Wisconsin; Savannah, Georgia; and Ybor City, Florida. As they say, what's old is new again.

At the Seashore Trolley Museum, part of the fun is hearing the *clang clang clang* of the bell, the *whoosh* of air as the brakes are released, the loud *toot* of an air horn, and the *ding ding ding* that warns pedestrians and other vehicles that a trolley is approaching a crossing. But traveling the rails, electric cars themselves are quiet.

According to John Middleton, an avid historian and museum volunteer who serves as vice president for business administration, the old streetcars were so quiet in their day that many were designed with wide, low fenders in front, like a steam engine's "cowcatcher," to scoop up pedestrians on the tracks before they could be knocked down by an approaching train.

"Streetcars were much more reliable than automobiles," said Middleton. "They moved on tracks instead of muddy roads, so they didn't get stuck, and revolutionized how people got around. Before their time, people walked or maybe rode horses, which were mostly owned by farmers, not city dwellers. Streetcar lines enabled people to live in the country and commute to town for work."

During your visit, take a leisurely country ride aboard a restored streetcar on 2 miles of track built for the Atlantic Shore Line, an interurban line that closed in 1927. Before a conductor calls "All Aboard," step into the vestibule of the waiting trolley and let a friend take your picture at the controls. Then take a seat. During your short journey, you can hop on and off at stops to see trolleys up close in three exhibit barns. In the Highwood Barn are 17 streetcars including a San Francisco cable car and an 1800s Omnibus modified for use as a sheriff's wagon. Another barn contains experimental subway cars from the 1970s and trucks used to service rapid transit and other lines.

Middleton, a retired physicist, said his favorite is identical to the one he rode as a student. The one he calls "his" is a 1924 Boston Elevated car. It has 44 orange-painted wood seats that flip to allow four passengers to face one another. Boston had hundreds of these and they all looked alike, he said. They had white wood-lathing ceilings and floors, sturdy hanging straps for standing passengers to hold, and bare light bulbs.

When you visit, your trolley ride will be aboard one of 10 cars used in rotation. Depending on the day, perhaps it will be an open-air car, known as a "breezer," or "1901 air conditioning," as Middleton called it. Or it might be the one from Australia, or the *Liberty Bell Limited*, which ran from Allentown to Norristown to Philadelphia, Pennsylvania, in 1935. Maybe you'll board a horse-drawn streetcar from about 1896 that's the oldest in the collection.

"The magic happens in the Town House Restoration Shop," said Middleton. Six or seven projects are usually underway and it takes years to restore the relics. Most of the work is done by volunteers who bring to the task their skills as carpenters, electricians, painters, plumbers, steelworkers, upholsterers, and other tradesmen.

Everything here is acquired for the specific purpose of national preservation. In 2009, a 1906 electric locomotive became the brightest star in the museum's constellation. As the last electric locomotive to operate in Maine, ASL-100 is listed on the National Historic Register. With funding from the State of Maine and Federal Highway Administration, several historic railway organizations, local businesses and individuals from nearly 20 states, the three-year, $180,000 project restored the locomotive to its condition circa 1935 when ASL-100 operated on the Atlantic Shore Line until 1949. A small staff and more than 50 volunteers contributed 3,500 hours of labor to the restoration project, which also involved creation of an indoor and traveling exhibit, "History in Motion: Public Transportation Connecting Maine Communities." In partnership with the Maine Department of Education and a Boston Museum of Science program called "Engineering is Elementary," the ASL-100 project inaugurated professional development workshops for elementary school teachers. The workshops incorporate science, technology, social studies, and visual arts for students in kindergarten through eighth grade who learn how electric transportation affected people and their work in southern Maine.

USEFUL INFORMATION

• Two of the trolley cars used for visitors' rides are handicapped accessible. If you call in advance with a request, they can schedule these to run on the day you visit.

• A small snack shop sells pre-made deli sandwiches, ice cream, and beverages. Benches for picnics are outside.

• Boy Scout troops as a group can earn merit badges for railroading during four special scout weekends a year.

Time to allow: 1–2 hours
Admission: Includes unlimited 30-minute rides on authentically restored streetcars.
   $8 Adults
   $6 Seniors (60 and older)
   $5.50 Ages 6–16
   Free Ages 5 and younger
   $4 Sunset rides, all ages, includes ice cream
   Guided group tours at discounted rate; reservations required.
When it's open: Memorial Day–Columbus Day,
   Daily, 10 am–5 pm (last ride at 4:15 pm)
   May and Oct., Sat. and Sun. only
   Sunset/ice cream rides: Wed. and Thurs., July–Aug., at 7 pm
   Christmas Prelude rides: first two weekends in Dec.
Directions: From Portland: I-95 South/Maine Turnpike to Exit 32 (Biddeford). After the toll booth, straight across to ME-111. Go 1 mile. Turn right onto US Route 1 South. Go 3 miles. Turn left at traffic light onto Log Cabin Road. Museum is 1.7 miles on the left.
   From Boston: I-95 North/Maine Turnpike to Exit 35 (Kennebunk). Left onto ME-35 into downtown Kennebunk. Left onto US Route 1 North for 2.8 miles. Right at the light onto Log Cabin Road. Museum is 1.7 miles on the left.

FUN FACTS

• Pumpkin Patch Trolley Rides on weekends in late September and early October include stops to pick pumpkins in a field close to the track. Children can decorate their pumpkins with paints supplied by the museum, then "check" their pumpkin with volunteers who transport them back to the Visitor Center, where they can be picked up for the trip home. No extra charge.

• It often costs just $1 to buy an aging streetcar from a municipality, but it might cost thousands to truck it to the museum. One double-decker car arrived by ship from Great Britain.

• You can be a motorman. By reservation only, you can operate one of the museum's antique streetcars following a brief introduction about how streetcars work and operating instructions. Then you'll take the controls, guided by an instructor, and your immediate family can come aboard for the ride. The program, a fundraiser for the museum, costs $50 for one hour.

Wells Auto Museum
Route 1, Wells
www.wellsautomuseum.com
207-646-9064

WHAT YOU'LL FIND HERE: Eighty antique automobiles, most pre-1955. Vintage motorcycles and trucks. Large display of nickelodeons and antique arcade games in operating order. Gift shop.

Janet Mendelsohn

WHY GO: Glenn Gould always loved cars. When he returned home in 1946 after serving in World War II, he told his uncle he wanted to restore an old one. His uncle offered Gould his early Stanley Steamer, launching a collection that kept him busy until his death in 2005. Gould never stopped working on cars, tenderly bringing them back to original condition, doing most of the work himself even when in his 80s.

The Wells Auto Museum's 80 cars built between 1894 and 1955 are almost entirely from Gould's collection, which took him more than 50 years to build. If you love antique cars, there are some real jewels here. Many were rich men's toys, meant to be entertainment, and they look like fun if only you could get them out on the road. Frustratingly, however, the collection is displayed in crowded rows that don't present the Brass Era beauties and other classic cars in their best light. On the bright side, scattered about are fully operational old-time arcade games, nickelodeons, penny picture shows, kiddie rides, and music machines. Bring a pocketful of quarters and play to your heart's content. One among several tempting arcade games entices, "See Rhonda's revealing balloon dance!"

Gould was an electrical supplies salesman. His work took him all over New England and everywhere he went, he looked for cars. He traveled with an empty trailer and would often return home with a vehicle that recently resided in somebody's barn or field. "He was one of the early pioneers in the hobby, well before others got into it as an investment," said manager Ken Creed, who has worked on the collection since 1975. Many of the cars predate 1912. Gould's gems include a handsome 1928 Auburn Boattail Speedster featuring a small "golf club door" behind the passenger door, just big enough for your clubs. From England, there's a 1935 Lagonda perfectly suited to Jay Gatsby. Nearby are a 1918 Stutz Bearcat, a sporty red and black 1911 Maxwell, and a 1908 Baker Electric originally built for John D. Rockefeller to his specifications, with rear seats on which his children could sit facing each other, like on a train. The Baker's electric charger hangs beside it on the wall. Some cars are more functional than flashy. Mixed in is a seven-passenger 1940 Bombardier snowmobile, one of only 50 built, with skis in the place of front wheels and powered by a continuous track in the rear. One hard-to-define 1909 vehicle was manufactured by Sears Roebuck and originally sold for $410. It's more farm vehicle than family car. In the back room, among Willys Jeeps and vehicles in various states of repair, there's a 1941 Dodge command car and 1927 Reo fire truck. You'll see a 1915 Adams Indy racer and the kids might recognize a stainless steel 1982 DeLorean MC-12 from its twin in the film *Back to the Future*. Tucked here and there are vintage radios, toy train sets, lots of rusting license plates, and old car parts for spice, but by and large, it's mostly about the cars without much information.

Gould, who lived in Shirley, Massachusetts, first kept his cars in a barn near his home. By 1950 the collection had outgrown that space, so he moved the cars to Meredith, New Hampshire. Meanwhile, he was still actively selling on the road. For three years, he leased the cars to an amusement park in Myrtle Beach, South Carolina, but he took them back when he purchased the building in Wells, where he could work on the cars and put them on display himself. Reportedly all but seven of the vehicles are operational, and about six go out on the road for parades and car meets.

USEFUL INFORMATION Photography is permitted. No credit cards accepted. All the arcade games and nickelodeons are ready to play, most for 25 cents.
Time to allow: 45 minutes
Admission: $7 Adult
 $4 Ages 6–12
 Free Ages 5 and younger
When it's open: Late June–Labor Day
 Daily, 10 am–5 pm
Directions: On US Route 1 in the center of Wells.

CHAPTER 2 CASCO BAY & PORTLAND

CHILDREN'S MUSEUM MAINE

Children's Museum & Theatre of Maine
142 Free Street, Portland
www.kitetails.org
207-828-1234

WHAT YOU'LL FIND HERE Interactive exhibits and programs for children ages six months to 10 years. Children's Theatre of Maine productions for kids, by kids. Museum outreach programs for classes pre-kindergarten to fifth grade. Camera Obscura with guided tours of panoramic views of Portland. Snack tables. Outdoor garden of musical instruments and pirate ship. Gift shop.

WHY GO Don't be alarmed if there's a big red ladder truck out front and Portland fire fighters in full gear when you arrive at the museum. On Fire Safety Fridays, twice a month, kids can climb aboard the truck and pretend they're fighting a blaze while adults get tips on creating fire-escape plans. It's just one of a zillion ways the Children's Museum and Theatre of Maine turns learning into fun.

Have a little ham in the family? Follow that youngster to the "Dress Up Theatre" where she or he can slip into costume and enter imaginary lands on a junior-sized stage in front of bolster seats for the audience (you!). Arts education, always important here, took on new dimensions in 2008 when the museum merged with the professionally run Children's Theatre of Maine, which was founded more than 80 years ago. Not only did the new partnership expand audiences for both, but the museum's theater got a makeover in readiness for more than a dozen plays and puppet shows put on by cast and crew, ages 7–16, each year. CTM also offers acting classes geared for ages 3–5, 6–9 and 8-15.

Can we climb inside the whale? Yes, indeed, if Istar the humpback whale is in residence. The real Istar swims in the Gulf of Maine and Atlantic Ocean, where marine scientists have observed her activities since the mid-1970s. Istar's life-size, inflatable double travels to schools throughout New England as part of a whale education program but periodically she's back "home," suspended above the first floor for an extended stay. Twice a day she's lowered so visitors can step inside for a guided tour that explains how whales communicate, travel, eat, breathe, and play.

Science education is big here. Instead of the whale exhibit, you might get a chance to walk in the shoes of archeologists tracking dinosaurs or . . . well, who knows what you'll find? Shows change during the year but there are always three floors of fun stuff to do that oh-by-the-way teach children (and adults) about science. Sit in the cockpit of a mini-spaceship. Gaze at the stars in a mini-planetarium; shows are twice a day. Hold a starfish or one of its friends from a tide pool touch tank full of live critters from Casco Bay. Climb a tree house. Meet Bizzy Bob, Eloise, Dill, and Nigel, the turtles at the Ranger Station where future Maine Guides can try to identify plants and animals native to the Pine Tree State. Crank the conveyor belt of a saw mill to turn rough pine into smooth wood. Roll balls on tracks, make them speed up, slow down, and jump from lane to lane in "Have a Ball." It just happens to demonstrate basic physics.

Everything is designed so children and their families or caregivers can learn through playing together. Science is often the focus but arts education and our multicultural world get equal attention, and sometimes an activity involves two or all three. For the youngest visitors, an enclosed, safely padded Toddler Park, for ages three and younger, has a rainbow to climb and an infant area tucked into the corner. When the whole place begins to feel too hectic, head for the quiet Book Nook to read a children's book in English, Braille, Spanish, Vietnamese, Cambodian, Russian, Farsi, or Somali.

Another catch-your-breath corner, We Are Maine, is a place to sit and watch videos of 20 Maine kids whose families have roots all over the world. Each child shares a story about what makes his or her family both different and the same as everyone else's. Nearby, the food, clothing, and traditions of another culture are featured, a different country every six months.

Most of the first floor is Our Town. It's like a village where children can do all the jobs. At the fire station, they shimmy down a fire pole and crawl through a "low smoke" area. At the car repair shop, would-be mechanics tinker with a scaled-down auto and pump gas. Before buying groceries next door, kids might want to withdraw money from a replica ATM; the activity provides a good opportunity to talk about how people earn money and why we need it. The town has a veterinary clinic to practice taking care of farm animals and pets, and a small-scale lobster boat with traps to haul. On the outskirts, a dairy farm's cow needs milking, eggs need sorting, and mini bales of hay need loading onto a conveyor belt. Many stops have cardboard cards and letters ready for delivery to mailboxes by young postal carriers in borrowed uniforms. None of it is real, of course. Look for signs in each area with suggestions for helping kids learn something extra while having fun.

Weather permitting, don't miss the unusual experience of watching what's happening live outside in Portland from a room with no windows. It's called a Camera Obscura, and there are guided shows throughout the day.

USEFUL INFORMATION:

• More than 150 children's museums and science centers in the United States and Canada offer free admission for visitors who participate in the Association of Children's Museums (ACM) Reciprocal Membership program. Complimentary entry benefits vary by museum but at least one adult named on the membership must be present. For a list of participating museums or to purchase memberships, inquire at this or another children's museum's admission desk or website or visit the ACM online at www.childrensmuseums.org/visit/reciprocal.htm.

• Clean and Safe: CMTM has a lead-free policy for toys in its exhibits and store and avoids potential choking hazards in exhibits. To reduce the spread of germs, a cleaning crew works every night. All plastic food is washed and sanitized daily. Hard props are cleaned in a dishwasher and soft props, like stuffed animals and dress-up clothes, are laundered in a washing machine on a rotating schedule. Visitors who see a toy go into a child's mouth can place the dirty toy in a drop bin in the toddler park.

• Downloadable exhibit guides on the museum's website have great tips for interacting with your child at the museum and fun learning at home. Also online is a list of favorite children's books.

Time to allow: 1 hour or more

Admission: $9 per person

    Free Under age 18 months

    Group discounts available with advance reservation.

    $4 Camera Obscura only

When it's open: Labor Day to Memorial Day

    Mon., 9–11 am for members only

    Tues.–Sat., 10 am–5 pm

    Sunday, noon–5 pm

    Holiday Mondays, 10 am–5 pm but closed New Year's Day, Easter, July 4,

    Thanksgiving and Dec. 24 and 25.

    Open every day during Maine school vacation weeks.

    Memorial Day to Labor Day

    Mon.–Sat., 10 am–5 pm

    Sun., noon–5 pm

    All year: First Friday of the month, 5–8 pm, $1 per person.

    Free for members and age 17 months and younger.

Directions: From I-295, Exit 61 (Forest Avenue South), bear right at the light onto ME-77 South, go up the hill and turn left onto Congress Street. Go 0.2 mile, cross High Street and immediately bear right onto Free Street. In Portland's Arts District, next door to the Portland Museum of Art.

Courtesy of Children's Museum and Theatre of Maine

SPOTLIGHT

Camera Obscura: the original reality show

What if you could stand in a room with no windows yet clearly see outdoors? Imagine observing wildlife or people going about their daily business without them knowing you are there. It's possible with an optical instrument called a camera obscura, meaning "dark room" in Latin. The term was first used in the early 1600s by the German astronomer Johannes Kepler. Portable versions of the instrument eventually evolved into what we know as a camera and led to the development of photography and movies. But for centuries, scientists, artists, and ordinary folks have been fascinated by images that appear when a camera obscura projects outdoor light through a small hole into a dark enclosed space. A recent revival of interest has led to several locations around the globe where visitors can observe its use today.

    In New England, only one camera obscura is available to the public. It's in Portland, at the Children's Museum of Maine, possibly the only children's museum in the world to have one. When you enter its big box of a room, about 14 feet by 20 feet, with walls 12 feet high, there's nothing to look at. Everything is painted the deep blue of a night without stars, except for two carpeted risers on which visitors can sit or stand, and a round, white-topped table with mechanical controls attached. To see how the camera obscura works, you need to join a guided tour. Suzanne Kahn Eder led ours, and she introduced young visitors to the experience by comparing it to standing inside an eyeball.

Our tour on a Friday morning included an unusually quiet group of three- to five-year-olds from a nearby nursery school, their adult chaperones and two families who timidly filed into the room. Eder calmed a few children afraid of the near-dark by telling us we were about to see something magical. And she was right. At the far end of the room, she slid the cover off what the museum calls its "natural camera," a room-sized pinhole, or shoebox, camera that is simply a small hole in the otherwise solid wall. When she uncovered the hole, sunlight spilled in, casting a soft-focus moving picture high on the wall. There was Free Street, outside the museum, at that very moment.

"I see cars! I see people walking!" youngsters shouted, pointing above our heads. One adult gasped. The entire scene—cars, trucks, pedestrians, buildings—was upside-down, the same way images enter our eyes before our brains flip them upright. This

Janet Mendelsohn

simple version, which gives only a fixed view, works just like the one used by early experimenters before a lens and angled mirror were added during or before the 17th century.

Eder redirected our attention to the table in the center of the room and above it, a hole in the ceiling containing the elements of the camera obscura. When she slid the cover off the hole, we could see partway up a long tube. At the top, sunlight streamed through windows in the cupola on the roof, struck a 20-inch diameter mirror, flowed through a 12-inch lens and down 15 feet (its focal length). Where the light landed on the white tabletop, suddenly, in full color, we saw seagulls flying, pigeons strutting on a rooftop, and vehicles moving down the street. It was like watching an HD movie, so real it seemed we could touch the birds. Sure enough, little hands reached out as if to grab them.

Gradually, Eder rotated the rooftop mirror 360 degrees to give us a full-circle panoramic view of the Portland landscape. Remember: We were indoors inside a windowless room. We watched pedestrians on the sidewalk and trucks making deliveries. We tried to look into windows across the street from the museum but failed. The scene gradually moved from the buildings of the Old Port district out to Portland Head Light and followed oil tankers and tugboats crossing Casco Bay. The images were silent and compelling.

Kids often grasp that it's like looking through a submarine's periscope, Eder said. Camera obscuras can project images from as far as the eye can see. The day was slightly overcast yet we could identify Peaks Island across the harbor. In the opposite direction, on a clear day, mountains in New Hampshire are visible.

Everyone was handed index-card-size pieces of white paper, but before our guide could demonstrate what to do, the children figured it out. They "lifted" trucks and people by raising the paper as much as a foot above the table, which created a sort of 3-D illusion. When shown how to place folded sheets in the path of "oncoming cars," we delighted as the vehicles appeared to ride up and over the paper peaks. It was simultaneously silly, immediate, and engrossing.

"One day, a man on the tour saw a pedestrian drop something as he was getting into a car," said Eder. "He ran out of the room. We saw him run across the street, pick up something, and hand it to the person before he drove away. When he came back, he said it was a hat. Recently, a woman was worrying aloud about feeding the parking meter when her five-year-old saw a ticket flapping on the windshield of his mom's car."

People have been fascinated with the effects throughout history. Mo-Ti, a Chinese philosopher during the fifth century B.C., was the first to record seeing an upside-down but otherwise accurate image in a dark enclosure with a pinhole in its side. The following century, during a solar eclipse, Aristotle noticed the crescent shape of the sun where light rays shined through dark foliage onto the dark ground. An Arabian scholar in the 10th century, Alhazen (Abu Ali al-Hasan Ibn al-Haitham), noted that the larger the aperture of the hole, the fuzzier the image that formed. In 1490, Leonardo da Vinci made one of his most important observations when using a camera obscura. He noted that objects reflect rays of light in all directions, which led him to explain how the eye works. Later, camera obscuras were used by Renaissance painters as basic drawing tools; by fortune tellers and magicians who fooled audiences into believing they were looking at the future; and in Victorian England, at seaside resorts where they were popular entertainment, often located in small octagonal buildings near beaches or on piers.

During the Renaissance, artists struggled to make their paintings realistic. Many used the instrument to learn accurate perspective because the projected image is proportionately correct. Our guide demonstrated how, using portable camera versions in a studio or outdoors, they would place a blank sheet or canvas directly on top of the image and trace it. The Dutch painter Johannes Vermeer (1632–1675) was reputed to rely on one in his studio. In the novel named for Vermeer's masterpiece, *Girl with a Pearl Earring*, author Tracy Chevalier imagines a conversation in which the painter explains its purpose to his puzzled young assistant, Griet: "The camera obscura helps me see in a different way, to see more of what is there." Which is why sometimes it's better to look at the landscape from inside a dark room when you could just go outside.

Camera Obscura in the Children's Museum & Theatre of Maine
Portland
www.kitetails.org
207-828-1234

Guided tours of the camera obscura are free with general admission and given sporadically daily. Photographers, astronomy clubs and others get a special admission rate for the camera obscura tour only. Call at least 24 hours ahead for group reservations.

International Cryptozoology Museum
661 Congress Street, Portland
www.cryptozoologymuseum.com
207-518-9496

WHAT YOU'LL FIND HERE: Unconfirmed species of animals as depicted in stories, art, and reported sightings. Large and small replicas including action figures, stuffed animals, and models as big as 8 feet tall. Newspaper accounts and maps of alleged sightings. Plaster casts of footprints. Videos, films and related memorabilia.

CaddyHead closeup

WHY GO: Do Bigfoot, the Loch Ness Monster, and the Abominable Snowman exist? Maybe. Cryptozoology is the study of hidden animals, or "cryptids," for which there is not (yet) proof of existence, or which are presumed to be extinct. Some people take this quite seriously. One of them is Loren Coleman, lecturer and author of numerous books on the subject and director of the museum that contains his personal collection of cryptid materials acquired over a lifetime of active pursuit.

Coleman gives visitors a 15–20-minute tour that includes a short course on the history of what he says is a "very recent science." He says this is the only cryptozoology museum in the world, that the word itself has been used since 1961, and that there is now a boom in interest thanks to documentaries on TV.

Bigfoot, or Sasquatch, is a tall hairy humanoid said to roam the Pacific Northwest United States. Hunters have tried to track the creature for hundreds of years. There are numerous first-person accounts, collected samples of Bigfoot's feces and hair, and a blurry 1967 video of an apparent sighting in the woods. Yeti, also known as Abominable Snowmen, have reportedly been seen many times in the Himalayas, but never captured. Then, of course, there's Scotland's Loch Ness Monster, for which the largest body of so-called evidence exists, including photographs, videos, and sonar soundings made in 1972. In Maine, there have been more than 200 sightings of a sea serpent in the water between Kittery and Casco Bay, and about 30 sightings of Bigfoot in the state's forests, most reported in the mid-1970s. Coleman has a map indicating the Maine Bigfoot locations with pins. Does he believe these creatures are really out there?

"Belief is not part of cryptozoology," said Coleman. "I've been studying this for 50 years. As a cryptozoologist, I accept or deny evidence. About 80 percent of cases I investigate I have to throw out as mistakes. About 1 percent are hoaxes, but that's what the media focus on. There's a lot of compelling evidence. We don't need to believe; we need to be open-minded as scientists."

And maybe there's something to it. The elusive giant squid for centuries was portrayed as a dangerous sea monster in mythology, literature, legends, and popular culture. Occasionally the carcass of a giant squid washed up on the shore, but in December 2006, researchers in waters off Japan filmed a live giant squid in the wild for the first time. Little is known about them to this day but respected scientists are beginning to study these marine animals that reach nearly 60 feet in length and live 650–2,600 feet below the ocean's surface. Similarly, National Geographic says deadly komodo dragons have lived on the Sunda Islands in Indonesia for millions of years, but humans only confirmed their existence 100 years ago.

Fantastical or factual, rumors of cryptids' existence provide fertile material for artists as well as writers and researchers. A 2006 exhibition and symposium at the Bates College Museum of Art, "Cryptozoology: Out of Time Place Scale," explored the convergence of science and art in what was referred to as a desperate quest to have a visual encounter with the unknown.

Coleman considers cryptozoology a "gateway to science" for children and adults. His collection combines artifacts of natural history with toys and popular culture representations, all crammed into an area at the back of the Green Hand Bookshop in downtown Portland.

Time to allow: 20 minutes
Admission: $5 per person (no credit cards)
When it's open: Wed.–Sat., 11 am–6 pm
    Sun., noon–5 pm
Directions: From I-295 South, take Exit 7 to Franklin Street/US-1 A. Merge onto Franklin Art/US-1 Alt. North, then right on Congress Street.

FUN FACT: The hairy, 8-foot-tall "Crookston Bigfoot" model was created by a Wisconsin taxidermy artist named Curtis Christensen and named for the Minnesota town that in 1995, after a series of reputed local sightings, apparently (and briefly) proclaimed itself the "Bigfoot Capital of the World." The title has more recently been claimed by Willow Creek, California.

Maine Historical Society Museum
Brown Library and Wadsworth-Longfellow House
489 Congress Street, Portland
www.mainehistory.org
207-774-1822

WHAT YOU'LL FIND HERE: Maine state history told through autographed letters; archeological artifacts; political memorabilia; paintings, portraits, and photographs; archival films and videos; industrial, domestic, and military objects; furniture; traditional Native American crafts and tools; glass and ceramics; early maps; architectural drawings; broadsides, newspapers, manuscripts, books, ships' logs, and diaries; period clothing; toys and ephemera. Corporate archives of several Maine-based companies. Brown Research Library with extensive genealogy facilities. Wadsworth-Longfellow House, home of Henry Wadsworth Longfellow and his family, with original furnishings and garden. Gift shop.

Online: Maine Memory Network, a vast, statewide collaborative database with close to 20,000 catalogued and annotated historical documents contributed by more than 210 partnering organizations. www.mainememory.net

WHY GO: Two years after Maine separated from Massachusetts and became a state in 1820, the Maine Historical Society was established. Many of the MHS founders were key figures in the new State of Maine, people in positions that enabled them to donate significant items that resonate with us today, such as a letter from Benedict Arnold that was contributed by Aaron Burr. For 175 years, the MHS collections grew but, except for the childhood home of poet Henry Wadsworth Longfellow, everything was largely hidden from public view.

"We had such terrific things and they weren't being seen," said Richard D'Abate, MHS executive director. Fortunately, in the early 1990s, that changed. "We wanted to turn ourselves inside out, show people what we have and get them interested in and proud of their heritage." In 1995, MHS first opened the museum.

You can count on seeing some remarkable pieces in major exhibits that change twice a year, as well as in smaller shows. Selections tend to be strongest on the documentary side—manuscripts, articles, items on paper, maps, and related materials—rather than objects. But there's plenty of historical diversity and a lot that's unexpected. You might find a life mask of Abraham Lincoln made shortly before his death, a carved wooden eagle from a former Portland synagogue, or a silk wedding dress worn in 1912.

In the adjacent Brown Library and of particular interest to the legions of genealogy researchers are vital records, town records, and biographies. Here, too, is access to 250,000 engineering drawings and an equal number of architectural renderings, along with archives of 17 newspapers, including the state's first printed paper, and 5,000 manuscript (hand-drawn) and printed maps. Among 6,000 manuscript holdings from the 15th–21st centuries are the entire personal library of renowned architect John Calvin Stevens (1855–1940), and a rare original copy of the Dunlap broadside of the Declaration of Independence, one of only 25 copies printed July 4, 1776.

As this book goes to print, the Maine Historical Society had just completed a major expansion of the library and was beginning a three-year plan for a new, larger museum.

Wadsworth-Longfellow House, adjacent to the museum and library, was the childhood home of poet Henry Wadsworth Longfellow (1807–1882), whose father was a founder of the historical society where, in 1834, Henry worked as a librarian. The house was built by the poet's maternal grandfather, General Peleg Wadsworth. It was occupied by three generations of the family from 1786 until the death of Henry's younger sister in 1901, when, according to her will, it was bequeathed to the Maine Historical Society as a memorial to her brother and their family, making it one of the earliest house museums in the United States as well as one of the earliest literary shrines. The first fully brick home in Portland, its interior is almost entirely furnished with the family's possessions. Guided tours of the meticulously renovated house and its Colonial Revival-style garden are given May through October. The Historical Society maintains an excellent resource for teachers and anyone interested in Longfellow's life and writings at www.hwlongfellow.org/life_overview.shtml.

Time to allow: 30 minutes for the museum only; longer if touring the Wadsworth-Longfellow House

Admission: Museum
$5 Adults
$4 Seniors and students
$2 Children

Wadsworth-Longfellow House guided tours (includes museum admission)
$8 Adults
$7 Seniors and students
$3 Ages 5–17
Check the website for discount tickets.

When it's open: Museum:
Mon.–Sat., 10 am–5 pm
Sun., noon–5 pm
Brown Research Library:
Tues.– Sat., 10 am–4 pm
Closed Sun., Mon., and some holidays.
Wadsworth-Longfellow House:
Guided tours May–Oct., on the hour
Daily, 10:30 am– 4 pm
Sun., noon–4 pm
Weekend and holiday hours, Nov. and Dec.

Directions: I-295 to exit 7 (Portland/Franklin Street). Take Franklin 0.5 mile and turn right at Congress Street. MHS will be on the right in the center of Portland's arts district.

SPOTLIGHT

Maine Memory Network: Where the Past Meets the Future Online

"We're coming to realize what museums of the future will be," said Richard D'Abate, executive director of the Maine Historical Society. "We feel we're on the cusp of important discoveries."

D'Abate wasn't discussing some abstract idea. He was talking about the Maine Memory Network, a statewide, collaborative, digital museum that MHS launched in 2001. The online collection of more than 20,000 historical photos and documents, contributed by more than 200 participating organizations, is available to anyone, anywhere, at any time. All you need is an Internet connection.

D'Abate's professional life is dedicated to preserving the past. He heads up the third-oldest historical society in the nation, one with an extensive archive of old photographs; handwritten letters, diaries, and logs; crinkling newspapers; aging town hall records; books; artifacts; and maps that are kept in MHS's storerooms, research library, and brick-and-mortar museum. He and his colleagues are keenly aware that not only within their own walls but also at some 223 local historical societies, 288 libraries, five archives, and nearly 80 museums in Maine, treasures are locked away where only a handful of people know they exist. And because many of these organizations are seasonal, their collections are available only a few months a year and then only to those able to travel, often to remote parts of the state. The Maine Memory Network enables organizations to take advantage of the MHS resources to reach a wider audience.

This extraordinary network is used by close to 300,000 unique visitors a year. At your fingertips is an easily searchable, rapidly growing database of catalogued and annotated historical materials, a timeline of events in state history over more than four centuries, and online exhibits that take advantage of the contributors' diverse collections.

A student doing homework in Kittery or Caribou, an author in Oregon researching the Civil War, and a genealogist looking for her family's Swedish ancestors in Maine can search historical collections in Rangeley, Eliot, Portland, and Presque Isle without leaving their desks. They can view clips of early home movies that captured scenes of ship launchings or winter logging. They can read a Western Union telegram sent in January 1880 by General Joshua Chamberlain in which he asked the Brunswick selectmen to keep an eye on his family and home while he and his troops guarded the state capitol during a rebellion, without worrying his wife.

To the surprise of its creators, the Maine Memory Network has also become a catalyst for community projects.

"What we didn't anticipate is that as organizations began to contribute material, people in their towns would begin to take interest, schools would want to use it to further their work, and people would suggest new directions," said D'Abate. "Spontaneous collaborations have been stimulated by this new ability to get local history on the Web."

One of the most successful offshoots is the Maine Community Heritage Project, a partnership between MHS and the Maine State Library, launched in 2008. Initially, teams from 16 communities digitized local historical collections in an intensive effort to create custom-made websites about their towns. Since then, additional teams of students, teachers, and local history experts have continued to add to the project. Their websites reflect their own communities' priorities and personalities. D'Abate said that as the teams start using the technology, it becomes an occasion for people to get together and gain a greater sense of themselves.

Some unexpected historical discoveries have been made. Students and teachers on the Bangor team were startled to find photographs from 1937 of a shootout in their city. The pictures showed two dead bodies lying in the street. Investigating the event, the team learned that both men belonged to the Brady Gang, wanted for multiple murders and robberies in the Midwest. They had come to Bangor to purchase firearms and ammunition in a place where they thought they would be undetected, but the owner of Dakin Sporting Goods Co. on Central Street alerted authorities when he became suspicious about strangers asking about a machine gun. The FBI staked out the store and the shootout took place when the gangsters returned to buy the gun. One of the dead men was Al Brady, whom the FBI had previously declared Public Enemy Number One.

Another unexpected outcome resulted when Skowhegan students became activists. Working on a Maine Community Heritage Project team, they scanned old photographs of houses near their homes. Having read letters between a Civil War soldier and his sweetheart back in Skowhegan, they began to notice that a lot of the hotels and buildings from that era were gone, and they began asking why. When they heard that the Skowhegan Grange hall also might be torn down, they started calling town officials and key managers at the bank that had bought the site and planned to raze the building. The students mobilized to save the Grange.

Any organization collecting historical items related to Maine history is eligible to contribute materials to the network. Participants run the gamut from Maine Forest Service to Camp Winnebago and from the National Archives Northeast Region to the Millinocket Fire Department, Portland Public Library, Lubec Historical Society, and the corporate archives of L. L. Bean and Hannaford Bros. Co. The cost to contribute is zero. The only tools required are a scanner and a computer, which means scanning and uploading items can even be done by one person working from home. Training is provided by Maine Historical Society staff. Especially for small, all-volunteer organizations, the value of this easy way to share collections is impossible to calculate. Posting selected materials might ultimately bring more visitors to their doors but even if it doesn't, pieces of our shared past can now be shared in ways unimagined not long ago.

Maine History Online, a major new interpretive section of the Maine Memory Network, was launched in May 2010. Stories about the state and its people are told through essays, images, anecdotes, and documents provided by the network's contributors. It is organized by themes, time periods, and intellectual discussions called "Thinking About History." Topics are as diverse as how the forests and oceans influenced Maine's development and how unemployed and rural Mainers coped during the Great Depression. One exhibit is about Dexter Cooper, a young engineer in the 1920s whose plan to generate power for Washington County by harnessing the tides gained the support of Franklin D. Roosevelt. His dream of tidal power is still timely but unfulfilled.

Museum of African Culture
13 Brown Street, Portland
www.museumafricanculture.org
207-871-7188

WHAT YOU'LL FIND HERE: Traditional and contemporary art and ceremonial objects from sub-Saharan Africa. Masks, costumes, and tools, some dating back thousands of years. Sculpture, baskets, jewelry, textiles, paintings, and photography. Workshops and performances for children and adults. Film and video presentations. Demonstrations of spiritual and healing ceremonies.

WHY GO: When Chief Oscar O. Mokeme first came to Portland from Nigeria 20 years ago, he found a city steeped in art but lacking in understanding about African art and culture. In New England, he found collections that identified objects only by their country of origin, not their symbolic roles in the lives of those who made them. He was mystified by museum exhibits that lacked the sensory experiences vital to appreciating how traditional African arts communicate ideas and are central to spiritual and healing ceremonies. Since 1976, he has collected thousands of masks, costumes, musical instruments, tools, and other objects. More than 1,500 are in the collection of the museum he founded as an educational gateway to understanding the people and cultures of Africa. It's a small gem with a big mission.

Three distinct sections focus on art from sub-Saharan Africa—a gallery for rotating shows of contemporary works by artists of the African Diaspora; Heritage Hall, filled with ritual and utilitarian objects including bronze and carved figures, textiles, and

Courtesy of Museum of African Culture

photography; and the Mask Room, a permanent exhibition of traditional masks, regalia, and ritual objects from the nine villages of Obaldemili people of southeastern Nigeria.

Several bronze figures are more than 1,000 years old and a few ivory flutes and clay pots are twice that age. One mask dates back to 1600 A.D. Another is Mokeme's initiation mask, given to him when he was 12 years old as part of a rite of passage known as *I'ma-muo*. Mokeme said the mask was made from a tree planted on top of his umbilical cord when he was born and, in the tradition of his ancestors, when his body dies it will be buried under this same "tree of life."

Mokeme, the museum's director and curator, descends from a long line of Igbo royal family practitioner healers. Beyond his traditional priesthood title, you get the sense that his heritage fires his passion for helping others learn about the diversity of ideas and experiences among cultures. Mokeme is a

Oscar Mokeme, director of the Museum of African Culture.

natural teacher. Ask him questions and he will explain how an object is made and its role in agricultural, marriage, or funeral ceremonies, rites of passage, or enforcement of laws and moral codes. A "mask of the month" is selected as the focus of gallery talks and performances that revolve around such themes as renewal; forgiveness; the roles of women, mothers, or grandparents in African culture, men in the spirit world, and ancestors in belief systems; symbols of power; springtime; or letting go.

One recent theme, "The Harvest Spirit of Dryness," featured a dark, forbidding mask with black netting that drapes over the wearer. Beside the mask was an explanation that read, "In African world view, every problem is spirit related; in that sense, the current financial crisis is also a spiritual predicament, that people of the world have let down their guard, followed their ego, and are wandering in search of happiness and materialism. They have committed crimes against nature. But seasons die. There will be turnover and change. With patience and humility, fruitful seasons will return."

According to Mokeme, "Masks are meant to be worn in dance and ceremonies, not kept in cases. Other implements are made for healing and divination. They are meant to be practical. Our purpose here is to make these objects come alive."

On weekends at the museum, as well as in programs at schools, prisons, retirement homes, hospitals, and youth centers, Mokeme and others demonstrate healing and spiritual ceremonies, conduct educational workshops and perform African music, drumming, and dance. The cultural programs often feature local musicians and dancers of African descent. At retirement and nursing homes, Mokeme said the subject often turns to the process of dying or the role of elders in African communities, where they are respected as mentors for youths, advisers to tribal leaders, and loving caregivers for children.

Evening and weekend events welcome families for a variety of programs such as an Ethiopian coffee ceremony or mask-making for children. Adults attending a Cape Verdean wine-tasting might go beyond the beverage to discuss the impact of slavery on the lives of those who remained when their neighbors and loved ones were taken away. Given Maine's centuries-old nautical connections to the world, a Museum of African Culture in Portland suddenly seems logical.

USEFUL INFORMATION The Museum of African Culture is a member of Library Thing, an online source for recommended books on many topics of interest. View the museum's online library at www.librarything.com/catalog/MofAC.

Time to allow: 30 minutes
Admission: $5 per person
   $10 per family for Saturday family workshops.
   $10–$30 for events (includes admission)
When it's open: Tues.–Fri., 10:30 am–4 pm
   Sat., noon– 4 pm
Directions: I-295 to exit 7 (Portland/Franklin Street). At the fourth light, turn right on Congress Street. After 0.4 mile, turn left on Brown Street. In Portland's Arts District, one block west of Monument Square.

Portland Museum of Art
7 Congress Street, Portland
www.portlandmuseum.org
207-775-6148

WHAT YOU'LL FIND HERE The largest art museum in Maine. Focus on art from the 18th century to the present, especially 20th and 21st century art of Maine and the United States; and sculpture, painting, and decorative works by 19th-century European artists. Exhibitions in three buildings: McLellan House (1801), a fully restored Federal-era mansion; The L. D. M. Sweat Memorial Galleries (1911), fully restored Beaux Arts galleries; Charles Shipman Payson Building (1983), designed by I. M. Pei & Partners. Studio classes and workshops for children and adults. Museum Café. Gift shop.

WHY GO: Fine art museums can be intimidating or, like the Portland Museum of Art, they can be light, airy places of inspiration and discovery. PMA exhibitions often have a new take on their subject, and the museum itself feels human-scaled; seamless, despite multiple buildings; and not designed to impress.

Maine's largest and oldest public art museum, founded in 1882, owns more than 17,000 works of fine and decorative art from the 18th century to the present, with the largest collection of European art north of Boston by such masters as Degas, Monet, Picasso, and Renoir. Maine artists past and present are emphasized, including Marsden Hartley, Rockwell Kent, Louise Nevelson, and N. C., Andrew, and Jamie Wyeth, as well as such American masters as George Bellows, Childe Hassam, and Fitz Hugh Lane. The museum's collection of watercolors and drawings by Winslow Homer is one of the largest and best in the art world.

Homer's studio on Prouts Neck, 12 miles south of Portland, was acquired by the museum in 2006. Following a full restoration of the weather-beaten seaside structure, it will be open to the public on a limited basis, probably beginning fall 2012.

Mark Bessire, who joined PMA as director in 2009, said its exhibitions delve into three broad areas. "One of the narratives we tell is about the history of art in Maine. People might know Marsden Hartley and a few other artists but then they look at the roster and are blown away. Even Mainers don't always know how many great artists came here to paint." In the 19th century, when the urban world was evolving and Thoreau was thinking about transcendentalism, urban transformation, and factories, people were taken with his notion of back-to-nature. Maine defined wilderness. Its landscape became iconic. It was the place to go to fish or have camps when the American West was still such wilderness it wasn't even imaginable to most people.

"Artists started coming here, saw this coast, and began a 200-year tradition that in many ways began on Monhegan Island, the pinnacle of the art colony experience," said Bessire. Charles Woodbury founded an art colony in Ogunquit and artists began moving into the lakes region. "At one time, Katahdin was [like] the Grand Canyon. There were Native Americans. It was very spiritual, unspoiled, and Hartley and everyone had to come paint it. The landscape was more rugged and tough and had something they wanted. They were looking back at a time before society seriously encroached on nature." Next to arrive were the modernist painters from New York and Philadelphia around 1900. When photography became a new medium, those artists came to capture these stunning views. And all the while, local artists expanded the Maine artist tradition.

"Suddenly in 1883–1910, you have Winslow Homer, who already had a great career when he came to Prouts Neck. It was the anchor moment," said Bessire. "This place, this Maine, was his vernacular and everything in American painting changed. America was being defined and much of that identity was [captured by] Homer. He didn't just visit, like [Frederic] Church did, he stayed and it perpetuated the myth about Maine. Painters came to see what he saw."

Gradually the flow led to establishment of the Skowhegan School of Painting and Sculpture in 1946, and all that followed. "You have Alex Katz, Lois Dodd, David Driskell, and other artists mostly coming from New York and Boston. Driskell tells a great story of wanting to be an artist in the 1950s, of being well connected, but if you wanted to make it as an artist you needed a place in Maine for the summer, a camp where you could paint. It was part of the identity of being a successful American artist," said Bessire. "David arrived as an African American artist who came to Skowhegan from the south not knowing anything about Maine and he's been here ever since.

"I don't know of any other state with that kind of impact," he said. "Certain cities, yes, New York and L.A., but not an entire state. If you look back over a period in the 1820s and '30s, a lot of painting was going on Down East, on Monhegan, a little bit around Rangeley. Marsden Hartley painted around Kezar Lake. In southern Maine, you have Ogunquit, York, a little bit around Portland. Elsewhere in the country there have been moments and regions, but not an entire state like this."

Courtesy of Portland Museum of Art

N. C. Wyeth (United States, 1882–1945), Dark Harbor Fishermen, *1943, egg tempera on Renaissance panel, 35 x 38 inches. Portland Museum of Art, Maine. Bequest of Elizabeth B. Noyce, 1996.38.63. Photo by Melville D. McLean.*

In addition to the history of art in Maine, the museum spends a great deal of academic energy to tell the narrative of the rise of European modernism. "We're really presenting the art our community collected," Bessire said. A third story is that of taking shows that fill the gaps in the museum's collections because an institution this size—small compared to big art museums in major cities—cannot cover every area in depth. "That might mean an African or Chinese exhibition in which our community can see that we're addressing global issues and they don't always have to go to Boston or New York to see that type of work."

Although this may be the only museum in the country where you can see exhibits in three buildings designed in three architecturally significant styles, it is nevertheless a manageable size for a brief but satisfying visit. An hour meandering through galleries leads to new insights about both familiar and unfamiliar subjects, artists, and individual works. Acknowledging that most people spend only three seconds in front of a work of art, the education department installed three-sided kiosks throughout the museum to help us see deeper into the collections. These "Stop and Look Stations" contain printed gallery guides to read, and have three interactive panels. One panel has an iPod embedded so you can touch the screen and hear recorded messages from art experts, security guards, docents, and others about what the featured piece means to them. Another panel points out details created by the artist; a third has a door that allows you to get up close to something that otherwise is off-limits.

The Portland Museum of Art received its first permanent building as a bequest in 1908. In McLellan House, a three-story, Federal-era mansion, today's visitors learn about architecture and daily life circa 1801. The donor, Margaret Jane Mussey Sweat, also gave funds in memory of her husband, Lorenzo de Medici Sweat. The L. D. M. Sweat Memorial Galleries, designed by John Calvin Stevens and built in 1911, have been restored to their original Beaux Arts grandeur. The new core of the museum and its front entrance is the postmodern Charles Shipman Payson Building, designed by Henry M. Cobb of I. M. Pei & Partners, and built in 1983. In addition to the Winslow Homer Studio, PMA recently purchased two properties on Spring Street, adjacent to the campus, for long-range expansion. One of these, the Charles Quincy Clapp House (1832) is an outstanding example of Greek Revival architecture on the National Register of Historic Places. It housed the Maine College of Art in the museum's early years when, as the Portland Society of Art, the two institutions were one.

USEFUL INFORMATION:
- Wheelchairs are available. Call ahead to reserve.
- The Museum Café is a quiet spot with a seasonal menu for light lunches or coffee and dessert. Hours vary.
- No admission is required to enter the Museum Café and Store.
- Classes and workshops are frequently scheduled for teachers, children, and adults.

Time to allow: 2 hours
Admission: $10 Adults
$8 Seniors (65 and older) and students with ID
$4 Ages 6–17
Free Ages 5 and younger
$8 per person with a group of 15 or more. Contact the museum's education department at least three weeks in advance to schedule a group tour.
Free Fridays from 5–9 pm
When it's open: Tues., Wed., Thurs., Sat., Sun., 10 am–5 pm
Fri., 10 am–9 pm
Mon., 10 am–5 pm, Memorial Day–Columbus Day
Closed New Year's Day, Thanksgiving and Christmas.
Directions: From I-295, Exit 6A to Forest Avenue South. At the first light, bear right onto ME-77 (State Street). Drive through the park and up State Street. At the top of the hill, turn left onto Congress Street. The museum is on the right, after the next light, in the heart of downtown Portland's Arts District.

FUN FACTS:
- Download audio podcasts from the museum's website to learn about artists, exhibits, and programs in advance or on your iPod or mp3 player while in the galleries.
- Jazz Breakfasts are held Sundays in winter and spring from 10:30 am to noon. Concerts are free with museum admission. Breakfast items are available for purchase.

• The Biennial, a juried exhibition held alternate years, showcases new work by living artists connected to the State of Maine.

• Architalx is a lecture series on selected Thursday evenings at the museum featuring prominent architects from cities around the world. See www.architalx.org.

• A "Movies at the Museum" series features artful, foreign, alternative, and classic films. See www.moviesatthemuseum.org.

SPOTLIGHT

Winslow Homer, His Studio, and the Portland Museum of Art

Few artists have shaped our view of Maine more than Winslow Homer (born 1836), who lived and worked here from 1883 until his death in 1910. Homer's paintings, alternately ominous and awestruck, of waves crashing against boulders on the shore and fishermen toiling in small boats, expressed his respect for the ocean's power and the people who made its shores their home. Although his work covered a wider scope, the paintings inspired by the view from his studio on Prouts Neck are those most people associate with the artist. In 2006, Homer's studio was purchased by the Portland Museum of Art, which began an extensive restoration project to preserve for all time the place that was central to the artist's vision and which, in turn, has influenced the way countless artists approach nature. Prouts Neck, in Scarborough, is 12 miles south of the museum.

"The Portland Museum of Art exists, in many ways, because of Winslow Homer," said PMA director Mark Bessire. The connection perhaps began when Homer's work was exhibited at the museum during his lifetime. Homer was a successful freelance illustrator in Boston from 1857–1875, selling drawings for engravings that appeared in popular magazines of the day. As a Civil War correspondent, his increasingly vivid images, such as A Sharpshooter on Picket Duty, helped readers envision scenes from the battlefield.

Following the war, which took him across the American landscape, Winslow Homer abandoned illustration in 1875 to concentrate on painting en plein air, working outdoors in the manner of European painters. He sought isolated landscapes in Massachusetts, the Hudson River Valley, and England, where he lived in a fishing village in 1881. When his brother Arthur honeymooned on Prouts Neck in 1875, Winslow came to Maine for the first time. Eight years later, their older brother, Charles, purchased land on the rocky spit to build a summer compound for the family. They called it "the Ark," and when Winslow returned from his travels abroad, he moved to the property. Although the family offered to build him a room at the rear of the house in which to paint, he asked that the carriage house behind the Ark be converted to a studio. It was moved closer to the shore, where he could have the solitude he desired, and adapted to his needs, adding a viewing porch that wrapped around the second floor on the ocean side.

From his studio, Homer studied the sea's forces and the struggles inherit in living and working at the mercy of nature. He continued to travel south in the winter and to sporting camps in the Adirondacks and Canada, but Maine became his home.

A century later, in 1976, Charles Shipman Payson, a philanthropist and summer resident of Maine, gave the museum 17 works by Homer, including four oil paintings and 13 watercolors, plus $8 million to build an addition to house the collection. PMA's Homer collection includes his first oil painting, *The Sharpshooter,* and other works that helped shape an image of the growing nation as one containing small towns, quiet lakes for fishing and canoeing, and places to experience tranquility, even as society was becoming industrialized.

Courtesy of Portland Museum of Art

Winslow Homer (United States, 1836–1910), Sharpshooter, *1863, oil on canvas, 12¼ x 16½ inches. Portland Museum of Art, Maine. Gift of Barbro and Bernard Osher, 3.1993.3.*

In 1991, Peggy and Harold Osher donated 445 wood engravings by Homer to the museum. The illustrations form a nearly complete record of his career as a commercial artist. An online gallery on the museum's website presents a searchable and zoomable way to access more than 250 of the engravings, many of which had never previously been seen by the public because of the light-sensitive, fragile nature of works on paper. Most of the Homer graphics appeared in *Harper's Weekly,* a popular news magazine in the mid-1800s.

Like any wooden building on the coast, Homer's studio endured the ravages of time and weather. The museum has completely rebuilt and reinforced the structure to re-create the views and light that Homer enjoyed. Beginning in fall of 2012, when the restoration is completed, the public will be able to visit Homer's studio, but only at certain times of the year and through tours and programs offered by the Portland museum. The restrictions help maintain the integrity of experience, which would be altered by crowds of visitors, said Bessire, and because public access to the Prouts Neck community is limited.

Portland Museum of Art

www.portlandmuseum.org

207-775-6148

Among collections elsewhere in Maine that own work by Winslow Homer are the Saco Museum and most members of The Maine Art Museum Trail.

www.maineartmuseums.org

Portland Observatory
138 Congress Street, Portland
www.portlandlandmarks.org
207-774-5561
(Greater Portland Landmarks)

WHAT YOU'LL FIND HERE: Seven-story signal tower overlooking the City of Portland and Casco Bay. Guided walking tours of exhibits on the construction and history of the observatory and Portland. Harbor views from the top. Gift shop.

WHY GO: Today Portland Observatory on Munjoy Hill overlooks a modern urban landscape, but in 1807, when Captain Lemuel Moody (1768-1846) designed and built his wooden octagonal tower, it stood in a cow pasture. Never a lighthouse, as is often assumed, the observatory was always a privately owned signal tower, from the top of which you still get great views of Mount Washington, Back Cove, and Casco Bay, especially at sunset. In Moody's time, Portland was a city of 6,000 people that already had a busy harbor. Moody was a former sea captain turned businessman. In an era before telephone or telegraph, he sold shares in his new venture to 43 investors who appreciated the practical and marketable service he devised.

Janet Mendelsohn

From his vantage point atop the tower, using a powerful telescope, Moody was able to identify incoming vessels by name as far as 30 miles out, long before they entered the shipping channel at Spring Point Ledge. Merchants who subscribed to his service were alerted via signal flags so they could arrange for stevedores to unload cargo at the dock.

Moody was a mariner, not trained as an architect, so he applied what he knew of boats to building the structure. He set the 65-foot wooden tower on the ground, not in it, 141 feet above mean low water. His work crew filled the base with 122 tons of boulders, like ballast on a ship, and built an open three-foot deck surrounding the tower's top with an enclosed lantern 8 feet in diameter. Moody also developed a system to record weather for mariners and the local newspaper. He was the signalman for 40 years; his son handled the job for 30. Signal operations ceased in 1923.

In 1936, Portland Observatory was listed in the Historic American Buildings Survey. The Moody family gave the building to the city in 1937 and two years later, during the Great Depression, the tower was restored as a WPA project under President

Franklin D. Roosevelt. Portland Observatory has earned status on the National Register of Historic Places (1972), National Historic Landmarks (2006), and National Civil Engineering Landmarks (2006).

Maritime signal towers were once common along the coast. Now operated by Greater Portland Landmarks as a museum, Portland Observatory is believed to be the last maritime signal tower in the United States.

USEFUL INFORMATION:

• The seven-story tower is only handicapped accessible by lift to the first level. There are 103 steps up a winding stairway from the base to the lantern deck.

• Visitors are not permitted above the entrance level except on guided tours.

Time to allow: 45 minutes (guided tour)

Admission: $8 Adults
   $5 Ages 6–16
   Free Ages 5 and younger
   Portland residents:
   $5 Adults
   $2 Ages 6–16

When it's open: Memorial Day to Columbus Day
   Daily, 10 am–5 pm

Directions: From I-295, Exit 7 (Franklin Arterial), take Franklin to Congress Street and turn left (east). The Observatory is on the right, at the crest of Munjoy Hill.

FUN FACT: Men hired to build the Observatory were paid $2 per day; boys were paid 50 cents per day.

University of New England Art Gallery
University of New England
716 Stevens Avenue, Portland
www.une.edu/artgallery
207-221-4499

WHAT YOU'LL FIND HERE: Contemporary fine art photography, works by Maine artists, international themes. Annual Sculpture Garden Invitational, June–October. Small, diverse permanent collection including Impressionist oil paintings, watercolors, photography, sculpture, and works on paper.

WHY GO: This small museum has had its ups and downs since it was founded in 1977 to house a private collection of Impressionist masterpieces. Nearly all those great works are now elsewhere, but their spirit remains in the building itself. Tucked at the back of the University of New England's Portland campus, it is rightly referred to as "the little jewel" or "the cube," both of which describe the building's architectural design. Natural light floods the galleries from skylights at the peak and through tall windows on the

Janet Mendelsohn

Bloom and Blossom *sculpture by Jac Oulette, a Maine College of Art professor, at the entrance of the University of New England Gallery of Art.*

second and third floors. Even on a rainy day, the light has an unusual, almost magical, ability to flatter each piece on the walls. Not that the works need boosting.

The permanent collection now is small, about 500 works, but includes paintings by Maurice Utrillo and Alexander Bower, bronze plaques by William Zorach, sculpture by Louise Nevelson, and works on paper by Hans Hofmann, Paul Klee, Kaethe Kollwitz, Leonardo Lasansky, Leo Meissner, and James McNeill Whistler. Its strength is photography, by both contemporary artists in Maine and such masters as Berenice Abbott, Henri Cartier-Bresson, and Eugene Atget. Exhibitions change five times a year. An annual sculpture garden runs from June through October.

The museum's fluctuations are linked to a variety of college mergers and changes in ownership, including the closing of its first host, Westbrook Junior College, in 1991. The art gallery (a freestanding museum) reopened in 1998 with Anne Zill at its helm. "Institutional memory is still on index cards because the museum closed in an era pre-computers," said Zill. Catch-up is underway. Now that it is part of the University of New England, the focus is on making the museum more relevant to academic departments and exhibition subjects of interest to the wider community. "People now realize that art and learning are cross-disciplinary," she said. When students in UNE's Westbrook College of Health Professions visited the galleries, for example, they realized there is symmetry in art just as there is in the human body.

Time to allow: 30 minutes
Admission: Free
When it's open: Wed., Fri., Sat., Sun: 1–4 pm
 Thurs., 1–7 pm
 or by appointment
Directions: From I-95, take Exit 48 (Westbrook). After the tollbooth, turn left at the traffic light onto Riverside Drive and follow that about 0.25 mile to the intersection with Brighton Avenue (Route 25). Turn left onto Brighton Avenue, go about 1.75 miles and turn left onto Stevens Avenue (Route 9). After three traffic lights, the campus is on the left. The museum is a free-standing building behind the main campus.

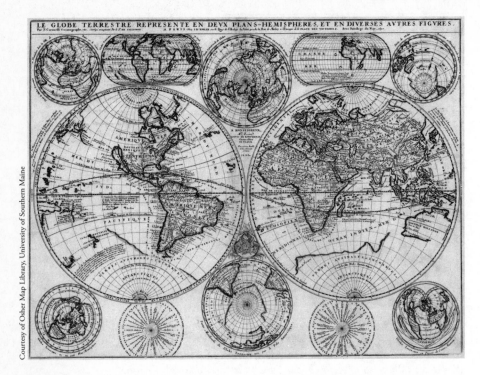

Courtesy of Osher Map Library, University of Southern Maine

Le Globe Terrestre Represente en deux Plans-Hamispheres, et en Diverses Autres Figures Coronelli, *V.M. and Jean Nicolas de Tillemon, 1690.*

Osher Map Library
University of Southern Maine
16 Bedford Street, Portland
www.usm.maine.edu/maps
207-780-4850

WHAT YOU'LL FIND HERE: Rare and antique maps and globes from 1475 to the present. Research library.

WHY GO: Antique maps aren't only about routes and terrain. A roomful of second graders made that discovery while on a field trip to the Osher Map Library, and it began with maps in a children's book, drawn with crayon and projected onto an overhead screen. As their teacher turned the book's pages, an imaginary mapmaker named Sarah crisscrossed her town and the children followed her route, shouting out the stops. They searched for objects hidden in Sarah's room and named relatives on her family tree. These junior explorers quickly understood that if you know how to read between the lines, maps can tell us about the people who made them and what was happening at the time.

The Osher Map Library (OML) and Smith Center for Cartographic Education at the University of Southern Maine reopened in October 2009 after a two-year closing for expansion. Two new public spaces—a contemporary gallery and a multipurpose room—are part of the $12.3 million, three-story renovation that quadrupled the library's size, from 4,500 to 19,500 square feet, adding advanced security systems and a 7,500-square-foot climate-controlled vault. On the building's façade are 104 aluminum panels etched with a 156-by-26-foot Dymaxion map, possibly the largest exterior map installation in the world. The map was invented by the futurist Buckminster Fuller in 1946 to depict the globe with minimal distortion and make a political statement about the interconnectedness of continents and peoples.

The gallery is open to the public only three afternoons a week. There are no docents to guide you. But anyone with a particular interest can make a specific request. If time permits, a staff member will bring selected maps down from the vault.

"Maps are universal documents," said Harold Osher, M.D., the retired cardiologist from Portland whose extraordinary map collection helped establish the library. "Maps encompass not just geography but also history, art, superstition, religion, dogma, warfare, any type of human activity, and furthermore they do it in a graphic fashion. Maps are worth a hundred thousand words. Instead of reading about an event written 100 years later, you can often see it through the eyes of a contemporary who was there or at least got a current account, not filtered by time."

The library has earned a national reputation for its commitment to the use of maps in kindergarten through college education. Workshops and online resources are offered for educators in addition to scholarly conferences and public lectures and panel discussions. Their exhibits of facsimile maps travel around New England, and the website has activities for fourth–tenth graders, as well as a wealth of information for adult map enthusiasts.

Matthew Edney, faculty scholar in residence since 1995, said the library's priorities for acquiring and preserving old maps form concentric circles, beginning with Maine, widening to New England, and then America. While most rare map libraries specialize, OML's education mission means they look for examples of different genres, periods, and methods of production.

Seen up close, in person, rare maps have depth and beauty that doesn't come across any other way. Do some homework before visiting and their history takes on new

Copernian Armillary Sphere, Charles Francois Delamarche, 1790.

meaning. The library's website has room to tell much more about maps in the current exhibit than fits on the gallery walls. Catalogue descriptions go back to the museum's first exhibit in 1996, "Jerusalem 3000: Three Millennia of History." Another featured American road maps printed by oil companies since the early 1900s, which seemed out of place until Yolanda Theunissen, curator and director of the Smith Center, pointed out that in a few years we'll all use global positioning systems and printed road maps will be things of the past.

An artistic and historical gem is "The Columbus Letter," which OML has made available online in the original Latin and English translation. One of Dr. Osher's most prized acquisitions, the letter is Christopher Columbus's account to Queen Isabella of his discoveries in America. Columbus wrote the letter during his return trip in 1493. It was soon printed in several versions, creating excitement throughout Europe. This rare edition, published in Basel in 1494, has woodcut illustrations that were the first stylized pictorial maps showing Columbus's ship in the West Indies, making it the first printed map of any part of the New World.

"Maps are not just geographic pictures, said Osher. "They're original historical documents, primary sources, encompassing all areas of human knowledge, culture, and civilization."

The library got its start in 1986 when Eleanor Houston Smith, in memory of her husband, Lawrence M. C. Smith, gave the University of Southern Maine a collection of antique globes, maps, and atlases she and her husband had acquired over three decades. Three years later, Osher and his wife, Peggy, donated their own large and diverse collection. Combined, with little overlap, the gifts totaled 20,000 maps printed before 1900. Some are separate sheets, others are in bound volumes. There also are explorers' narratives, early travelers' accounts, and books on navigation, history, geography, and astronomy. Many predate 1600. Since then, several smaller but significant collections donated by others have brought the total to 300,000 maps, and added surveying equipment.

The Smith Globe Collection includes more than 62 antique terrestrial and celestial globes. Altogether, the library has more than 100 antique globes by Dutch, French, German, English, Italian, and American cartographers, one of the most comprehensive globe collections in New England. Globes are complex scientific instruments that can be damaged by exposure to light, dust, smoke, heat, and abrasion, which is why they are displayed on glass shelves and protected by light-filtering screens. A staff member will be happy to raise the screens for you. The students on their class field trip seemed especially curious about a gentleman's pocket globe, only 3 inches in diameter, with a spherical leather case, and a perfume-bottle globe from the 1892 World's Fair. Another is a tabletop globe (circa 1800) painted with routes taken by Captain James Cook and other explorers, indicating what was known at that time about what the adventurers found while circumnavigating the planet.

Most of another collection was donated by Peter M. Enggass, professor emeritus of geography at Mount Holyoke College, in 1996. The Enggass Collection now comprises more than 100 sheet maps of the Iberian Peninsula and Spain, dating from 1486–1829.

A recent Osher Map Library exhibition, "American Treasures," is among those online. Its centerpiece is *Nova Totius Americae Tabula* (New Map of all America), made by the Dutch cartographer Frederick de Wit in 1672. The de Wit map, one of seven known to exist and one of only two in the United States, measures 60 inches by 77 inches, with an ornate banner and a border of Latin, Dutch, French, and English textual explanations. Engravings depict Dutch colonies in America, Spanish and Portuguese settlements in Central and South America, animals, allegorical figures, and Dutch merchants negotiating with Native Americans.

Edney noted that while the geography of Central and South America the de Wit map presents is fairly accurate, it also reflects misconceptions about North America that were believed to be true when the map was made: California is a large island and the northwest territories are blank. In contrast, other maps in the show were precise, including several pen and ink land surveys done in 1850 by Henry David Thoreau. Still others demonstrate attention to detail and beautiful penmanship by 11- and 12-year-old students who painted them with ink and watercolors in 1814–1816.

Edney used an ethnographic map in an 1885 atlas of Mexico to illustrate what is revealed by "reading between the lines." In the late 19th century, he said, codification of different groups and professions was part of an attempt to understand indigenous peoples. "Almost all of the vignettes [around the map's border] are part of a pictorial tradition of defining not only pure-blood Indians but also degrees of African, Indian, and white intermarriage. Regions are defined not by physical entities but by the peoples that dominate that place. It's interesting to see that indigenous peoples are shown in terms of their physical labor, except for the white race, at the top left, which is shown at leisure." From a historical point of view, the illustrations show the ways hierarchies were encoded.

USEFUL INFORMATION:

• Tours of the gallery are self-guided, but if you have a special interest that's not part of a current exhibition, make a specific request, preferably in advance. If time permits, a staff member will bring the selected map from the vault.

• Researchers are required to register for access to primary documents of the Osher Map Library and Smith Center for Cartographic Education. Scholars and the general public may examine primary documents in the consultation room.

• The University of Maine System library catalogue, URSUS, includes catalogued reference and other materials in the OML and Smith collections at http://ursus.maine.edu.

Time to allow: 45 minutes
Admission: Free
When it's open: Tues., Wed., Thurs., 1–4 pm
Closed when the USM Glickman Family Library is closed.
Directions: From I-95/Maine Turnpike, Exit 44, to I-295 to Exit 6B (US-302/ME-100/Forest Avenue). Turn right, go 0.2 mile and make a U-turn at Preble Street, and make the first right onto Bedford Street. On the Portland campus of the University of Southern Maine, the Glickman Family and Osher Map libraries will be the first building on your left. Continue to just past the Abromson Center (on your left, with the skywalk that connects to the other side of campus) and turn left into the parking garage.

PEAKS ISLAND

5TH MAINE REGIMENT MEMORIAL HALL.

Fifth Maine Regiment Museum
45 Seashore Avenue
Peaks Island, Casco Bay
www.fifthmainemuseum.org
207-766-3330

WHAT YOU'LL FIND HERE: Rustic reunion hall on the National Register of Historic Places. Civil War memorabilia related to Maine regiments. Peaks Island history including World War II and Peaks Island Military Reservation. Educational and cultural programs for children and adults. Civil War workshops for teachers. Gift shop.

WHY GO. When the first shots of the Civil War were fired in early 1861, thousands of men from Maine's cities, towns, farms, and coastal villages answered newly inaugurated President Abraham Lincoln's call to arms. Among the patriotic enlistees were 1,046 men from central and southern Maine who formed the Fifth Regiment Maine Volunteer Infantry, among the first to muster in. Later, another 500 joined them. More than 300 of the men came from areas around Portland ("the Forest City"), forming three of the 10 companies in the Fifth Maine and earning them the nickname "The Forest City Regiment." In July 1861, they traveled by train from Portland to Washington, where they were assigned to the Army of the Potomac and fought in 22 battles during the War Between the States, from the first Battle of Bull

Fifth Maine Regiment Museum Collection Peaks Island, Maine

General Aaron Daggett, the last Fifth Maine veteran to pass away.

Run (Manassas) to Petersburg. When they mustered out in July 1864, only 193 men remained in the Fifth Maine. Like thousands of soldiers on both sides, most had died of disease or been killed in battle; a few had transferred to other regiments.

The Fifth Maine is credited with capturing 1,200 Confederate soldiers, including several officers, and six Confederate battle flags, more than all other Maine regiments combined. When the Civil War ended in 1865, the regiment's survivors returned home to pick up their lives. But as civilians, they remained in close contact. As a group, they helped provide for the regiment's widows and orphans. And every summer the veterans and their families held a weekend reunion to enjoy friendships and remember those who died. They camped on Peaks Island, an easy boat ride from Portland, where Casco Bay breezes brought welcome respite from the heat. During the 1880s, Peaks was being developed as a major summer resort; there was plenty to do amid idyllic island views.

"By the 1880s, the ladies of the regiment (wives, mothers, daughters, and sisters) grew tired of camping out," said Kim MacIsaac, director and curator. "One of the ladies, Mrs. Anna Goodwin, purchased a small piece of land that was a very small portion of a large sheep pasture and donated it to the Fifth Maine Regiment Memorial Society. The ladies then persuaded the veterans to build a real building where they could be sheltered from the elements, sleep in beds, and cook in a real kitchen." The cottage built in 1888 as the regiment's headquarters and memorial hall had 15 sleeping rooms, plenty of indoor space for socializing, and wide verandas for dining outdoors. It was designed in Queen Anne style by a Portland firm, Fassett and Thompson, and built mostly by the veterans themselves.

In addition to the annual reunion, the families took turns vacationing here through the summer, a tradition that continued until 1949. By then, the building had deteriorated badly and the few descendants interested in returning couldn't afford to repair it.

In the 1950s, the cottage was on the verge of being demolished. Thanks to local efforts, it was saved and restored. Today the building is a seasonal social, cultural, and education center for Peaks Island residents in addition to serving as the Fifth Maine Civil War and local history museum. From late May through September, islanders and visitors enjoy concerts and lectures, art and crafts workshops, book signings, community breakfasts and suppers. One-day or one-week summer camps for children and young teens involve such activities as climbing aboard a schooner to sketch the rigging or joining Civil War–era activities on the home front.

The museum focuses on what led up to and followed the Civil War. The first floor features a large living room surrounded by memorial windows made of handblown glass. The window panes, clear or tinted amber, burgundy, or deep blue, bear the names of the Regiment's veterans, some with their rank. The rights to embed veterans' names or initials in the panes were a fundraiser for the hall when it was first built. Civil War uniforms, rifles, swords, chewing tobacco, bibles, documents, and 1890s portraits of the veterans are displayed in somber tribute, as are cases filled with battlefield pickups—hardtack, a bugle, bayonets, and rusty canteens, dented and shot with holes—and reunion souvenirs that were popular in the 1870s, right after the war, beginning at Gettysburg where locals gave battlefield tours. Overhead are replicas of several of the captured Confederate flags. In 1927, a flag exchange to heal the wounds of war was held in Washington, D.C., and the originals were returned to southern troops, said MacIsaac.

Towns were given recruitment quotas but often didn't want to send their most able-bodied men. Among the recruiting signs are advertisements seeking men willing to substitute for those who could pay them to take their place, a legal practice. "Usually for $300 you could find someone to go for you, but it created problems," said MacIsaac. "Many would go for basic training and then desert, sometimes repeating the transaction elsewhere."

A centerpiece of the collection is the large handmade silk regimental flag sewn in 1861 for the Fifth Maine by ladies in Portland. Flags were the primary means of communication, noted MacIsaac. They had to be big because on the officers' orders, the signal man used the flag to lead the men into battle. Silk was used for Union flags because cotton was unavailable in the north. The regimental flag shares a gallery with other prized possessions. Among them is the uniform of Adjutant George W. Bicknell, who found and wore a chaplain's cap bearing a red cross although he was not a chaplain. Through the cap is a hole from the bullet that wounded Bicknell at Fredericksburg, Virginia, in May 1863. "His great-grandson told me that after the war, Bicknell became a minister," said MacIsaac.

In one corner is a tribute to General Aaron Daggett from Greene, Maine, who died in 1938 at the age of 101. "He was the last Fifth Maine veteran to pass away and served in the Army for forty years," said MacIsaac, whose father knew the general. Daggett led the 25th Colored Regiment in Cuba. His descendants donated his dress sword, photos, and sharpshooter certificates. Daggett authored *America in the China Relief Expedition*, a classic history about that conflict.

Upstairs, several former "sleeping rooms" and hallways have exhibits honoring local men and women who served in the military as well as Peaks Island's pioneering families, many of whose descendants still live here. Of particular interest is a roomful of photographs and memorabilia from the Peaks Island Military Reservation in World War II, and another exhibit on the era 1880–1920, when Peaks flourished as a resort community with 16 hotels, an amusement park, and three summer theaters headlining nationally known actors.

USEFUL INFORMATION:

• Exhibits on the second floor are not handicapped accessible.

• Throughout Maine, the sesquicentennial of the Civil War is being remembered by more than 20 museums and historical societies. Exhibitions, battle reenactments, symposia, special events, and educational programs began in 2010 and culminate during the summer of 2013, the 150th anniversary of the battle at Gettysburg. Kim MacIsaaac, director of the Fifth Maine museum, is leading the commemoration, which is called the 2013 Maine Civil War Trail.

• Only three regimental halls remain in Maine. One of them is a stone's throw from here. The Eighth Maine Regiment Memorial Hall, at 13 Eighth Maine Avenue, is the summer home of descendants of that regiment, and a living history museum and lodge. The lodge operates communally. Guests cook their own meals and share chores like washing the dishes by hand and setting the tables, just as the veterans and their families did when the lodge was built in 1891. For information: Eighth Maine Regiment Memorial Association, Inc., 207-766-5086, or EighthMaineHost@EighthMaine.com.

Time to allow: 15–30 minutes
Admission: Free
When it's open: Memorial Day–July 1
  Sat. and Sun., 11 am–4 pm
  July–Labor Day
  Mon.–Fri., noon–4 pm; Sat.–Sun., 11 am–4 pm
  Labor Day–Columbus Day
  Sat.–Sun., 11 am–4 pm
  or by appointment
Directions: Peaks Island is a neighborhood of Portland and the closest island in Casco Bay. Take the Peaks Island ferry from the Casco Bay Lines terminal at Commercial and Franklin streets. (Parking garage on site.) There is no need to bring your car to the island. The Fifth Maine is a five-minute walk or three-minute bike ride from the wharf. On Peaks, walk up the hill from the wharf. Turn right onto Island Avenue. Take the third right onto Whitehead Street. The museum is a short distance ahead, on the right.

Umbrella Cover Museum
62-B Island Avenue
Peaks Island
www.umbrellacovermuseum.org
207-766-4496

WHAT YOU'LL FIND HERE: Covers that protect new umbrellas, and their stories. Gift shop.

WHY GO: Here's an odd one—but think about it. Nancy 3. Hoffman says her collection of more than 750 umbrella covers celebrates the mundane in everyday life. Yes, we're talking about those sleeves or tubes that cover a new umbrella, the nylon, fabric, or plastic cases (also called sheaths or pockets) most of us toss into the back of the closet and forget. "The world's first and only Umbrella Cover Museum" (and who can doubt it?) began on Hoffman's kitchen wall with seven specimens she found while

Janet Mendelsohn

A collection of umbrella covers in fabrics created by fashion designers.

cleaning house in 1996. She realized it was serious when she swiped just a cover, not the umbrella, from a dime store. When the collection grew too large to display at home, she moved it to this small shop just a five-minute walk from the town dock on Peaks Island, a Portland community in Casco Bay.

"It's about appreciating ordinary objects and sometimes ordinary lives," said Hoffman. "People send me their covers from all over the place. Many of them come with stories the donors tell that link to their own lives, their travels or observations. This gives everyone a chance to contribute to a museum."

National Public Radio, the Weather Channel, and the British press have featured the odd assemblage. A family in the Netherlands read about it and donated photographs and items related to their family's generations-old umbrella factory.

Stories sent with the covers are funny, poignant, or simply factual. One cover was found beside the Berlin Wall, another traveled from Nepal on a journey over four continents, although the umbrella itself was lost along the way. Hoffman posts the stories beside the covers in ever-changing groupings. In displays not unlike a school project on poster board, you might see an exhibit of several in fabrics by famous designers, or plaids, floral prints, or unusual materials. "Royal covers" includes one from the Buckingham Palace souvenir shop; its story is written from the perspective of the umbrella cover which claimed to be ripped from its happy home in (rainy) England, stuffed in a suitcase, and forced to sit through a James Joyce symposium. The "sexy" collection includes examples made of black mesh, transparent plastic, or bold red nylon.

Artist-designed covers are sculptural, not functional, and fashioned by admirers of the collection. They're made of porcelain, wood, recycled grocery bags, or braided gum wrappers. Visiting craftsmen have contributed pieces created from pony beads and pipe cleaners, or crocheted and decorated with buttons. One is shaped from x-ray film.

The smallest cover is for a Barbie doll's umbrella; the largest enclosed a patio umbrella. With the help of "interns," ages four and up, each cover is measured and tagged by donor, place of origin, and arrival date. "It teaches my helpers to take care of things, about being neat and collecting," she said.

Hoffman, who conducts an ongoing, informal "curiosity research project," loves observing people's reactions. "It's delightful to me to guide people through. If they're not already engaged in the subject, and most are not, I have to be a psychologist to get them to stay and ask questions. Some people stick their heads in for three seconds and say, 'Oh, it's really just umbrella covers' and leave before I can help them see that it's more." About 17 percent of the people who come in say they actually use their umbrella covers.

A professional musician, Hoffman ends most tours by accompanying herself on the accordion while singing the museum's theme song, "Let a Smile Be Your Umbrella."

USEFUL INFORMATION: Before you come, call or e-mail the director at 3nancy3@gmail.com to check when the museum will be open.

Time to allow: 15 minutes
Admission: Free
When it's open: Summer only
Hours vary but mostly 10 am–1 pm and 2–5 pm
Directions: From Portland, take the Casco Bay Ferry to Peaks Island, a 20-minute trip. From the Peaks dock, walk straight ahead to Island Avenue, turn left and the museum is on the left, several buildings down.

FUN FACT: Nancy 3. Hoffman sings and plays the accordion in a rousing rendition of the museum's theme song on YouTube at www.youtube.com /watch?v=GLciKBWjHvE.

CHAPTER 3

MIDCOAST

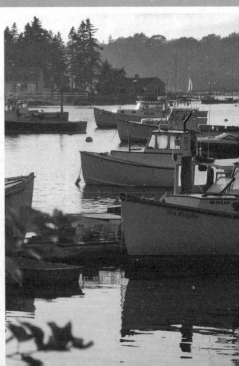

Bowdoin College Museum of Art
Bowdoin College campus, Brunswick
www.bowdoin.edu/art-museum
207-725-3275

WHAT YOU'LL FIND HERE: Paintings, sculpture, antiquities, prints, drawings, photographs, and other objects of American, European, ancient, non-Western, modern, and contemporary art. Among the oldest college art museums in the United States. Neoclassical building designed by McKim, Mead and White with contemporary additions. Five 9th-century stone panel Assyrian reliefs, specially lit at night and visible from the street. Gift shop.

WHY GO: First and foremost, this is a teaching collection intended to augment current academic programs at Bowdoin College, but its breadth and depth is a pleasure for students and non-students alike. Exhibits blend selections from a permanent collection of more than 15,000 works with loaned art from other institutions in diverse and enlightening learning experiences. Signage tends to present a foundation for further study, more detailed than the usual explanation of themes and specific works.

Bowdoin College Museum of Art, Brunswick, Maine, Bequest of the Honorable James Bowdoin III

Gilbert Stuart, Portrait of Thomas Jefferson. *ca. 1805–1807. Oil on canvas. 48 1/2 in. x 39 7/8 in. (123.19 cm x 101.28 cm).*

Especially notable are Bowdoin's ancient Greek and Roman vases and sculpture, Assyrian reliefs, the earliest collection of Old Master drawings in the United States, and American paintings, including portraits by Gilbert Stuart and John Singleton Copley. Other strengths are 15th- through 21st-century prints; photography by Robert Mapplethorpe, Man Ray, Eugene Atget, and Dorothea Lange; paintings by Marsden Hartley, Winslow Homer, Andrew Wyeth, Rockwell Kent, Alex Katz, and other Maine artists; and European sculpture, paintings, and decorative arts including works by Magritte, Corot, and Picasso.

Architecturally, the museum presents an interesting and, to my mind, successful approach to incorporating old and new while addressing the needs of the surrounding community. The building was closed for two years for extensive restoration and renovations. It reopened in 2007 with a new front entrance that helped improve climate control and use of space within the original neoclassical building by architect Charles Follen McKim. At risk was the future of the wide front steps, guarded by stone lions, that is the traditional site of Bowdoin College commencement ceremonies. Instead, a separate, freestanding, dark glass pavilion was erected to one side of the building. Visitors now enter the museum by going down into the lower level and working their way up. The rear façade of the building had been a forbidding brick wall. Now it is a glass-enclosed gallery showcasing the museum's signature collection of five substantial Assyrian reliefs, stone panels carved between 875 and 860 B.C. in what is now Iraq. At night, they are lit and visible from the street, in a sense becoming public art.

Linger to absorb details of the stone carvings. In *Relief of Winged Spirit* or *Apkallu Awaiting Ashurnasirpal II*, the king, wearing symbols of his royal status while being anointed by a protective spirit, is mutilated. His right hand is missing; his eyes, nose, and ears deliberately chiseled off; his beard, toes, and Achilles tendon chipped away. Perhaps most tellingly, the symbol of the king's power, his bow, is broken in half. The explanation provided points to these crude cuts and an obviously hastily added figure painted into the scene as if approaching the king, suggesting that we are looking at acts of revenge by late 7th-century Medes and Babylonians.

Galleries adjacent to the reliefs contain pottery, marble sculpture, and jewelry representing ancient Egyptian, Cypriot, Phoenician, Greek, and Roman cultures and their dependence on the sea.

USEFUL INFORMATION: Guided tours are available by appointment.

Time to allow: 1 hour
Admission: Free
When it's open: Tues.–Sat., 10 am–5 pm
  Thurs., 10 am–8:30 pm
  Sun., 1–5 pm
  Closed Mon. and national holidays.
Directions: From I-295, Exit 28 (Topsham-Brunswick) follow US Route 1 North/Pleasant Street to the light at Maine Street and turn right. Continue on Maine Street for 0.5 mile (passing the former Naval Air Station) to the Bowdoin College campus at the intersection of Maine Street and Bath Road. The art museum is on the quad in the middle of the campus.

FUN FACT: Overhead in the rotunda on the second floor are four beautiful murals commissioned when the museum opened in 1893. Each is an oil on canvas by an American painter depicting one of the great cities of Europe: *Florence* by Abbott Thayer, *Rome* by Elihu Vedder, *Venice* by Kenyon Cox, and *Athens* by John LaFarge.

Peary-MacMillan Arctic Museum
Hubbard Hall, Bowdoin College
Brunswick
http://academic.bowdoin.edu/arcticmuseum
207-725-3416

WHAT YOU'LL FIND HERE Exploration, history, and culture of the Arctic regions with an emphasis on Labrador, Greenland, Baffin Island, and Alaska. Equipment and photographs of Admiral Robert Peary's 1908-09 expedition to the North Pole. Gift shop.

WHY GO One of the few U.S. museums devoted to the Arctic region, the Peary-MacMillan was founded with collections from explorers Donald MacMillan and the more widely known Robert E. Peary. Although addressed by some large national institutions—the Smithsonian and New York's American Museum of Natural History, among them—encounters with the Arctic seem more personal and real on Bowdoin's campus, largely because both men were Bowdoin alumni and Arctic studies have received serious academic attention here both before and since the two men's student days.

Major exhibitions run for one year on such themes as Canadian Inuit Art (through October 30, 2011), which explores how Inuit artists express deeply held ideas about personal and community identity. An earlier show celebrated the centennial of Peary's 1908–09 expedition, when he and his team were the first to reach the North Pole. At least a partial account of that world-famous expedition is always on exhibit, with photographs, his equipment, and taxidermy mounts of polar bears, musk ox, caribou, seals, and walrus. Contemporary and historical photographs often present the Arctic's diverse cultures and natural environment.

Bowdoin's ties to the region originated in 1806 when a professor brought students to the Arctic to study along the coasts of West Greenland and Labrador. Today, Bowdoin faculty and students conduct field research on the environment and cultural traditions in northwest Greenland and Baffin Island. Ongoing research and the museum's growing collections inspire exhibits on topics that show the natural and cultural diversity of the Arctic regions through ethnographic and historic objects, images, and film.

Peary, a civil engineering major in the class of 1877, first crossed the Greenland Ice Cap in 1886. Not until his eighth expedition to the Arctic did he and his team reach the North Pole. When they succeeded on April 6, 1909, his assistant was Donald MacMillan. Over the next 45 years, MacMillan made 25 trips to the eastern Canadian Arctic and Greenland, where he introduced modern technology to the field of scientific exploration, and founded a school for Inuit children in Labrador.

With Peary for the last portion of the push to the North Pole were just four Inuit men and Matthew Henson, who spoke the Inuit language. But it took the full team of 24 men and 133 dogs to accomplish their goal. Despite formidable preparation and undeniable bravery, the team would never have succeeded without the Inuit men and women who lived above the Arctic Circle. The Inuit taught the explorers how to survive in a land where travel is possible only during brief periods of adequate daylight and sufficiently solid sea ice. Inuit women sewed caribou-hide parkas and knee-length pants made of polar bear fur for them, just as they traditionally did for their husbands. Peary said the clothing was "ideal . . . impervious to cold . . . almost indestructible" —and this from a man who understood the odds. On the front of his plain flannel undershirt, he added two red pockets into which he tucked his chronometers. It was the only way to keep the instruments warm enough to work so he could determine latitude and longitude when he reached the Pole. His team's supplies included piano wire to plumb the depths of the ocean. And to provide "all the comforts of home" aboard ship, he had a well-stocked library for the crew and drawing supplies for Inuit children who came aboard. The explorers brought with them a gramophone, which enabled them to make the earliest recordings of Inuit voices, in 1890, and journals in which they recorded their census of the native population, noting family relationships and communities.

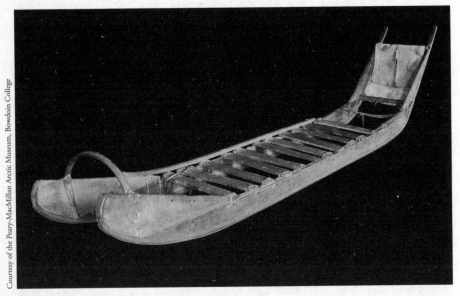

Courtesy of the Peary-MacMillan Arctic Museum, Bowdoin College

The Hubbard Sledge, one of five sledges used by Robert E. Peary on his trek to the North Pole in 1909. Made of oak lashed together with rawhide; runners are steel. Built by Matthew Henson to Peary's design, aboard the S.S. Roosevelt in 1908, the sledge was later presented to Thomas Hubbard, one of Peary's backers, and through him to Bowdoin College.

On your visit, borrow the museum's iPods for a free, 40-minute audio tour. It will help you navigate through galleries where you might see compelling news footage of expeditions, or stand in front of the U.S. flag Peary's wife sewed for him to raise when he reached his goal. A corner of the flag is missing; Peary ripped out a piece to leave behind.

Almost always on view is the centerpiece of the collection, the 14-foot sledge Peary's team constructed from wood and flexible rawhide. Peary adapted an Inuit sled design to build a stronger version capable of carrying 500 pounds of supplies. This is the sled their dog teams pulled on the final leg of the trip.

International honors were bestowed Peary for his achievement, but first he was forced to defend his reputation. Upon his return from the North Pole, he discovered a rival explorer was claiming to have gotten there before him, in 1908. Newspapers and magazines splashed the controversy across front pages around the globe. It was even debated in the halls of the U.S. Congress. But when the sparks subsided, Peary's accomplishment was widely celebrated. He became a marketing darling. His likeness appeared on trading cards, tobacco cans, and small dolls dressed like Peary the explorer. Our modern obsession with celebrity is not new.

USEFUL INFORMATION:

• A self-guided, 1.3-mile walking tour of Bowdoin's connections to the Arctic highlights 10 locations on campus related to members of the college community involved in exploration and research, 1860 to the present. Robert E. Peary, class of 1877, was an active member of Delta Kappa Epsilon. Donald B. MacMillan, class of 1898, belonged to Theta Delta Chi. Both fraternities' original houses, as well as several statues of polar bears, are along the route.

• The museum is handicapped accessible through Hawthorne-Longfellow Library in the same building.

Time to allow: 1 hour, including 40-minute audio tour
Admission: Free
When it's open: Tues–Sat., 10 am–5 pm
   Sun., 2–5 pm
   Closed Mon. and national holidays.
Directions: From I-295, Exit 28 (Topsham-Brunswick) follow US Route 1 North/Pleasant Street to the light at Maine Street and turn right. Continue on Maine Street for 0.5 mile (passing the former Naval Air Station) to the Bowdoin College campus at the intersection of Maine Street and Bath Road. The Arctic Museum is in Hubbard Hall in the center of campus.

FUN FACTS:

• People often confuse the Arctic with Antarctica. Both regions are very cold, but Antarctica is a continent, land surrounded by water, and the Arctic is water surrounded by land. They are at opposite ends of the globe.

• You can stand on sea ice at the North Pole, but the sea ice is always moving.

• The Inuit people live in the Arctic. Other than scientists, no one lives in Antarctica.

• Peary's expedition relied on five teams. The first group made a trail, set up camp, and stored supplies. Successive groups went farther to build igloos on the trail and move up supplies. The last was Peary's team, who used the camps set up by the others to save time and pick up supplies on their way to the pole.

• Peary started his career in Nicaragua as chief assistant on an expedition surveying a route being considered as alternative to the Panama Canal. He met his future assistant, Matthew Henson, while shopping for a sun helmet for the Caribbean.

• The Bowdoin College mascot is the polar bear.

Facts courtesy of The Peary-MacMillan Arctic Museum.

Fishermen's Museum
Pemaquid Point
Route 130, Bristol
http://lighthouse.cc/pemaquid/
207-677-2494

WHAT YOU'LL FIND HERE: Pemaquid Point Light. Former light-keeper's house with historical exhibits on the local fishing industry. Iconic coastline. Gift shop.

Janet Mendelsohn

The Fishermen's Museum in the former keeper's house at Pemaquid Point Lighthouse.

WHY GO: You've seen this lighthouse—it's on the Maine state quarter, along with the schooner Chimes, which sails out of Rockland. Pemaquid Point Light, built in 1827, was commissioned during John Quincy Adams's administration and placed on the National Register of Historic Places in 1985. It's set on granite cliffs whose marbled northwest-southeast patterns swirl into the ocean.

Pemaquid Point is one of the most popular tourist destinations in Maine, attracting some 100,000 visitors a year. Because of its elevation on the rocks, the lighthouse tower is relatively short, but climbing the steps to the lantern deck isn't easy. Diehards hike up 30 steps before reaching a narrow, 12-rung ladder for the last leg to the top. They're rewarded with a view that encompasses Monhegan Island, 10 miles offshore, and occasionally whales—when the fog lifts.

Most folks are content to stay at ground level, shoot great photos, or sketch the fabulous view and visit the Fishermen's Museum.

The collection began as a neighborhood project in 1972. Several women, including Mary Orick, who lived up the road, thought it was high time tourists learned about the lives of working fishermen. They persuaded some of the men to build display cases and neighbors to donate old fishing gear and other items from their attics. What they received predates technology and electronics.

"Before a fisherman could go out, he had to make his nets, hone his tools, and repair traps," said museum volunteer Barbara Marshall, who also served on the board. "Wives helped make the nets. Then the boats went out with only the use of a compass."

A Fresnel lens, on loan from the Coast Guard and formerly used at Baker's Island Light, is the centerpiece of the Navigation Room. Signs provide a good explanation of how a concentrated band of light is intensified and projected by the lens. Elsewhere are different nets for different methods of harvesting from the sea, fish hooks and buoys, and yellowing captains' logs and albums filled with bills of lading and the like; the penmanship is beautiful. The Fish House room replicates a lobsterman's work area with tools and gear, some of it obsolete. A real preserved 25-pound lobster is mounted in a glass case on the wall.

On a foggy day in August 1917, the two-masted schooner *Willis and Guy* wrecked just off the coast. The three-man crew was rescued by lightkeeper Clarence Marr, but the cargo, 216 tons of chestnut coal, scattered over the shore. Bristol residents collected the coal and used it to heat nearly every home in town that winter. One man reportedly gathered five tons. Look in the back room for photos and newspaper accounts of the event.

It's always fun to check the guest log to see where other museum visitors came from. The same day I was here, so were folks from Greece, Austria, Ireland, Germany, Scotland, Carthage, and many states beyond New England.

USEFUL INFORMATION

• Picnic tables are available along the water.

• Pemaquid Point Light is actively used by mariners in Muscongus Bay and John Bay. It is operated by the U.S. Coast Guard. A photovoltaic cell next to the lamp makes the light come on automatically at dark, flashing once every six seconds, and visible for 14 miles. The tower (but not the museum) is licensed to a local chapter of the American Lighthouse Foundation.

• A one-bedroom apartment on the second floor of the keeper's house is available for weekly vacation rentals.

Time to allow: 30 minutes
Admission: Free
When it's open: Memorial Day–Columbus Day
  Daily, 10:30 am–5 pm
  Lighthouse tower is closed on rainy days or when volunteers are unavailable.
Directions: From US Route 1 in Damariscotta, take ME-130 South to Bristol (about 14.5 miles) directly to the parking lot (small fee) at Pemaquid Point.

Maine Maritime Museum
243 Washington Street, Bath
www.mainemaritimemuseum.org
207-443-1316

WHAT YOU'LL FIND HERE: History of shipbuilding, maritime trades, and individuals and their families whose livelihood is tied to the sea. More than 20,000 artifacts, paintings, ship models and tools. Historic Percy & Small Shipyard (1896–1920) with active boatshop and 140 historic boats with Maine connections. Donnell House, a Victorian-era shipbuilder's home (seasonal). Grand Banks fishing schooner the *Sherman Zwicker* (seasonal). Full-scale contemporary sculpture representing the wooden schooner *Wyoming*. Summer camps for teens and children. Marine skills workshops for families and adults. Fifty-foot pirate play ship. Behind-the-scenes trolley tours of the neighboring Bath Iron Works (seasonal). Research library. Gift shop. Snack bar. Sightseeing cruises.

WHY GO: There aren't many places in America where the same industries important 300 years ago are still vital today. Yet in 1607, when English colonists at Popham Beach built their first oceangoing vessel in the "new world," they were already latecomers. Hundreds of years earlier, Native Americans in the region were already successfully fishing and building canoes capable of lengthy coastal voyages. Today, boat building, sail making, fishing, and maritime trade are still among the most obvious industries driving the state's economy and shaping its character.

"Maine has everything that makes for a great shipyard," said the museum's executive director, Amy Lent. "That's why so many ships were built here, more than anywhere else in the country." Part of the experience of visiting Maine Maritime Museum and Bath, the City of Ships, is getting a handle on that legacy. "You look north [from the museum] and see Bath Iron Works, where current employees are related to others who worked here building ships for generations. At the museum, we tie people to maritime history by exposing visitors to the whole web of things that go on around boat building, from surveying to logistics to global business; from engineers and accountants to the widening of the Panama Canal for giant ships."

A rare opportunity is available with advance reservations for the museum's behind-the-scenes trolley tours of Bath Iron Works, where ships have been built for the U.S. Navy since 1893. Inside the mammoth General Dynamics shipyard, a retired BIW electrician or mechanic is likely to be your guide for an up-close view of U.S. naval destroyers under construction. Prefer to get out on the water yourself? You can join any of the museum's sightseeing cruises (also seasonal), lasting one hour or a full day. They offer a relaxing way to photograph lighthouses, river wildlife and water views of Bath Iron Works or maybe fall foliage or Maine's windjammer sailing fleet.

The museum's 25-acre riverbank campus offers plenty to keep you busy for hours. In the modern, spacious main exhibition hall are highlights of collections that include 475 maritime paintings, 550 ship models, and what is believed to be the world's

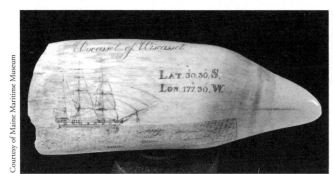

Courtesy of Maine Maritime Museum

Wiscasset scrimshaw.   *Sam Skolfield figurehead.*

largest collection of shipbuilding tools, as well as furniture, textiles, jewelry, and ships'
logs. Folk art includes scrimshaw and paintings. Visitors learn about whaling and
the days when trade in slaves, lime, wood, ice, and fish linked Maine to Asia, Africa,
China, and Europe long before railroads, trucking, or high technology "created" the
global economy. Temporary exhibits often blend storytelling, archival and recent photography, hands-on learning, and special programs with themes such as the economics
of Maine's fin fisheries or life aboard ship.

The Percy & Small Shipyard (1896–1920), America's only surviving shipyard where
large wooden sailing vessels were built, is now part of the museum. The yard is domi-
nated by a full-scale steel sculpture by Maine contemporary artist Andreas von Huene
that evokes the enormity of the *Wyoming,* built here, and said to be the largest wooden
sailing vessel ever built. Docents can answer questions about the historic shipyard and
the skills required to construct and maintain wooden ships. Notice how the land's
slope makes it well-suited to launching on the Kennebec River.

The *Sherman Zwicker,* a 142-foot wooden fishing schooner, awaits you at the dock.
Built in Nova Scotia in 1942 and active until the early 1960s, the schooner is still
seaworthy but doesn't leave her berth. In her day, officers and a crew of 24 made three
trips a year to the Grand Banks, a 35,000-square-mile area east of New England,
Nova Scotia, and Newfoundland that is one of the world's most productive fishing
grounds. The vessel's hold stored 320,000 pounds of fish in an era before refrigeration,
when salting was required to preserve the catch.

In 2010, the former Portland Harbor Museum, which focused on the Casco Bay
region, merged with Maine Maritime Museum. Mark Thompson, the ex-director of
the much smaller museum who became MMM's southern regional director, said that
while the Portland museum no longer exists, over the next several years Maine Maritime will have a bigger presence in the Portland area, with exhibitions and programs
presented in a variety of venues.

"This is the cultural heritage of our nation," said Lent. "We bring the past into the
present and the future."

USEFUL INFORMATION:

• Boaters can reserve Kennebec River moorings by calling 207-433-1316, extension 0. The Visiting Yachtsmen's Building has showers and washing machines. Mooring fee includes two admission passes to the museum. Located 10 miles up the Kennebec River from the Gulf of Maine (lat: 43 degrees 53.871 feet, long: 069 degrees 48.889 feet), the museum's mooring field, floating dock space, and 75-foot pier can accommodate vessels from 60–300 feet in length.

• "Notes from the Orlop," a blog written by the curator of exhibits, takes readers into the museum's back rooms to see some of the unusual treasures that are not currently on display. It is linked from the museum's home page.

Time to allow: Half a day
Admission: $12 Adults
  $11 Seniors (65 and older)
  $9 Ages 5–17 and students with ID
  Free Ages 4 and younger
When it's open: Daily, 9:30 am–5 pm
  Closed Thanksgiving, Christmas, and New Year's Day.
Directions: From the South: From I-95/Maine Turnpike, Exit 52, take I-295 to Exit 28. Follow US Route 1 North through Brunswick to Bath. Take the Historic Bath exit downhill to the traffic light and turn right onto Washington Street. Drive 1.2 miles, passing Bath Iron Works, to the museum.

From the North: Take the Maine Turnpike to Exit 103 (West Gardiner) onto I-295 to Exit 31A (Topsham) and turn right onto ME-196 East. Proceed to Route 1 North to Bath. Take the Historic Bath exit and turn right at the traffic light onto Washington Street. The museum will be 1.2 miles down, on the left.

FUN FACTS:

• At the entrance to the indoor galleries, look for the familiar likeness of Benjamin Franklin as a figurehead (circa 1850) from the bow of the steamer Franklin, which sailed between New York City and France.

• Indoors, children (and adults) can play captain and sound the horn of a replica tug boat pilot house (circa 1955). Outdoors, they can climb all over a fully rigged brig, Pirate Paradise, in the spirit of real pirates who frequented New England's coastline during the early 1700s.

Inside the Gates at Bath Iron Works

Nowhere is the maritime history of this state and the nation more dramatic than on a guided tour of Bath Iron Works, where ships have been built for the U.S. Navy since 1893.

"Shipbuilding is absolutely the number one influence on the economy and character of Maine in history and today," said Amy Lent, executive director of Maine Maritime Museum, which runs the tours in partnership with its neighbor, the General Dynamics-owned shipyard. The one-hour guided trolley tour begins in front of the museum. In recent years, despite increasing the number of weekly tours during the 22-week summer season, most tickets sell out well in advance.

Courtesy of Maine Maritime Museum

Trolley tour of Bath Iron Works.

Minus cameras, cell phones, large purses and backpacks, forbidden for national security reasons, we entered BIW's south gate on an old-fashioned green trolley that looked ridiculous beside mammoth assembly buildings and towering cranes. Before September 11, 2001, it was relatively easy to see behind the scenes if you knew a shipyard worker, but now precautions are strict. The names and citizenship of all 20 tourists were required for a list the museum submitted to BIW before they let us in.

"After 9/11 we stopped all visits other than those directly related to our business with the U.S. Navy, even veterans' groups," BIW communications manager Jim DeMartini told me later. "But it didn't feel good. A lot of us are Navy veterans and reservists and we're all proud of what we do. When the museum came to us about reinstating the tours, we agreed, but with new rules to deal with windshield issues. When the trolley comes through, visitors wave and we wave back. It gives us the opportunity to show the public what we do and how proud we are of the tremendous skill it takes to build a Navy warship."

Unless you've lived aboard a ship, you don't understand the complexity of what goes into it, said DeMartini. Even what's visible from the trolley boggles the mind. We rolled slowly past assembly buildings that resemble airplane hangars. Each is 110 feet wide, 236 feet deep, and 72 feet high. Our eyes grew larger by the minute. We got pretty close to the action, though not indoors and never off our seats. At the time we took our tour, BIW was still building destroyers in modules called Mega Units, a system that required significantly fewer hours and lower costs than previous methods. Each module, one-third of a ship, weighs 100 tons and looks sliced as if cut top to bottom, giving us cutaway views. By the time this book is published, construction will be done in Ultra Hull Units up to 176 feet long and 50 feet high. We waved at welders, pipe assemblers, and electricians and they, indeed, waved back. The color of their hardhats—white, purple, green, brown, yellow, gray—identified their trades.

Bath Iron Works built its first U.S. Navy ship, the gunboat USS *Machias*, in 1893 and its first commercial ship a year later. Among 425 shipbuilding contracts have been 245 military ships and more than 160 private yachts and commercial vessels, including the yacht *Ranger*, winner of the America's Cup race. During World War II, crews worked three shifts around the clock building 82 destroyers for the Navy. At the peak, they delivered one ship every 17 days. BIW recently completed its contract for AEGIS guided missile destroyers, underway since 1985. In 2009, they began building the Navy's newest model, the Zumwalt (DDG-1000) destroyer. You're likely to see several ships in various stages of construction.

Ray Ingraham, a tour guide and retired destroyer engineering manager, described the fabrication process, the old launch systems, and the current Land Level Transfer Facility that enables workers to complete 85 percent of construction on dry land and move the nearly complete ship to dry dock before it's launched in the Kennebec River.

From the time steel is delivered to Bath by rail, it takes 42 months to build a guided missile destroyer. A single AEGIS class destroyer requires 48 miles of piping, 254 miles of electrical cable, 6,500 light fixtures and 6,200 tons of steel.

"People want to know what powers the ship," said Ingraham. "They ask what weapons are installed and how that's managed. The AEGIS's radar assembly was visible on the bridge structure. It doesn't move and visitors want to know how it works." We were floored to learn the 750-foot long dry dock was built in China and, with three giant cranes lashed inside, traveled by ocean on a six-month journey, through two typhoons and a storm in the Gulf of Maine.

Bath Iron Works trolley tours depart from
Maine Maritime Museum
243 Washington Street
Bath, Maine
207-443-1316
www.mainemaritimemuseum.org
Advance reservations strongly suggested.
May–Oct., Mon.–Fri., 12:30 pm and Sat., 10 am (subject to change)
Photography is prohibited. Cell phones, cameras and large bags are not permitted on the trolley and must be secured in your own vehicle prior to the tour. Visitors will be asked to sign in and state their country of citizenship.
Tickets are non-refundable, except by BIW in the event of a national emergency.
Trolley tours are not cancelled in inclement weather.
$20 Maine Maritime Museum members
Ticket price includes museum admission for two consecutive days.
$30 Adults
$15 Ages 3–15
Free Younger than age 3 (infants must be held on lap)

Marshall Point Lighthouse Museum
Port Clyde
www.marshallpoint.org
207-372-6450

WHAT YOU'LL FIND HERE Lighthouse in an iconic coastal setting. History of the light, local industries, and the working lives of people on the St. George Peninsula. Gift shop. Picnic tables.

Janet Mendelsohn

WHY GO If you arrive on a summer afternoon before the museum opens, bring a picnic to enjoy behind the keeper's house. Listen to the rumble of lobster boats entering and leaving Muscongus Bay and, more than likely, the steady sound a distant fog horn. The ocean air will be fragrant with pink-blooming rosa rugosas near raspberries in a big unruly patch. Tourists put on a show of their own, posing for pictures on the long ramp to the lighthouse, with Monhegan Island in the distance. Over the years, Marshall Point Light has been the setting for BMW ads and fashion spreads in *Vogue* magazine.

Rugged rocks along this shore are more than four million years old. How old they are is among the questions answered on the first floor of the white shingle house where keepers lived until 1971, when the 150-year-old lighthouse was automated. The St. George Historical Society has given its museum more than the usual personal touch by honoring the working people who have made Port Clyde their home. On one wall are rows of miniature buoys painted the colors that belong to every active and deceased lobsterman, identified by name. The Dana A. Smith Room was named for the museum's late director, a local schoolteacher who compiled the archive where you can browse through 50 volumes of letters, newspaper clippings, old photographs, and other materials about the area.

In 1970, the Port Clyde Packing Co., a sardine cannery, was destroyed by fire, devastating the community; 150 jobs were lost. Pieces of the building reportedly still wash up on the shore. In the former summer kitchen you'll read about the disaster, as well as lobstering; the now-gone sardine, clam, and granite industries; and the daily lives of keepers' families. A small old wooden desk recalls the classrooms where children once learned and dreamed about the sea. You can learn how the tide is driven by the pull of the moon and about lighthouse operations yesterday and today.

Time to allow: 30 minutes
Admission: Free
When it's open: May
    Sat. and Sun., 1–5 pm
    Memorial Day–Columbus Day
    Daily, Sun.–Fri., 1–5 pm
    Sat., 10 am–5 pm
    Grounds open sunrise–sunset all year.
Directions: From Brunswick or Rockland: Marshall Point is 15.2 miles from the intersections of US Route 1 and ME-131. Follow Route 131 for about 14 miles, past Route 73, to where the road bears left at the top of a hill. Turn left at the blue Marshall Point sign and right on Marshall Point Road. The final quarter mile is narrow and winding, with a parking lot just before the lighthouse.

FUN FACT: In the 1994 Oscar-winning movie *Forrest Gump,* Marshall Point Lighthouse is the last stop on Forrest's long-distance run up the coast. Actor Tom Hanks and the crew filmed here for two days in October 1993. Look for an album of photos capturing the event.

A Conversation with Painter Barbara Ernst Prey, National Council on the Arts

Barbara Ernst Prey juggles a busy travel schedule, dividing the year between summers in Port Clyde, Maine, and winters in Oyster Bay, New York. Prey has lived and painted in Europe and Taiwan. She attended shuttle launches at the Kennedy Space Center when NASA commissioned her to paint four watercolors, including a tribute to the ill-fated *Columbia*, and another of the *X-43,* the world's fastest aircraft. In 2003, she met with the first lady when President and Mrs. George W. Bush invited her to paint a scene for their White House Christmas card. Her work hangs in prominent corporate and museum collections, including the Smithsonian American Art Museum, Farnsworth Art Museum, The Brooklyn Museum, and the private collections of such luminaries as Nobel Laureate Dr. James Watson and his wife and actor Orlando Bloom. More than 30 U.S. embassies and consulates, from Caracas to Athens and Rangoon, exhibit her work. And although she finds subjects elsewhere in New England, on Long Island, New York, in space and out west, her work is especially admired for the way she captures the quiet beauty and true nature of Maine.

During the winter of 2007–08, an elegant Old World cultural center in Paris was transformed with L. L. Bean Adirondack chairs, a handmade quilt, fishing nets, and multicolored lobster buoys imported by the sponsoring foundation to accompany "An American View: Barbara Ernst Prey," her first major international show. Art lovers came from all over Europe to see Prey's work despite a French transit strike. Surrounded by purely American objects and scenes—the red Adirondack chairs were a big hit, said Prey—they responded to her vivid, saturated colors and universal themes: the quiet dignity of lobster

fishermen at work; the simplicity of clean wash fluttering on a clothesline; the timeless beauty of wooden boats and old houses; coastal villages at dusk; autumn meadows and the roiling sea.

Prey now serves on the National Council on the Arts, the advisory body of the National Endowment for the Arts. Previous council members include Leonard Bernstein, John Steinbeck, Marian Anderson, and Isaac Stern. It was a total surprise, she said, when a phone call from the Bush White House informed her of the nomination in 2008. Before confirmation by the U.S. Senate, the FBI conducted a lengthy background search, giving her the same scrutiny that U.S. ambassadors receive.

Barbara Ernst Prey by Deborah Feingold.

One of only two visual artists on the 14-member board, she is serving a six-year term that ends in 2014. But in reality, Barbara Ernst Prey has been an artist-ambassador for quite some time.

As an artist, how have you worked and traveled in so many places?

BEP: I lived in Europe for three years on a Fulbright fellowship that I received in 1979, and painted and exhibited in Taiwan on a Henry Luce Foundation grant in 1986. Since then, more than 30 pieces of my artwork have been selected for the U.S. State Department's Arts in Embassy Program which has added them to their embassy and consulate collections worldwide including Paris, Madrid, Seoul, Baghdad, Abu Dhabi, Bogotá, Buenos Aires, Mexico City, Lima, Tunis, Vilnius, and Cairo. As part of that program, I gave lectures on American art in France, Spain, Norway, and the Czech Republic. In Washington, D.C., I've given lectures on Winslow Homer at the National Gallery and for the John Singer Sargent exhibit at the Corcoran Gallery of Art.

What have you learned from participating in the Arts in Embassy Program?

BEP: Every country is proud of their own art, and most countries have been producing art a lot longer than we have. Art creates a universal language and builds bridges and crosses boundaries. I think because we live in a global century, there is a strong awareness of American modern and contemporary art. Everyone knows [Robert] Rauchenberg's name and sees contemporary art in books, on the Web and in museum shows. In the U.S. Embassy exhibit in Paris, which includes one of my paintings, there are also paintings by Winslow Homer, John Singer Sargent, and the American Impressionists. I was a bit anxious as to how my lecture on American Impressionists, as well as how my concurrent solo show in Paris, would be received because of tensions between the U.S. and France at that time. Both were extraordinarily well embraced. People came from all over France and the world to see my exhibit in Paris. That was an example of how interested people are in seeing how an American views her country and how a nation other than their own sees itself.

Do art collectors, curators, and the general public outside Maine have an accurate picture of this state's art scene?

BEP: Maine has always had an important place in American art from the perspective of museums and artists, with its long history of artist colonies in Ogunquit, Mount Desert, and Monhegan. In the Paris lecture I gave with [Corcoran Gallery] curator Sarah Cash, we did a walk through American landscape paintings, and mentioned many paintings painted in Maine as well as art pockets in Cos Cob, Southampton, Gloucester, and the Adirondacks. I spoke about the influence of Hopper and Homer on my artwork. The tradition, the weather, the beauty, the light of Maine for a landscape painter is very inspiring. But it is not just landscapes, there are also well-known figurative painters, such as Alex Katz, who paint in Maine. Artists still come to Maine either to live full-time or to work in the summer, including some of our most well-known American painters.

I go to museums for fun and the art museums in Maine are true gems. I go to the Farnsworth often in the summer; they have a wonderful permanent collection of late 19th- and early 20th-century American paintings that has always been such a part of me. The Colby Museum is well known for its contemporary art and American folk artists. The Center for

Courtesy of Barbara Ernst Prey

Family Portrait, *watercolor, 22 x 28 inches. Collection: The Brooklyn Museum*

Maine Contemporary Art is a beautiful space and they have very current contemporary exhibits. Maine Maritime Museum, which people may not think about as an art museum, resonates with me because I've been painting the working waterfront for years. Bowdoin, Colby, and Bates colleges all have great teaching museums, each with its own niche. Bowdoin has an encyclopedic collection. If you don't want to go to New York City, you can get a good short snippet there. Bates has an incredible works-on-paper collection that I particularly appreciate as a watercolorist working on paper. Ogunquit, long associated with the local arts colony, is in a beautiful setting. One of my favorite small museums is Marshall Point Lighthouse (which also has one of my paintings on exhibit). It is right around the corner from where I have an exhibit every year so I spend a good deal of time in the museum. Be sure to ask questions, as the volunteers are both knowledgeable and helpful. It has rooms full of regional history about the community and fishing. I particularly like the small exhibit of all the buoys of the local lobsterman.

In the art world, Maine's museums are all very well respected for museums of their size. They are able to attract top-notch professionals. There's such a diversity of collections, they don't compete with each other. Having worked with a number of curators and curating exhibits myself I appreciate how the exhibits are presented, from the choice of colors to how the exhibits are hung. The Farnsworth, Portland, and college museums might be regional but they're really national. You could have a great vacation around the museums.

What draws you to paint in Maine?

BEP: Maine is a source of inspiration for my landscapes and water has always been important to me. I grew up on the water and now live in fishing communities on Long Island and in Maine. My mother was a very gifted artist and head of the Design Department at Pratt Institute in New York. Although I first visited Maine with a friend from Williams College, I always knew of the Portland Museum of Art's Winslow Homer collection because the Paysons [whose gifts to the museum include 17 Homer paintings] lived down the road and my parents knew the collection. When I went to Homer's studio in Prouts Neck it gave me goose bumps. Only after I came here did I discover I have family roots in the midcoast area, around Vinalhaven, that go back to the 1700s on my mother's side. I've been painting here for more than 30 years. Maine speaks to me on many levels. Sometimes it takes years for a painting or a theme to develop. I am now very interested in the islands, sustainability, and the working waterfront and continue to be an advocate for the environment. Many of the people and fishermen I paint are my neighbors and friends.

What is involved in serving on the National Council of the Arts?

BEP: The National Council on the Arts advises the chairman of the National Endowment of the Arts (NEA) on agency policies and programs. It reviews and makes recommendations to the chairman on applications for grants, funding guidelines, and leadership initiatives. I was appointed as an artist from New York. As an artist, it is an opportunity to experience the incredible breadth of the arts in America and to be an ambassador for the NEA. Personally, there is only room to grow both as a person and in my work. I hope that my being involved in the Arts in Embassies program and on the National Council of the Arts will help give more people exposure to American art and a greater understanding of American culture.

What might your role on the National Council mean for Maine?

BEP: Every year, the NEA gives out more than 2,000 grants totaling more than $100 million to fund the arts in all 50 states and six jurisdictions. The magnitude of what they do has been so amazing for me to learn about. They support folk and traditional artists, writers, dancers, musicians, visual artists, actors and organizations that perpetuate the arts, like "Jazz Masters on Tour." I really like "The Big Read," which makes books and resources available to people across the country and encourages them to read and discuss books. In Maine, what I'd like to see is a continued and greater emphasis on arts education, K through 12. I'm often asked to speak to PTAs and school boards on the importance of the arts at a time when arts programs are being cut in the schools. Arts organizations and artists are really struggling everywhere, of course. In Maine, we're fortunate to have the Maine Arts Commission, which is exceptional.

The Musical Wonder House
18 High Street, Wiscasset
www.musicalwonderhouse.com
207-882-7163

WHAT YOU'LL FIND HERE: Close to 5,000 fully restored antique music boxes, phonographs, player pianos, and mechanical musical home décor and instruments custom-made by expert craftsmen between 1800 and 1920. A sea captain's mansion (circa 1852). Period furnishings. Gift shop.

WHY GO: "Most visitors are shocked," says Joe Villani, co-owner of this house of antiques that play music. "People don't know what to expect. Men, especially, come as a favor to their wives then discover the collection is mechanical." People have been known to stay for hours, intrigued by how the diverse, often complex, pieces work and charmed by their simple melodies, natural birdsongs, or full orchestral sound.

In our age of disposable music players, when new technology makes the latest handheld device obsolete almost overnight, it is especially delightful to explore this Victorian mansion where 11 public rooms are filled with custom-made, finely crafted Old World music boxes, wind-up phonographs, decorative accessories, and museum-quality instruments from around the world. The sheer number and variety is astounding. You'll see and hear musical teapots, candy dishes, beer steins, wind-up phonographs, player grand pianos, and ornate, desk-size music consoles whose metal cylinders and disks are intricately stamped in patterns that play folk tunes, hymns, and favorites by composers of the day—Gilbert and Sullivan, Mozart, Verdi, Bach, Liszt, or Chopin.

Nearly every piece on display has been expertly tuned and its case restored to original condition in the museum's workshop by Michael Everett, resident technician since 1982. Most were made between 1800 and 1920 in Europe, China, and Japan.

To see and hear the collection, you have to choose between a one-hour guided tour geared to general audiences or more extensive versions that include the second floor. It is well worth the price to see the second story, where some of the most unusual pieces are found, including an Edison phonograph and a Dutch barrel organ flute clock (circa 1830). A musical mirror is in the Bird of Paradise Room, which contains a bedroom suite that belonged to Austrian Archduke Franz Ferdinand, whose assassination triggered World War I; the furniture was inherited by the museum's founder, Danilo Konvalinka, through his grandfather, who was the archduke's in-house composer.

There simply isn't time enough to take in everything. Lifelike porcelain birds in brass cages sing sweetly. Musical salt and pepper shakers would enliven any meal. A rare Louis XV–style inlaid wood round table shaped like a drum would complement the most elegant formal salon. The handsome table conceals an instrument: a 20-inch short bedplate Regina music box that plays symphonies recorded on metal disks.

During the late 19th and early 20th centuries, especially in Europe, people surrounded themselves with all kinds of beautiful things that were often passed along from generation to generation, says Villani. It was fashionable to surprise guests or simply entertain one's own family with unusual items that played music. These hand-crafted pieces often were inlaid with abalone, ebony, and rare woods; some were auto-mated. Wealthy Victorians competed to see who could commission the most elaborate and unusual mechanical musical instruments. One such wonder is the Ducommun Girod box (circa 1868). On its beautiful rosewood and gold-trimmed table rests a matching cabinet. Interchangeable cylinders inserted into the cabinet trigger musical combs that produce a concert hall sound.

Konvalinka, a native of Austria, moved to Wiscasset with his wife, Lois. In 1963, they began rescuing musical pieces, mostly European, from flea markets, barn sales,

and antique shops. Villani, a vocal music teacher, first saw the collection in 1964 and was spellbound, returning year after year. After he retired in 2005, he and Paulo Carvalho purchased the 32-room house and the musical treasure it contains, becoming trustees of the museum. The entire house is devoted to the collection, a workshop, a restoration service, and gift shop.

Many of the pieces contain secrets. Ask to see a tabletop "mosque" veneered with ivory that hides brandy glasses. A sleek Swiss-made accessory from the 1930s opens to reveal cigarettes, the perfect touch for a Bette Davis movie. Ornate gold-framed dioramas and pictures on the walls become minia-ture private theaters when a cord is pulled; skaters dance on frozen ponds or figures dance on stage.

Ducommun-Girod interchange-able cylinder musical box with six cylinders (circa 1868).

By the end of your tour, what may at first have seemed like a silly name for the museum has become an accurate description.

Courtesy of Musical Wonder House

USEFUL INFORMATION:

- All tours are guided because the docent plays the instruments for you.
- Still cameras are permitted but video cameras are not.

Time to allow: 1 or 2 hours for a guided tour
Admission: Guided tours, per person
    $10 Half (two rooms downstairs and the hallway)
    $20 Full (four rooms downstairs and the hallway)
    $40 Grand House (nine spaces on two floors)
When it's open: Memorial Day weekend–Oct. 31
    Mon.–Sat., 10 am–5 pm
    Sun., noon–5 pm
Directions: US Route 1 to Wiscasset. In the center of town, near a white church and a courthouse on the hill, turn left onto High Street.

Thompson Ice House Museum
Route 129, South Bristol
www.thompsonicehouse.com
207-729-1956 (winter), 207-644-8551 (summer)

WHAT YOU'LL FIND HERE: Replica of the ice house that operated here for 159 years. Vintage tools and heavy equipment. Video and exhibits on past ice harvests on Thompson Pond. Two special events: Annual ice harvest in February and ice cream social in July. Gift shop.

WHY GO: This is the only place we know where every July a community-wide ice cream social features the old-fashioned taste of creamy summer favorites hand-churned from ice that was harvested on the same spot in February by bundled-up volunteers. It's where every winter, as many as 450 people in one day slice the surface of frozen Thompson Pond into 300-pound blocks of ice using tools and techniques handed down through five generations of one family.

At its peak in the 1800s, ice harvesting was among Maine's biggest industries. It was as important to the state's economy as fishing, granite, and lumber. Small operations like the Thompson Ice House provided an essential community service. In an era before refrigeration, imagine what it meant to storekeepers and homemakers to get a regular delivery of 25- or 50-pound blocks for their kitchen ice boxes. Yachtsmen bought ice when they provisioned. For New England's fishermen and dealers, ice opened up markets near and far.

The Thompson Ice House Museum keeps that piece of Maine's past frozen in time.

The industry's most famous merchant was Frederic Tudor, a Massachusetts entrepreneur who found that large quantities of ice could be kept solid during lengthy journeys in the hold of oceangoing ships. Harvesting ice from ponds near Bath and Boston, in 1820 Tudor reportedly introduced iced beverages to the Caribbean and subsequently became the first to ship fresh fish from northern waters, predating the frozen food industry by a century. By 1860, he had customers from South Carolina to Singapore and Brazil. Competitors sprang up quickly, including many on the Kennebec River, vying for business in South America, India, and China. Even small operations like this one were important not so long ago. Photos of the Thompson Ice House prior to 1980 show trucks from Boston lobster wholesaler James Hook & Co. being loaded with crushed ice for the trip to markets in Florida.

The industry as good as folded in the early 1900s when electricity was introduced, making artificial refrigeration possible. Still, some fishermen prefer natural ice today because the lower air content makes it last longer than mechanically made ice.

Proud of his heritage, the late Herbert Thompson often told the story of his great-grandfather, Asa, who entered the trade in 1826 when a home-improvement project turned into a business opportunity. On a farm founded by his grandparents in 1752, Asa dredged a stream, built a dam, and created a pond to supply his family with ice to preserve fish and other perishables. Beside his pond, he built an ice house to hold the ice. That first winter, with more than enough stored for his needs, he had plenty left over for his neighbors, many of whom were fishermen. The horse-drawn Thompson Ice House wagon became a familiar sight as the company grew, delivering ice to the region's growing summer community for a penny a pound.

For 159 years, Asa and his descendants used picks, chisels, tongs, poles, and busting bars forged from iron, relics of tool design that changed little over 200 years. But they were not averse to modernization if it improved efficiency. They rigged a Model A Ford with a snowplow to clear the pond and attached a four-cylinder motorized buzz saw to a sled to make deep cuts in the ice. When electricity sliced profit, Herbert Thompson installed an ice crusher for the region's fish packers and truckers. Ultimately, when age and its ills caught up with him, he contracted with others to do the work. Ken Lincoln was the last to manage the operation.

"My dad worked the ice harvest," said Lincoln, whose roots are deep in South Bristol. "When us kids were big enough to move ice in the channel, we went to work. I started in 1968 when I was about eight years old. A lot of us did—my dad, kids, siblings, cousins and friends. It was a big commercial operation until 1981. Unfortunately, ice harvesting is a lot of hard work with little pay." Lincoln switched to construction.

In 1974, the Thompson Ice House was listed on the National Register of Historic Places, making headlines in the *New York Times, Wall Street Journal, Audubon* magazine, and elsewhere as the only commercial house on the register to have stored naturally frozen ice harvested in the traditional way from a nearby pond.

Credit for the museum idea is given to Erica Mather Welter. Beginning in the 1940s, she stopped by twice a week all summer as much to hear Herbert Thompson's stories as for the burlap bags of ice he loaded into her car. Some folks feel a personal loss when the old ways fall by the wayside. Welter was among them.

"Herbert Thompson's enthusiasm was contagious," wrote Welter in her account, *My 40 Year Dream.* It would be a fitting memorial to a disappearing industry, she told him, if, when the old building collapsed, as they knew it would, a smaller replica could be built with salvaged lumber. He agreed. Her grassroots efforts kept the idea alive for 40 years. South Bristol school children made "Save the Ice House" posters. Welter met with preservationists in Augusta. In 1964, her husband, Amthor Stone Welter, photographed the ice harvest for the Lincoln County Cultural and Historical Association. Some of his photos, now fading, are displayed in an outdoor display named for him, beside Thompson's Pond. The Thompson Ice House finally closed in 1985.

"Mr. Thompson wanted someone to turn his business into a museum so the ice industry would be remembered," said Barbara Hamlin, whose husband, Norman, helped Thompson develop the plan. "He refused to sell his family's land to someone who would put up vacation condos." Norman Hamlin, a retired professor of naval architecture, had spent every summer in Christmas Cove and shared Thompson's belief that Maine's past is too important to forget. When Herbert and Gwen Thompson deeded their property to a newly formed nonprofit, the Thompson Ice House Preservation Corporation, Norman Hamlin agreed to steer the project as president of a board that would include preservation experts and neighbors who shared their love of history. A local architect was hired to tackle rebuilding the dilapidated structure. A smaller replica opened as the museum in 1990.

Thompson Ice House Museum.

One August afternoon, Barbara Hamlin and another trustee, Judith Manchester, were out front arranging souvenirs for sale on folding tables—old photos, postcards, mugs, a DVD of Welter's history, an activity book for children. They stopped to give me a tour.

We strolled behind the barnlike building on one of those clear coastal days you wish would last forever. A warm breeze chased away most mosquitoes. The whole pond rested before us, surrounded by birch and pine. A dragonfly lit on swaying reeds by the water's edge. Birds sang, oblivious to the occasional burping of frogs. Every so often, I heard a low groan.

"What's that?" I asked, puzzled by the oddly familiar sound.

"Ice shifting in the storage house," said Manchester. *Aha.* The voice of the previous harvest was a rumble I knew from winter walks along our tidal creek.

"Ice houses don't last long," said Hamlin. "They either burn or get torn down. As the sun moves across the roof, the ice begins to slowly melt. The heavy blocks shift, putting pressure on logs that hold up the wooden walls. Ice houses all lean to the south and, in the end, this one was sagging badly."

A fairly new and sturdy-looking wooden ramp rises from the water's edge, looking like a little ski jump abutting the ice house ending just short of the roof. Platforms at two midpoints press against shuttered openings in the building's back wall. In February, when the whole contraption is put into action, a pulley system carries the blocks of ice in cradles that drop their load from three staggered heights onto a chute indoors. Experienced hands maneuver the heavy blocks into place. But none of that is visible from the road.

"You could drive by this place and it looks like nothing," said Manchester, "but if you stop, you'll likely be surprised." When she opened the door to the ice storage room, I expected a blast of cold air. I was wrong. Even in summer, the ice house remains a cool 40 degrees Fahrenheit thanks to double walls insulated with 10 inches of sawdust between them and salt-marsh hay spread over the top layer of ice. It was nearly Labor Day and the room still held enough solid 300-pound blocks to fill a good-sized backyard pool.

USEFUL INFORMATION:

• The annual Ice Harvest, usually on the Sunday of President's Day weekend, welcomes hundreds of volunteers for the better part of one very cold day to help cut heavy blocks of natural ice using the same methods and many of the same tools used here for 159 years. Everyone is welcome. Most volunteers arrive between 9 and 10 am and stay until 2 pm. Dress in layers and come ready to pitch in.

• The annual ice cream social is usually held on the Sunday closest to the Fourth of July. It also attracts hundreds of kids and adults who come for creamy treats made from natural ice.

• During the summer, ice blocks are sold on the honor system: $1 for a 25-pound block, from a cooler in the yard.

Time to allow: 30 minutes
When it's open: July and Aug.
    Wed., Fri., Sat., 1–4 pm
    Sunday of President's Day weekend for the ice harvest.
Admission: Free
Directions: From Route 1 in Damariscotta, take ME-129 South for 12 miles. Look for a sign on the left.

HARVESTING POND ICE

Ice is ready to harvest when it is about 12 inches thick. A 30-foot wooden straightedge is laid on the pond, at this point called a "field," to draw a grid. During the Thompson Ice House's annual ice harvest, Ken Lincoln and his brother usually handle the buzz saw that's mounted on a sled to cut grooves in the surface along the grid. Other workers use hand saws to cut "rafts," long sections of ice that are broken into 250- to 300-pound blocks with busting bars. Volunteers with poles push the rafts along a channel, or canal, to the base of a wooden ramp from the pond to the ice house. With busting bars, needle bars, and picks, the blocks are moved into cradles on the ramp where a pulley system hauls them indoors. Inside, a crew of experienced hands do the dangerous work of stacking them six tiers high. Finally, an insulating layer of salt-marsh hay is placed on top.

The annual event at the Thompson Ice House Museum is real work made festive with hot food and cocoa, and maybe ice skating on the far side of the pond. First-time volunteers can cut ice with hand saws and feed it down the canal.

Montpelier—The General Henry Knox Museum
30 High Street, Thomaston
www.knoxmuseum.org
207-354-8062

Collections of Montpelier, The General Henry Knox Museum

Aerial photograph of Montpelier by Ben Magro, Collections of Montpelier, the General Henry Knox Museum

WHAT YOU'LL FIND HERE: Colonial Revival mansion recreating the home of Henry Knox, Revolutionary War general and the nation's first Secretary of War. Early American furnishings. Tour guides in period costumes. Gift shop.

WHY GO: In the gentlemen's room, or library, of this stately hillside mansion, it is easy to imagine the 6-foot, 5-inch, 280-pound General Henry T. Knox and his long-time friend George Washington discussing politics and military strategy in oversized chairs by a fire. Picture Knox's wife, Lucy, descending the dramatic, two-pronged "semi-flying" staircase (which seems to have no structural support) and crossing the spacious oval room where receptions were held. Dressed in a gown of Chinese silk or colorful cotton from India, she's headed to one of two kitchens in the basement to check on dinner preparations. It was a time of elegance in Maine.

When Knox built Montpelier as his summer retirement home in 1794, it rivaled the deluxe mansions of the young nation's elite in Philadelphia and Boston. Each of its 19 rooms had a fireplace and mirrors to reflect available light. Montpelier was said to be the largest home in Maine, with nine outbuildings including a smokehouse, barn, and workers' housing. It soon became the family's full-time home.

This reproduction of the original mansion was built in 1930 by the local chapter of the Daughters of the American Revolution to honor the soldier-patriot for whom Fort Knox, Kentucky; Fort Knox, Maine; and numerous other forts and counties are named.

Although details of his early life differ with each account, Henry Knox (1750–1806) was born into poverty in Boston and left home at a young age to work and help support his mother. He apprenticed as a bookbinder. At age 21, Knox opened his own book-shop. Largely self-educated, he had a passion for military strategy and taught himself French so he could read military books in that language. Later, his fluency enabled him to converse with another Revolutionary War hero, the Marquis de Lafayette. On a wall near the home's entrance is a framed muster of troops under Brigadier General Knox's command (he would be promoted to major general in 1781). It was a gift from Lafayette, a major general, who signed and dated the muster on September 3, 1779, at West Point.

Knox acquired such expertise in artillery that soon after Washington inspected ramparts Knox designed, he named Knox his chief of artillery. During the winter of 1775–1776, when Knox was 25 years old, he engineered the transport of 59 can-nons from Fort Ticonderoga, New York, across the Berkshire Mountains to Boston, enabling Washington's army to drive the British out of Boston Harbor. Throughout the war, the two men worked side-by-side and in1785, Knox was appointed Secretary of War in Washington's first Cabinet.

After 10 years in that post, and almost 20 in military service, Knox longed to retire so he could spend time with his family and live the life of a gentleman farmer. Lucy's parents were staunch Tories who had fled the country during the war, leaving her the sole heir to land acquired by her grandfather, Brigadier General Samuel Waldo. On that property, Knox built Montpelier. A map made for him of the land he acquired from Waldo indicates 576,000 acres across what is now Waldo and Knox counties. Thereafter, he was involved in a variety of enterprises, not always successful, including cattle-raising, shipbuilding, brick-making, politics, and real estate speculation.

Knox died of an infection three days after swallowing a chicken bone while visiting a friend. Lucy struggled financially after his death and was forced to sell much of the land. It was not enough. The house began to fall into disrepair. When she died, first one, then another grown daughter lived at Montpelier, but it proved too expensive for them as well. Eventually the house fell to the Knoxes' ne'er-do-well son, who had neither interest nor money to provide for the upkeep. The furnishings were either dis-persed among descendants or sold at auction. Decayed and abandoned, the house was demolished in 1871 to make way for the Knox and Lincoln Railroad.

This close replica of Montpelier was designed from original sketches and letters, although the original blueprints were lost. Tour guides, some in Colonial costumes, describe the home and its period furnishings, and weave anecdotes through their history of the American Revolution and Henry Knox's role in the war. One guide discussed the finer points of that conflict with a history teacher and his family as our tour moved through the rooms. In the girls' bedroom, pointing out the rope beds, she told us the ropes supporting the mattresses had to be tightened often because they stretched, giving rise to the expression, "sleep tight," and the straw mattresses themselves harbored insects so the children were tucked in with the familiar warning, "Don't let the bedbugs bite."

USEFUL INFORMATION

• Guided tours are the only way to see the house. They run continuously so you can join and exit at any point.

• Concerts, classes, Fall Harvest weekend, an annual Holiday Open House, Revolutionary Encampment, and lectures are among the special events throughout the year.

• The Center for the Study of Early American Life holds a Summer Teacher Institute in July for teachers of history and social studies. For information, call 207-354-0858 or e-mail center@knoxmuseum.org.

Time to allow: 45 minutes for guided tour
Admission: $7 Adults
 $6 Seniors
 $4 Ages 5–14
 $18 Family rate
 Discounts for groups of 10 or more. Call ahead for reservations.
When it's open: Memorial Day–Columbus Day
 Guided tours Tues.–Sat., 10 am–3:30 pm
 Closed Sun. and Mon.
 Open by appointment Oct.–Dec.
 Closed Jan.–March
Directions: At the Intersection of US Route 1 and ME-131 in Thomaston.

FUN FACT

Running water for Montpelier's kitchen was diverted from a nearby stream using a system of wooden pipes that Henry Knox devised. The pipes were logs with holes drilled through the middle. Plugs were inserted to stop the flow.

Owls Head Transportation Museum
117 Museum Street, Owls Head
www.owlshead.org
207-594-4418

WHAT YOU'LL FIND HERE

Antique automobiles, airplanes, carriages, engines, bicycles, and motorcycles, including a full-size replica of the Wright Brothers' 1903 Kitty Hawk Flyer. Energy exhibit of more than 30 vintage engines. Monthly special event weekends. Annual auto auction. Ground vehicle and aviation restoration workshops (limited public access). Research library. Gift shop.

WHY GO

Drip pans under the cars and the smell of fuel near the planes tell you what's special about this collection: Nearly everything is fully restored to operating condition and demonstrated at special events.

Owls Head is *la crème de la crème* of Maine's transportation museums. Not only do the vintage automobiles and aircraft exemplify great engineering and design, but the place itself captures the pioneering spirit that moved horse-drawn carriages and high-wheeled bicycles into the age of great motorcars and spurred the evolution of aircraft from the Wright Brothers through the 1930s. Special events are held on more than a dozen weekends all year, from a foreign auto festival to vintage motorcycle meets and a midsummer Spectacular featuring the best of everything. All events are highlighted by the museum's Antique Aeroplane Show, except the annual New England Auto Auction. And any day, all year, you're likely to find volunteers and staff mechanics working on vehicles and planes in the shop. Drop by to watch and say hi.

"This is a museum with a heart," said co-founder Steven Lang. "After 9/11, we were open for the rest of that winter for free so people had a something to do, a place to go and be happy. When we started in 1972, our goals were to create a cultural center for the region that would be a better use for the land next to the airport than what others had proposed and create a way for younger and older generations to communicate better. We didn't know anything about operating a museum but we went to see how it

Janet Mendelsohn

Early bicycles at the Owls Head Transportation Museum.

was done all over the state and took their best ideas. We run it like a business, but it will never feel that way to the public. Early on, we found that the restoration workshops, where volunteers work on the cars and planes, bring generations together. After a while working side-by-side, young guys would ask the older ones questions that puzzle them about marriage and old guys would ask them why so many young people do drugs. Communication opens up and mechanical know-how that would otherwise be lost gets passed along.

"We're open all year and kids are always free," said Lang. "At events, we have a special children's area where only kids and their parents are allowed. We encourage parents to leave them alone to enjoy the pedal cars and make planes from kits so they get the satisfaction of making things with their hands."

Similarly, it's not unusual to see multiple generations admiring vehicles in the spacious showroom, talking about when these cars ruled the road. Emphasizing the late 19th and early 20th centuries, the automotive collection includes Karl Benz's 1885 Tri-Car, the first vehicle designed to be powered by an internal combustion engine; a 1935 Stout Scarab, considered the first mini-van and one of only six produced; and such magnificent machines as a 1913 Rolls Royce Tourer, 1939 Packard Town Car, and 1955 Ford Thunderbird, from a catalogue too long to list.

"Today's 16-year-old is interested in anything that has motion," said Charles Chiarchiaro, executive director, "but they've grown up in a push-button world. Most kids in Maine haven't been in an airplane but they can navigate a space shuttle in a computer game. We demonstrate real things [rather than interactive substitutes]. People come

Janet Mendelsohn

Wright Brothers' first flight (replica)

here to see the mix of wings and wheels. We show them the evolution of transportation so they leave appreciating that what they are driving or flying in today is better than the Duesenberg you see here, no matter how beautiful it is."

USEFUL INFORMATION

• Owners of pre-1990 vehicles are welcome to exhibit free of charge at any event except the Annual New England Auction. No pre-registration is required. Exhibitor gates open at 8:30 am.

• Events often include family-oriented activities such as rides in the museum's Model T Fords.

• *Spark Plug*, a newsletter for children, is available online at the museum home page.

• Virtual collections feature highlights from past shows, on the website under Exhibitions.

• Coastal plane rides aboard OHTM's 1978 Piper Super Cub, and 1941 Stearman and 1933 Waco biplanes are available to museum members for an additional fee. Riders must be age 18 or older.

Time to allow: 1 hour, or more for special events
Admission: $10 Adults
  $8 Seniors (65 and older)
  Free Ages 18 and under
  Rates vary for special events
When it's open: All year, daily, 10 am–5 pm
  Closed Thanksgiving, Christmas, New Year's Day, and Volunteer Banquet Day in November.
Directions: Off ME-73 in Owls Head, adjacent to Knox County Airport. Museum Street is 2 miles south of Rockland, and 2 miles from US-1.

PENOBSCOT BAY
REGION

Farnsworth Art Museum
16 Museum Street, Rockland
www.farnsworthmuseum.org
207-596-6497

WHAT YOU'LL FIND HERE: Permanent collection of more than 10,000 paintings, sculptures, watercolors, and fine art objects in 12 galleries. Works by many of America's finest 19th-, 20th-, and 21st-century artists with connections to Maine. MBNA Center for the Wyeth Family in Maine, showcasing the works of N. C. Wyeth, Andrew Wyeth, and James Wyeth. Two historic properties: Farnsworth Homestead (21 Elm Street, Rockland), a 19th-century Greek Revival house; and Olson House (Hathorn Point Road, Cushing), the subject of numerous paintings by Andrew Wyeth. Summer art program for teens. Large gift shop.

WHY GO: It may come as a surprise to some that an art museum of this caliber and size exists on Penobscot Bay, but in recent years a thriving arts community has emerged with the Farnsworth at its center, helping to stimulate Rockland's growth.

Courtesy of Farnsworth Art Museum

George Bellows, The Teamster, *1916, oil on canvas. Bequest of Mrs. Elizabeth B. Noyce, 1997*

"Maine in America," the museum's permanent collection, is impressive in the depth and breadth of its emphasis on works by artists who have lived or worked in the state. They include many of the 19th century's most beloved portrait and landscape painters— Thomas Eakins, Winslow Homer, and Gilbert Stuart among them, as well as such Impressionists as Frank Benson and Childe Hassam, who repeatedly sought to capture the light and beauty of Maine. In the Rothschild Gallery, where visitors have been known to gasp when they recognize George Bellows's *The Teamster* or Rockwell Kent's *Maine Coast,* selections from the permanent collection rotate so that you may encounter works by Fitz Hugh (Henry) Lane or Marsden Hartley, among others. An extensive contemporary art collection includes pieces by Sam Cady, David Driskell, Yvonne Jacquette, Alex Katz, Fairfield Porter, Neil Welliver, and Robert Indiana, a longtime resident of nearby Vinalhaven Island. Equally renowned is the photography of Berenice Abbott, Paul Caponigro, Elliott Porter, and many others. A major donation of Louise Nevelson sculpture was received from the artist, who grew up in Rockland, and her family.

The Wyeth Center is one of only two centers dedicated to the work of artists N. C., Andrew, and James (Jamie) Wyeth. (The other is Brandywine River Museum in Chadds Ford, Pennsylvania). N. C. Wyeth was a tremendously popular illustrator of such classic children's books as *Treasure Island* and *Robinson Crusoe.* His drawings appeared in most of his era's popular magazines, including *Harper's Monthly, Saturday Evening Post,* and *Ladies Home Journal.* His son, Andrew, spent nearly every summer of his life in Maine and is best known for his haunting work *Christina's World*, one in a series painted over three decades in Cushing. When Andrew Wyeth died at age 91 in January 2009, the *New York Times* wrote, "He was a reclusive linchpin in a colorful family dynasty of artists whose precise realist views of hardscrabble rural life became icons of national culture and sparked endless debates about the nature of modern art." Andrew's son, Jamie, who lives near Rockland, is admired for his portraits of prominent figures, people in Maine, and life on nearby islands. *Inferno,* a large-scale painting of scavenging gulls that is part of Jamie Wyeth's "Seven Deadly Sins" series, is examined in a short film narrated by the artist about his work process and views on Monhegan Island that inspired the painting's vision of hell and fiery destruction. That documentary, *Infernal Monhegan,* is screened beside the painting in a gallery primarily devoted to his work upstairs in the "church" building on the museum campus. Downstairs galleries focus on N. C. Wyeth's work, while Andrew Wyeth's paintings are more often in the main building. Across the street from the "church" is a house now dedicated to research, collecting, exhibiting, and programming related to all three generations of the family, but especially James Wyeth, whose office is here.

The original Farnsworth Homestead is a 12-room Victorian house on the museum campus. Built by William Farnsworth in 1849, it is authentically preserved with original furnishings, as stipulated in the will left by Lucy Farnsworth, the last of her family, who lived here until her death in 1935. Farnsworth left a sizable estate and instructions that the bulk of it be used to establish a library and art museum as a memorial to her father. The house is an elegant example of how an upper-class family in Rockland lived during the 19th century.

Another historic property, the Olson House in Cushing, is depicted repeatedly in Andrew Wyeth's work, including *Christina's World*. His drawings, watercolors, and tempera paintings of the saltwater farm owned by his friends Christina Olson and her brother, Alvaro, portray the location's isolation and the sparse life of its occupants. To Wyeth, the house and Christina, who was paralyzed from the waist down, symbolized Maine and New England. He could not stay away. The property is now a National Historic Site administered by the museum.

USEFUL INFORMATION: Julia's Gallery for Young Artists, an after-school and summer program for ages 13–17, gives teens opportunities to curate, create, and critique art. Free to students. Applications and information: www.farnsworth museum.org/julias-gallery-programs, or 207-596-6457 ext. 146.

Time to allow: 2 hours minimum
   Allow extra time for Olson House, 14 miles from Rockland.
Admission: $12 Adults
   $10 Seniors
   $10 Students with ID
   Free Children 16 and younger

Andrew Wyeth, Turkey Pond, *1944, Tempera on panel, Farnsworth Art Museum, Gift of Mr. and Mrs. Andrew Wyeth in memory of Walter Anderson*

Free Wednesdays 5–8 pm
Free Rockland residents
Olson House and Farnsworth Homestead included in price of admission.
$5 Olson House only
When it's open: Memorial Day to Columbus Day
Daily, 10 am–5 pm
Wed., 10 am–8 pm
Olson House 11 am–4 pm
Winter Hours: Wed. –Sun., 10 am–5 pm
Closed Mon. and Tues.
Wyeth Center closed Jan. 4–May 15
Homestead and Olson House closed Columbus Day to Memorial Day weekends.
Closed Christmas Day, New Year's Day, and Thanksgiving.
Directions: Museum Street is just off US Route 1 (Main Street) in the center of Rockland. Free parking for museum visitors is available on campus in four lots including a large parking lot opposite the main entrance and another behind the Wyeth Center. A street entrance to the busy gift shop is on Main Street.

FUN FACTS

• Christmas has long been important to the Wyeth family. From Thanksgiving through December, the Wyeth Center's "church" building is decorated to share the wonder of the holiday with a lavish train set, art, and a tree decorated by museum docents.

• The first three weekends in December, the Farnsworth Homestead is open for a High Victorian Christmas.

• Even before the museum opened, in 1944, when Andrew Wyeth was 21 years old, the Farnsworth purchased several of his watercolors. In 1951, the museum mounted his first solo museum retrospective, in collaboration with the Currier Gallery (now the Currier Museum). Today, the Farnsworth owns 25 works by the artist.

SPOTLIGHT

Olson House

A soft gray rain stopped falling as I turned off the pebbled lane into the driveway of a house that seemed familiar, and yet not. The unadorned saltbox, cloaked in weathered gray-brown shingles, rested on a hilltop closer to the road than I expected. The simple lines of a traditional New England house with small-pane windows on only the lower floors spoke to the house's age. Above a steeply pitched roof, two tall chimneys aligned with two dormer windows. There were no shutters. Each pair of windows looked stark and cold, like eyes focused somewhere I could not see. Nor was the structure's plain exterior softened by shrubs or garden, save two small areas near a one-story addition on

the right, near the barn. Daisies in one patch, orange day lilies in the other. A pine ridge formed a backdrop to the scene. Despite the deep green of that wet summer, I expected the lawn to be brown, and its slope steeper, the way it appears in *Christina's World*. But the pull of Andrew Wyeth's painting remained intact. A lone woman in a dusky pink dress lying on the ground, using only the strength of her arms to pull herself toward the front door. It was more than the afternoon's milky whiteness or the memory of seeing this place in so many Wyeth paintings. It was the stillness of the Olson House itself.

Janet Mendelsohn

The drive from Rockland had taken longer than expected. I arrived shortly before closing to find a half-dozen visitors inside and a museum docent annoyed when another opened the door. "Why do people always come right before four o'clock?" she murmured, looking at me. I apologized, begging her to let me take a quick look around. She softened. I rushed to the next room, where I stopped and briefly held my breath.

There was a white Shaker-style bench, an occasional wood chair, and fading stenciling on some walls, but little else inside the house that Christina Olson (1893–1968) and her brother, Alvaro (1894–1967), inherited as the last generation to live on their family farm. In 1743, one of their seafaring ancestors built a simple cabin on 100 acres he received as a land grant above the St. Georges River. Over several generations, his descendants replaced the cabin with a frame house, which they altered in 1871 to the house that remains today. Floorboards and door trims are worn from use. Decades-old paint fades on the walls, but in the kitchen a hefty cast-iron stove sits ready to prepare meals.

Curtains no longer dress the windows, and yet they seemed to flutter gently in a nonexistent breeze. I know these rooms and the way the late-afternoon light filters through departing rainclouds, washing across the wooden floors. I've been here many times, though only in my mind's eye. Fingering the lens of my camera, I wanted to stay, for hours, to capture this sense of the past and the lives lived in this place, just as Wyeth did. Over three decades, he developed a friendship with the Olsons. They let him wander through their home at will and gave him a room on the third floor to use as his studio. Christina, who was crippled from the waist down, was his frequent model. For Wyeth, her life and the house itself symbolized Maine and New England. He was often quoted, "I just couldn't stay away from there. I did other pictures while I knew them but I'd always seem to gravitate back to the house . . . It was Maine."

Olson House—A National Historic Site
Historic Property of the Farnsworth Art Museum
384 Hathorne Point Road, Cushing
207-354-0102
www.farnsworthmuseum.org/historic-properties

Admission: $5 per person or free with admission to the Farnsworth Art Museum in Rockland.
Limited wheelchair access; contact the museum in advance for assistance.
Note: Andrew Wyeth's painting Christina's World is in the collection of the Museum of Modern Art in New York.
When it's open: Memorial Day–Columbus Day
Daily, 11 am–4 pm
Bus tours by reservations only.
Directions: From US Route 1 in Thomaston, at the Maine State Prison Showroom, turn onto Wadsworth Street. Drive over a metal bridge after which Wadsworth becomes River Road. Follow this for 6 miles. Bear left just after passing Fales Store in Cushing. The road becomes Pleasant Point Road. Follow this for 1.5 miles and turn right onto Hathorne Point Road. The Olson House is about 2 miles farther, on the left.

Maine Lighthouse Museum
One Park Drive, Rockland
www.mainelighthousemuseum.org
207-594-3301

WHAT YOU'LL FIND HERE: The largest collection of lighthouse artifacts in the United States. A 292-year record of lighthouse operations. Dozens of Fresnel lenses. Large-scale models of light stations beloved for their architecture. Stories of keepers and their families. Gift shop.

WHY GO: *Blink . . . blink . . . blink . . .* Day and night, in rain, sunshine, snow, and especially fog . . . Merchant mariners and recreational boaters alike depend on Maine's 65 lighthouses for navigation. Their scenic locations and romantic image lures tourists of all ages, cameras at the ready. Some are stationed in remote offshore places like Matinicus Rock, Franklin Island, Egg Rock, and tiny Boon Island in York. Others are a long drive from most population centers—West Quoddy Head Light in Lubec comes to mind. And some are places where the timid fear to tread. Ghosts are said to haunt Wood Island in Biddeford, Hendricks Head in West Southport, and Owls Head, among others. A few light stations have museums of their own, including Pemaquid Point, Marshall Point, and Grindle Point, but if you want the big picture, it's hard to beat the Maine Lighthouse Museum at Rockland Harbor.

The extensive collection of Fresnel lenses, foghorns, blinking buoy lanterns, scale models, personal items, maps, and lore does an admirable job of describing their importance along the coast for hundreds of years. The essential Fresnel lens, for example, was a 19th-century technological innovation that took the light of an oil lamp and made it visible to mariners 20 miles out. And there's much to discover amid the fog horns in all shapes and sizes; keepers' hats, insignia, and contracts; and buoy lanterns that blink throughout the spacious hall, lending an air of festivity to the historic exhibits.

Today all but one of New England's lighthouses are automated (the exception is Boston Light Station) but that hasn't diminished their mystique. "At one time I would have told you people think lighthouses are romantic," said Dot Black, whose late husband, Ken, aka "Mr. Lighthouse," founded the museum. "But since knowing Ken and working here, I now see that visitors recognize the hard work people had to put into keeping the light going and what it took to save their families in hard conditions." As interim director of the museum, "Mrs. Lighthouse" runs the large gift shop, loaded with every imaginable lighthouse souvenir, and oversees the collection.

Ken Black was commander of the Coast Guard Station in Rockland when he began collecting lenses, lamps, and objects in the late 1960s. Black realized the historical value of the optical and mechanical systems that were being thrown away as lights nationwide were gradually automated. Obtaining official permission to save the gear, he amassed a display too large for its first home at the Coast Guard Station in Rockland. Black retired in 1973 and passed away in 2007, but the expanding exhibits ultimately arrived in their current location inside the Chamber of Commerce Visitor Center, where in 2008 alone the museum logged 39,000 visitors from all over the world.

Responsibility for lighthouses in this country has changed over time. After the Civil War, a Lighthouse Board was created to turn the nation's career civilian lighthouse keepers into a professional organization and oversee the advent of complex lighting and fog signaling equipment. Keepers were closely supervised by senior Naval officers. For the first time, they were trained and had to follow instructions, but the regimentation also meant their stark living quarters were improved, uniforms were issued in the 1880s, and even fine china and other amenities were provided for their families' use. Keepers became part of the Civil Service System around 1890, receiving a paid retirement plan for the first time in 1918. From 1939, when the 150-year-old Lighthouse Service was disbanded, to the mid-1990s, lighthouses were run by the U.S. Coast Guard and keepers could choose to remain civilians or become military personnel. Civilians were retired in World War II. Soon after, automation relegated the job of lighthouse keeper to the past.

Memorable stories here include those of a 17-year-old heroine who in 1856 kept the lighthouse working at Matinicus Rock during a powerful winter storm, and the Flying Santas, who for more than 75 years every Christmas flew to distant light stations to drop boxes of presents to Coast Guard families.

USEFUL INFORMATION:

• The museum is inside the Maine Discovery Center, headquarters of the Chamber of Commerce in downtown Rockland, adjacent to Buoy Park. Numerous waterfront summer festivals are held in the park, attracting huge crowds. The visitors' center lobby contains a wealth of information about the Midcoast region as well as an interesting one-eighth scale, tabletop diorama depicting Rockland Harbor on August 24, 1907, when the six-masted coasting schooner *Mertle B. Crowly* was launched amid 10 other boats afloat or in the Cook & Butler Co. shipyard.

• A coastal map on the floor in front of the Chamber's information counter indicates the location of all 65 lighthouses in Maine, plus three in Canada. They are all numbered. Ask for a free copy of the Lighthouse Legend to match each number with its name.

• Since 2009, Maine's annual Open Lighthouse Day welcomes the public to tour most of the state's lighthouses on a Saturday in September. www.lighthouseday.com.

Time to allow: 30 minutes
Admission: $5 Adults
    $4 Seniors (60 and over)
    Free Ages 12 and under
When it's open: June 1–Nov. 1
    Mon.–Fri., 9 am–5 pm
    Sat.–Sun., 10 am–4 pm

FUN FACTS A U.S. Coast Guard cutter is named for Abbie Burgess, the teenage heroine who kept Matinicus Light operating when her father, the keeper, was kept ashore by a winter storm in 1856. Matinicus Rock lies 25 miles out from Penobscot

Bay. Years after her impressive and doubtlessly lifesaving feat, she became the lighthouse keeper. Abbie Burgess Grant is buried in Forrest Hill Cemetery, off Route 73 in Spruce Head. A little lighthouse marks her grave.

National Audubon Project Puffin Visitor Center
311 Main Street, Rockland
www.projectpuffin.org
207-596-5566

WHAT YOU'LL FIND HERE: Educational exhibits on efforts to restore puffin colonies. Live video of seabird activity on Seal Island (seasonal). Small gallery of contemporary art and photography by international artists. Full-size replica of an observation hut. Gift shop.

WHY GO: While not a true museum, this is a good place to learn a lot about those adorable seabirds with orange feet and triangular, multi-colored bills. Many people assume these cold-climate birds are related to penguins, but they're not. Puffins are part of the auk family, like razorbills and black guillemots; unlike penguins, puffins can fly. They are smaller than you might think, only about 10 inches tall. Where puffins migrate in winter is something of a mystery, but in summer they love the Gulf of Maine. Project Puffin Visitor Center focuses on nesting seabirds, especially puffins, on Eastern Egg Rock, Matinicus Rock, and Seal Island National Wildlife Refuge (NWR), which is managed by National Audubon and its conservation partners.

Since 1973, as part of National Audubon's Seabird Restoration Program, Project Puffin has studied nesting pairs in the Seal Island NWR. The visitor center opened in 2006 to educate the public about the work.

Atlantic Puffins thrived in the mid-1880s, but nearly became extinct during the Victorian era when the birds were hunted for their feathers, a popular fashion accessory for ladies' hats, and for their eggs, which were considered a delicacy. Since puffins lay only one egg a year, they were unable to reproduce as fast as the eggs were taken. In 1901, only one nesting pair remained on Matinicus Rock. There were none at Eastern Egg and Seal islands when the restoration project was launched.

Beginning with five chicks transferred from Newfoundland, the project has successfully reintroduced puffins to Seal Island NWR. Hundreds of pairs now nest in hidden burrows under boulders, migrate in winter, and return here each spring. Thousands have formed colonies in the Gulf of Maine. Almost nothing is known about their winter home but researchers assume they migrate somewhere in the North Atlantic, floating on the sea surface.

In summer, there's a "Puffin Cam" in the front window of the visitor center. Passersby can watch live video of the seabirds' Seal Island habitat.

But if you come inside and follow the orange puffin footprints on the floor you'll come to a family-oriented exhibit area in the back. A "puffin burrow" for little kids might be big enough for courageous adults to crawl into, and inside they can watch a video of chicks interacting with adult seabirds. Elsewhere are samples of puffins' favorite foods—fish, mostly herring—and banding materials used by researchers to track the birds. In a full-size replica of an observation hut (a "blind"), you get a sense of what field investigators see and do on location and get answers to their typical questions. You can even read real data-gathering sheets.

USEFUL INFORMATION: Puffin cruises with Audubon naturalists as guides are offered by two companies. One departs from Boothbay, the other from New Harbor. Each summer, thousands of visitors view the puffin colony at Eastern Egg Rock. Although the boats go close to the island, binoculars are a must since puffins are fairly small. Also possible are views of the endangered roseate tern, common and Arctic terns, common eiders, laughing gulls, and other seabirds, as well as harbor seals and minke whales. Contact the visitor center for information, fares, and schedules.

Time to allow: 30 minutes
Admission: Free
When it's open: May: Wed.–Sun., 10 am–5 pm
　　June–Oct.: Daily, 10 am–5 pm and Wed. 10 am–7 pm
　　Nov. and Dec.: Sat. and Sun. only, 10 am–5 pm

FUN FACT: The "Puffin Cam" is also available online at http://projectpuffin.org/PuffinCam.html.

WHILE YOU'RE IN THE ROCKLAND AREA . . .

Two new museums are just getting started in the same building at Sharp's Point South, the old Snow Shipyard, on the harbor:

Coastal Children's Museum
For ages 2–9 and their families
75 Mechanic Street
www.coastalchildrensmuseum.org
207-975-2530

Sail, Power and Steam Museum
Maritime history of the Midcoast region
75 Mechanic Street
www.sailpowerandsteammuseum.org
207-594-2230

Center for Maine Contemporary Art
162 Russell Avenue, Rockport
www.cmcanow.org
207-236-2875

WHAT YOU'LL FIND HERE: Works by living artists with ties to Maine. Paintings, photography, digital media, craft, and installation art. Annual art auction. Biennial juried exhibition (alternates with the Portland Museum of Art Biennial). Annual "Work of the Hand" juried craft show and sale. Educational workshops and professional development programs for artists. Gift shop.

WHY GO: Much as open studio events invite us to see what artists are working on now, the Center for Maine Contemporary Art (CMCA) allows us to feel the vibrancy of the state's current art scene. CMCA is neither a true gallery nor a true museum. It represents no individual artists. It has no permanent collection. But throughout the year, temporary exhibitions present outstanding works by artists connected to Maine either because they were born here, studied in the state, or live here part-time or year-round. Art is curated or juried without concern for its commercial appeal but with the dual intent of exposing the public to emerging and established artists and increasing public understanding of artistic expression.

Fog-white barn-wood walls, floors, and rafters make the space restful and draw the eye to each work of art without fanfare. Shows are never predictable. A group exhibition might invite unconventional definitions of self-portraiture or examine the influence that comics, animation, and other popular imagery have had on the making of art.

CMCA was founded in 1952 as Maine Coast Artists, a Rockport-Camden artists' cooperative. Early members included two founders of prominent art schools in the state: Francis Merritt of Haystack Mountain School of Crafts and Willard Cummings of Skowhegan School of Painting. Over the past 60 years, exhibiting artists including Bernard Langlais, Alex Katz, Neil Welliver, and Fairfield Porter have achieved national recognition and CMCA has expanded its scope statewide. The name was changed in 1998. Professional development programs for artists focus on such topics as marketing strategies, grant-writing, and legal issues. In addition to showing the work of more than 400 emerging and established artists each year, from late spring to early summer CMCA holds a Distinguished Artist Exhibition focusing on a single artist's body of work. Previously these have showcased such notables as Alan Magee, Linden Frederick, and Yvonne Jacquette.

With a new director who arrived in fall 2010, watch for possible changes in seasonal dates and hours, and a focus that sets CMCA apart from other contemporary Maine art venues.

Time to allow: 30 minutes
Admission: Free
When it's open: Late spring–early Dec.

Summer hours
Tues.–Sat., 10 am–5 pm
Sun., 1–5 pm
Closed Monday

Winter hours
Thurs.–Sat., 10 am–5 pm
Sun., 1–4 pm
Closed Tues.–Wed.

Directions: From the south: Take I-295 north to Brunswick and continue north on US Route 1 to ME-90 East. Follow ME-90 to the end. Turn left on Pascal Avenue, go through Rockport Village and up the hill. At the Opera House, bear right. CMCA is on the right.

From the north: Take US Route 1 South through Camden. Turn left onto West Street at the junction of Route 1 and ME-90. Turn left onto Pascal Avenue. Go through Rockport Village and up the hill. At the Opera House, bear right. CMCA is on the right.

Penobscot Marine Museum
5 Church Street, Searsport
www.pmm-maine.org
207-548-2529

WHAT YOU'LL FIND HERE: Thirteen buildings, including eight on the National Register of Historic Places. Regional, antique watercraft, from birchbark canoes to lobster boats. Authentic sea captain's home furnished with items local mariners brought home from the Orient. Activity yard. "Pirate's hideway" and indoor activity center for children. Folk art and marine paintings. Research library. One of the largest collections of historical photographs in Maine. Picnic area. Gift shop.

WHY GO: Driving by on Main Street, it would be easy to mistake this for just another cluster of historic buildings like others in New England. But there's more than meets the eye at the oldest maritime museum in Maine.

"The story I've heard often enough to believe it's true is that in 1936, several descendants of local sea captains were driving through town talking about ways to preserve the past when they came upon a man throwing half hull models onto a fire," said Niles Parker, former executive director. "They immediately stopped and said 'Whoa, wait, we have to save these early objects. They have stories to tell.'" And that's when they founded the museum. The compact campus in the heart of Searsport feels much as this seaport village must have been at its peak during the Age of Sail.

"For such a small town, Searsport has had an outsized impact on shipping in this country," said Parker. "Unofficial reports indicate during the mid-1880s Searsport men represented 10 percent of all active men in the nation's fleet. Whether the number is accurate or not, it speaks to the fact that Searsport men built contacts and had knowledge that was so extensive, it branded the town. Major companies wanted to hire 'Searsport men' because they were considered the best. It was said that this town's captains were as at home on the streets of Hong Kong as they were in Searsport."

For a long time, people associated the museum with those sea captains but, as Parker observed, it's close to a beautiful bay with one of the busiest deepwater harbors in the state and one of the biggest fisheries in the world. That's why new exhibits draw parallels between those captains and work currently underway around Penobscot Bay.

But much of the focus is on life in the region during the 19th century and what it was like to sail to China when the Orient was a mysterious distant land. You'll learn about the skills required and the economic ups and downs of ice harvesting, granite, lumber, and fishing, all past or present industries in the region. "Gone Fishing" covers the fishing industry from handlining to lobstering and invites children and adults to board a replica lobster boat and sometimes the sardine carrier *Jacob Pike*. "Rowboats for Rusticators" dips into the traditional ties between local guides and visiting sportsmen.

While the founders' goal may have been to preserve and share the treasured possessions of local families, it's equally likely they hoped to give their town due recognition for its dual roles as a bustling shipbuilding community and anchor of early America's expanding global trade. Searsport today is a quiet, picturesque community of about 2,500 permanent residents, but during the mid-1800s it was a busy port. Captains often brought their families with them as they traveled around the globe. Children learned first-hand about other cultures and experienced the realities of life at sea. It's the stuff of classic novels and movies that conjure images of romantic and intriguing adventure, as well as hard work under trying conditions.

Sea captains' families enjoyed other benefits, as evidenced inside the museum's Victorian era Fowler-True-Ross House. The Federal-style, two-room farmhouse (circa 1805, with a two-story addition added in 1825) was occupied by a captain's descendants until 1967, when it became part of the museum. The kitchen's spacious fireplace is blackened from centuries of cooking. Rooms are graciously decorated with objects from the attics and parlors of several old Searsport families. Portraits, toys, hooked rugs, and musical instruments are scattered amidst 19th-century furniture, china, and glassware. A piano with mother of pearl keys and silk gowns was brought back from the Orient.

In the Nickels-Colcord-Duncan Barn and Boat House (circa 1841–1845), the eight small boats include a Herreshoff 12½ sloop; a North Haven dingy (1903), representing the oldest active racing sailboat class in America; and a Wee Scot Class sloop (1925) that's a 15-foot macaroni-rigged keel sloop. Nearby, the exhibit "Working the Bay" explains how loggers, farmers, ice harvesters, ship builders, and mariners in the Penobscot Bay region used tools unique to their trades.

A prominent shipbuilder's former home now is the "Peapod," a lively drop-in center where children can play dress-up in period clothing, pretend to work and live in a 19th-century town, or imagine themselves at sea. A former schoolhouse and the Congregational church vestry have been converted into a marine science center with a touch tank and other hands-on activities for children. In the yard, visitors can hoist sails, crank a capstan to raise and lower an anchor, use a block-and-tackle, and imagine they are aboard tall ships.

PMM experts also take the museum to the people by bringing slide shows and talks to churches and libraries in towns across Maine. Leading the emerging off-campus initiatives, in late 2008 PMM formed a partnership with Local School District No. 56's after-school program. Funded by a federal grant, the program enrolled nearly 90 children at three elementary schools who were taught a new curriculum that combines maritime themes with literacy skills and hands-on activities. An expansion grant in 2009 enabled museum educators to visit six elementary sites each week, participate in the district's summer school program, and work with the middle and high schools in Searsport to establish a new program there, as well. Elementary school students attend Down-Easter Days, the museum's summer day program, and a new elementary school curriculum integrates topics in maritime history from the museum's education website, www.penobscotbayhistory.org, relevant "Maine State Learning Results," hands-on activities, and literacy skills and practice.

"We hope to expand these programs further, in part because, like other seasonal museums, we have several old buildings that are not winterized and have to be shut down," said Parker. "Education outreach is an important way we are becoming a year-round museum."

USEFUL INFORMATION:

• Most buildings are wheelchair accessible except for the second floor.

• Searsport mooring No. 55 may be reserved by calling the Searsport Harbormaster at 207-548-2722 or on VHF channels 9, 10, 71, or 78.

Time to allow: 1–1½ hours
Admission: $8 Adult
    $3 Ages 7–15
    Free Ages 6 and under
    $18 Family (2 parents + children under 18 yrs in same household)
    $5 Groups, per person for parties larger than 10 people.
When it's open: Late May–late October.
    Mon.–Sat., 10 am–5 pm
    Sun., noon–5 pm
    Call in advance to arrange a tour for groups of 10 or more.
Directions: US Route 1 (Main Street) at the corner of Church and Main streets in the center of Searsport. Free parking on site and across the street.

FUN FACT: Sharing the museum's campus is First Congregational Church of Searsport, an active congregation. Eight of its 11 tall windows are authentic Tiffany stained glass (protected by bullet-proof glass). The vivid colors and floral patterns are exceptionally beautiful. Their richness contrasts with the simplicity of the sanctuary, creating a quiet, uplifting space for meditation. Visitors are welcome to enter the sanctuary during two 20-minute periods daily.

A Sea Chest Full of Photography Treasures at the Penobscot Marine Museum

More than 100,000 images from the past—prints, slides, daguerreotypes, glass plate negatives, postcards, cabinet cards, and albums—form an archive at the Penobscot Marine Museum that is one of the largest photography collections in Maine. Nine significant collections and dozens of wonderful smaller ones capture a wide range of places and moments connected to the Penobscot Bay region by their subject, photographer, or publisher. With the help of volunteers and the latest technology, photo archivist Kevin Johnson and his staff are cleaning and scanning the often-fragile images one by one, and entering each in an online database for use by researchers, writers, and the general public.

Modest fees are charged for fine art reproductions or licensing for commercial, artistic, or personal use in projects that range from illustrating books and creating historical murals to finding a single photo of a grandparents' store or the boat shop where a beloved skiff was built.

Ruth Montgomery Collection, Penobscot Marine Museum

The largest collection in many ways is also the most evocative. The museum owns more than 40,000 glass plate negatives shot and printed as specialty postcards by Eastern Illustrating & Publishing Co. between 1909 and 1947, when postcards were all the rage. In 1909, R. Herman Cassens, a young go-getter with an eye for opportunity, started the company down the road in Belfast when he realized there was money to be made by filling the gap between personal or amateur postcards and mass-produced postcards of big cities. His idea was to capture scenes of small-town America that told the true stories of people at work, children at play, and local events, and print these images as "real photo postcards."

Cassens and his small crew of photographers set out to shoot in every state, from Maine to California. They didn't reach them all but they covered New England and New York. Immediately after each shoot, they sent the exposed negatives back to the "factory" in Belfast for processing and printing. Then the postcards were shipped back to the local general store, which sold them for two to five cents apiece.

Long after the company folded, much of the Eastern Illustrated collection ended up in cartons that were almost destroyed in a 2007 flood.

Real-photo postcards today are a hot item among collectors, said Johnson, who noted there are gaps in the museum's collection that he'd love to fill. Whole towns in Maine are missing, most likely in private collections. Almost daily on eBay he finds 50 to 100 new listings, asking anywhere from $10 to $50 apiece for the glass plate negatives; one Eastern Illustrated postcard sold for $100.

Johnson, who seems to live with one foot in the present, one in the past, said: "We live in such a visual age that photography can capture even young peoples' minds. It's so literal. The Eastern Illustrated collection shows us how people dressed and what their churches, stately homes, shops, and main streets looked like in the first three decades of the 20th century. And our other collections tell us different things." Everett "Red" Boutilier, a freelance photographer and journalist from Bremen who died in 2003, went to almost every boat launch in midcoast Maine. He was friends with all the boat builders in this region and would often follow a boat from its beginning to launch. Charles Coombs, an undertaker in Belfast who took up the hobby in the 1890s, loved photographing Belfast and neighboring towns, family, friends, animals, and hunting and sailing trips. Frederick Ross Sweetser, a music teacher and organist, often returned to his native Searsport, where he photographed loved ones and family outings. The Sweetser and Coombs collections offer a nice picture of upper-middle-class family life around Pen Bay a century ago. Other small collections focus on Maine's working waterfronts and ships or maritime trades. Close to 1,000 negatives and prints in the archive documented the northeast fishing industry for *Atlantic Fisherman* monthly between 1919 and the mid-1950s.

"We're at the perfect time period now to be able to scan and then share these old collections over the Internet, which gets them to people who want to use them in so many ways," said Johnson. "I constantly hear from people looking for a picture of their boat or house or island." Make a request. For $1 per negative, archive volunteers or staff will scan appropriate photos and send a CD of low-resolution thumbnail images from which you can choose the prints you want. The fee finances the work which, except for the largest communities, usually takes 7–10 days.

The old black-and-white or sepia-tone photographs have become catalysts for education opportunities, said Johnson who presents slideshow talks to crowds at libraries, churches, and social halls around the region. There is enough material for at least a dozen books.

Glass plate negatives deteriorate over time due to oxidation, said Johnson. To slow down the process as much as possible, the plates are stored individually packaged in acid-free envelopes stacked on end, on weight-bearing shelves in climate-controlled, low humidity rooms. If they drop, they shatter.

Authors and researchers make rather specific requests. One wanted pictures of old-style ferries, when they were still simply rafts pulled across rivers by rope. Another needed early scenes of Mount Desert Island; a third wanted every town on Lake Champlain for a book published for the 400th anniversary of the lake's exploration by Samuel de Champlain.

But most requests are more personal—lots of folks just want to relive old memories.

Bryant Stove and Music Museum and Doll Circus
27 Stovepipe Alley, Thorndike
www.bryantstove.com
207-568-3665

WHAT YOU'LL FIND HERE: Hundreds of antique stoves, dozens of mechanical music players, antique cars, and an antique button collection. Doll Circus, an extravagant, animated display of vintage dolls, porcelain babies, Barbies, and furry creatures that dance, march, and fly.

WHY GO: You approach a rundown, rural warehouse and enter an office that hasn't been updated in decades. You ask to see the museum and friendly employees usher you through a windowless door into a dark room, saying "Tell us when you're all inside." You do, and wham! The lights come on, a circus calliope blares happy music, and everywhere you look dolls and furry critters whirl into action. They're riding tabletop Ferris wheels, dancing on miniature stages, tap dancing, or posing in rows with scores of their doll friends, grouped by style and era. From floor to ceiling and wall to wall, there are thousands of dolls, some genuine antiques, and many are moving. Marionettes walk in a "waddling parade" of animals. Teddy bears fly airplanes. There's a hopscotching dance show of clothespin dolls and others that play in a band. This amazing doll circus fills a room the size of a two-car garage. When I visited with two friends, our eyes popped, our jaws literally dropped, and we couldn't stop laughing.

Some things must be experienced to be believed, and this is one of them. It's what happens when two people with a passion for collecting and a talent for mechanical restoration merge their interests over 50 years. Joe and Bea Bryant put this astounding collection together and the doll circus is merely the beginning.

The heart of the operation is Bryant Stove Works, a family-owned business that repairs and sells coal- and wood-burning stoves, most built between 1846 and 1930. But the Bryants' favorite ornate cast-iron beauties, the ones they won't sell, are in the museum. Tear yourself away from the doll circus and walk past a collection of 31 model steam engines designed and made by Henry Stark on his porch in Zephyr Hills, Florida, each different and in working condition. That will bring you to a warehouse crammed like a New England antiques barn with old cars and trucks and fabulous antique stoves.

But wait, there's more. If you come when Joe Bryant can give you the tour, he'll sing songs of bygone days and play his mechanical instruments for as long as you're willing to stay. It's a grand show. There's a Nickelodeon from 1922; a Seeburg player piano with a wooden xylophone, mandolin rail, and stained-glass eagle on the front; a huge calliope; and five band organs that once played on carousels. A hurdy-gurdy street piano, or barrel organ, is programmed with 10 songs that played when someone tossed a coin to the guy who cranked it on Boylston Street in Boston. A tabletop Reginaphone music box and phonograph plays both metal disks and LPs. Bryant said the Regina music box company sold 100,000 metal disks between 1894 and 1920,

Janet Mendelsohn

but business tanked when records were introduced, so the company started producing those, too, and made players that could handle both.

When you're ready to move on, Bryant will tell you the history of some fabulously ornate cast-iron stoves that line the perimeter of the room. From there, you enter the business end of the building, an immaculate showroom displaying hundreds of reconditioned antique cook stoves and parlor heaters for sale.

"Bea got us into this stove thing," said Bryant. "I had a steel fabrication business and repaired trucks and fire truck bodies for about 11 years. We had a chicken house to help support our family and we always liked old things. When we acquired the old farmhouse across the road, we heated our part and the apartment above with wood stoves. Bea said we should start a company that combined her passion for antiques and my mechanical skills. I didn't think there would be 20 old stoves in the whole state of Maine, but when people heard we'd buy them or take them in trade, the whole thing mushroomed." Today they have close to an acre of stoves in several outbuildings and store parts outdoors on their 100-acre farm.

"One thing leads to another," said Bryant. "When I was in high school, there were two player pianos on stage. I'd go watch them work. I always loved mechanical things." During winters in Florida, he built almost all the animated circus toys and whirligigs, often using bicycle wheels to make them go. When they bought an old organ in Canada only to discover that mice had eaten through it, he adapted the instrument as a runway for a Barbie Doll fashion show.

During more than 60 years of marriage enlivened by a slew of children, grandchildren, and great-grandchildren, Bea Bryant has sewn hundreds of quilts and acquired an impressive variety of buttons, displayed in organized sets in one hall. She designed and sewed clothes for the dolls she found at flea markets, fairs, and garage sales from northern New England to Florida. How many dolls are there? "Who has time to count them?" she said, laughing.

Joe Bryant has a fine, strong voice and loves to belt out tunes while accompanying himself on his remarkable musical collection. He's like a big kid having fun and there's a story to go with nearly everything that came from another place and time.

"We're modern. We recycle," he said.

USEFUL INFORMATION: The museum is open all year but Joe and Bea Bryant leave Maine for the winter. Try to visit when Joe is available to give a guided tour. Although he suffers from a medical condition that requires him to use a wheelchair, he'll slide right onto a piano bench like a spry youngster to perform.

Time to allow: 45 minutes, but allow an hour or two for stories and musical entertainment if Joe Bryant gives his guided tour.
Admission: Free
When it's open: Mon.–Sat., 8 am–4:30 pm
Directions: Thirty miles east of I-95, exit 132, via ME-139; or 30 miles west of Belfast via ME-137 to ME-220, and turn right. At the junction of ME-139 and ME-220, near Unity.

FUN FACTS:
• If you've been inside a Cracker Barrel restaurant or store, you've probably seen one of the Bryants' restored stoves. They're part of the retailer's country decor nationwide.
• Bryant has also sold antique stoves to customers all over the world and several have been used in Hollywood movies.

CHAPTER 4

DOWN EAST

Abbe Museum
Downtown: 26 Mount Desert Street (Route 3)
Trailside, Acadia National Park: Sieur de Monts Spring
Bar Harbor
www.abbemuseum.org
207-288-3519

WHAT YOU'LL FIND HERE: Art, crafts, and history of the Wabanaki people of Maine, past and present. Two locations: The main building in downtown Bar Harbor displays works by Native artists, a timeline of the Wabanaki presence in Maine, archeological artifacts, special art and history exhibitions, Circle of the Four Directions gathering space, and year-round programs for interaction, exchange, and learning between Native and non-Native people. Original trailside museum in Acadia National Park contains early- to mid-20th century dioramas of Native life and archeological artifacts. Gift shops in both.

WHY GO: For close to 12,000 years, the region now called Maine has been home to the Micmac, Passamaquoddy, Penobscot, Maliseet, and Abenaki people, known collectively as the Wabanaki Tribes. Their first interactions with Europeans, in the 1500s and 1600s, dramatically altered the lives of both Native people and new arrivals. Each was introduced to the others' tools and technologies, religions, and agricultural and cultural practices, but contact also increased warfare and spread disease. The Abbe Museum does more than present the history of the Wabanaki and beautiful work by past and contemporary Native artists, although it does both well. In the oral tradition that is part of their heritage, first-person voices and visual images tell life stories, helping people of all backgrounds connect across cultures and learn to think differently.

In archeology, every object has a story. Even displays of stone-age tools and pottery remnants tell how an object was used. "Layers of Time," a hands-on exhibit with digging tools and magnifiers for children, explains what archeologists do and what we can learn from the things people left behind. Adults can tap into their inner Indiana Jones while holding literal pieces of the past, like ancient pottery shards and arrowheads found on Mount Desert Island. Several objects are rare and captivating finds, including a flute carved from the bone of a swan, estimated to have been made 2,000 years ago.

The museum successfully joins old and new, beginning with its two locations. The original museum in Acadia National Park was built in 1928. Essentially a single charming, eight-sided room, it has a high domed ceiling, glass-enclosed display cases, and tall windows that may have some of the prettiest woodland views of any on the National Register of Historic Places. Its somewhat dated exhibits—four basic dioramas depicting scenes of Passamaquoddy encampments in the four seasons—were built around 1973. Display cases contain archeological artifacts—stone projectile points, knives, fishing weights or harpoons, needles, combs, and the like, carved from bone—found in heaps around Lafayette National Park before it was renamed

Acadia. According to a docent, the museum's founder, Dr. Robert Abbe, was an avid collector who thought the tribes that carved the tools were extinct and was unaware that their descendants had their own advanced culture. He founded the museum as a private venture to preserve archeological artifacts for the public to enjoy. The institution immediately became the first in Maine to sponsor archeological research. Today, a popular ongoing program is the museum's Archeology Field School, one week each summer when participants can work alongside professional archeologists, conducting excavations, mapping sites, and analyzing artifacts.

In 2001, the Abbe opened a modern museum centrally located in Bar Harbor. Its spacious galleries present permanent and temporary exhibitions on nature and cultural identity, as when Native artists use various media to express what it is to "walk in two worlds." An extensive collection of traditional and fancy baskets made of ash, sweetgrass, birch, and other natural materials illustrates how basket making and other traditional Native crafts bring people and generations together.

Courtesy of Abbe Museum

Flute made from a swan bone, from the Tranquility Farm site. Abbe Museum collections.

"The Abbe Museum has long had a close relationship with the Wabanaki in Maine," said Cinnamon Catlin-Legutko, the museum's chief executive officer. "Members of the tribes serve on our board, as staff, and as guest curators. We bring artists, scholars, and political leaders to the museum throughout the year to interact with our visitors and lead workshops, demonstrations, and discussions. The Abbe has continued to expand our relationship with the Wabanaki, and be a leader in the field, through [their] increased participation in the exhibits process and by addressing contemporary issues that can, at times, be contentious."

A 2011 exhibition, "Indians and Rusticators: Wabanakis & Summer Visitors on Mount Desert Island," is a perfect example. Based on an extensive study by two prominent anthropologists, Bunny McBride and Harald E. L. Prins, the show is character-driven, using photographs, historic maps, and drawings to describe cultural threats and economic opportunities that confronted the Wabanaki when tourism began to surge in the region during the 19th century. Clothing decorated with beadwork and elaborately carved clubs made from roots were among items made specifically for the tourist trade. They were sold in tents and sheds that the museum is replicating for the show. Another exhibit, in 2010, used actual news headlines over a recent 20-year period and the voices of Wabanaki leaders to examine issues covered by the news media and of critical importance to the tribes, including recognition of Native veterans in the U.S. military, retention of traditional languages, environmental management of territorial land, hunting and fishing rights, international border disputes that divide families, and positive and negative stereotypes. Although that exhibit, "Headline

News: Wabanaki Sovereignty in the 21st Century," has ended, several of its themes will likely reappear in other forms.

At the entrance, a 12,000-year timeline of Wabanaki history in Maine (also available online in abbreviated form) introduces visitors to the museum's focus and its welcoming approach. By design, the interactive timeline's position on the wall and its signage make it accessible to those in wheelchairs, children, and short adults, but it's not so low that adults of average height cannot read the descriptions. Catlin-Legutko said larger font sizes make displays easier for people to read from a greater distance, or with below-average vision. Perhaps better than any other museum in Maine, without fanfare, the Abbe downtown is simply accessible to all.

The annual Waponahki Student Art Show is popular with all ages. The Circle of the Four Directions is an architecturally and culturally significant structure inside the building that Catlin-Legutko said fascinated locals while under construction. "It was created in response to Native focus groups' desire to see a circular space in the museum, representing traditional Wabanaki world views about the circular nature of time and the seasons." The Circle is used as a performance space and for demonstrations of techniques such as birch bark basket making and etching, paddle carving, crooked knives, and chip carving. The room is where public tours and education programs finish, and is used as a place where visitors can discuss and reflect on what they've seen.

The Abbe often collaborates on exhibitions with the Penobscot Nation Museum, the Hudson Museum at UMaine-Orono, and the Passamaquoddy Museum, and occasionally with local island museums and Maine's major art museums, including the Farnsworth and Portland Museum of Art.

The museum's founder, Dr. Abbe (1851–1928), was a pioneering surgeon, an avid student of many things, and a summer resident of Bar Harbor. Abbe is credited with the first use of radiation to treat cancer and is considered the founder of radiation therapy. He was also an artist, poet, and maker of three-dimensional plaster maps. In 1926, he persuaded other prominent summer residents who shared his interest in archeology, including John D. Rockefeller, Jr., to establish a museum for their collections, including his own early Native American artifacts from around Frenchman Bay. He died just months before the privately owned museum opened in what was then called Lafayette National Park, at Sieur de Monts Spring. That is the trailside museum, which was built as a stop for hikers along the trail.

Time to allow: 1 hour downtown
    15 minutes trailside
Admission: Free for Native Americans
    Abbe Downtown (includes Sieur de Monts admission):
    $6 Adults
    $2 Ages 6–15
    Sieur de Monts only:
    $3 Adults
    $1 Ages 6–15
When it's open: Downtown
    Summer hours:

Late May–early Nov.
Daily, 10 am–6 pm
Winter hours: Mid-Nov.–Dec. and Feb.–May
Thurs.–Sat., 10 am–4 pm
Closed Jan.
Trailside at Sieur de Monts Spring
Late May–mid-Oct.
Daily, 9 am–4 pm
Directions: *Downtown museum:* From Ellsworth, take ME-3 onto Mount Desert Island into Bar Harbor. The museum at 226 Mount Desert Street (Route 3) is opposite the village green. *Trailside:* Follow ME-Route 3 through Bar Harbor and south toward Otter Creek. Just past Jackson Lab, turn right at the Sieur de Mont Spring entrance to Acadia National Park and follow signs to the nature center, Wild Gardens of Acadia, and the Abbe. From the parking lot, take the path behind the nature center and up the hill.

Bar Harbor Whale Museum
Downtown Bar Harbor
www.barharborwhalemuseum.org
207-288-0288

Note: Beginning October 2010, this museum is temporarily closed while its former building is being redeveloped. It is expected to reopen for summer 2012 in downtown Bar Harbor near the waterfront. Check the website in 2012 for opening date and location.

WHAT YOU'LL FIND HERE: Marine mammal skeletons. Educational and interactive exhibits on the marine environment, especially the Gulf of Maine; climate change; conservation; history of whaling; and the life cycle of marine mammals. Whale bone puzzle, computers games, audio recordings of the Gulf of Maine. Gift shop.

WHY GO: This is the state's only museum solely focused on whales and seals in the Gulf of Maine. The museum offers an impressive introduction to its subject. Suspended in midair, as if swimming, are skeletons of animals that died of natural causes, including a dolphin, a seal, and a 22-foot minke whale that was entangled in lobster gear and drowned near Harpswell. Educational exhibits in most cases are accessible to all ages. They have been developed in partnership with scientific researchers and educators at College of the Atlantic and its marine mammal research group, Allied Whale, and the tour boat company, Bar Harbor Whale Watch Co.

A few panels display serious academic research but most are designed to answer questions you're likely to ask: Which whales live off the coast of Maine? What do they eat? Why are they mammals and not fish? Without revealing all that we learned here, we now know that finbacks, humpbacks, and minkes are the most common whales in this region, and that baleen is a series of fringed plates, "whale bone," that hang like vertical blinds from the whale's upper jaw to filter food from the ocean. Thanks to baleen, whales can strain mouthfuls of shrimp or schools of fish at one time. We also learned that like all mammals, whales are warm-blooded and have hair, although just a few bristly strands on their heads. Also like us, mother whales carry their young internally until birth and then nurse the youngsters with milk from mammary glands.

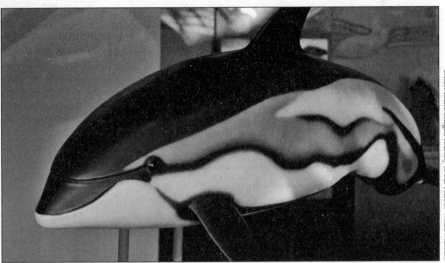

Desert Island Images, courtesy of Bar Harbor Whale Museum

Atlantic white-sided dolphin model at the Bar Harbor Whale Museum.

Time to allow: 45 minutes
Admission: Free
When it's open: Summer hours
    June
    Daily, 10 am–8 pm
    July–Aug.
    Daily, 9 am–9 pm
    Sept.–Oct.
    Daily 10 am–8 pm
    Winter hours
    Subject to staffing availability
Directions: Take US-1A-East, which becomes ME-3 East (Bar Harbor Road), into downtown Bar Harbor.

FUN FACT: Adopt a fin or humpback whale or a mother-calf pair to help researchers study their lives in the North Atlantic, a project that's been ongoing since the 1970s. Using photo-identification techniques, Allied Whale has been tracking individual whales identified by dorsal fin shape, natural color pattern, and acquired scars (fin whales) or fluke pigmentation patterns (humpbacks). The College of the Atlantic–affiliated program program maintains catalogues with thousands of photographs so researchers can learn more about whales, including their feeding habits and migration. Learn more about the program at www.coa.edu/html/adoptawhale.

George B. Dorr Museum of Natural History
College of the Atlantic
105 Eden Street, Bar Harbor
www.coa.edu/museum
207-288-5395

WHAT YOU'LL FIND HERE: Lifelike taxidermied mammals and aquatic creatures. Natural science specimens. Contemporary art reflecting environmental themes. Touch tank of marine life. Gift shop.

WHY GO: "The museum is designed for anyone who is curious," says Scott Swann, curator of collections. "Often people stop in when they find eggs or damsel flies, for example, and want to know more. They might end up tagging along with a staff member on a behind-the-scenes tour." Neither stuffy nor old-fashioned, this natural history museum is an integral part of College of the Atlantic campus where undergraduate and graduate students focus on the relationship between humans and the environment. It's a taste of what they learn in classrooms and field studies that make the most of their proximity to Acadia National Park and the Atlantic Ocean.

Intricately detailed dioramas are built and produced by COA students. A red fox is caught in midair leaping to capture a mouse; a black bear cub covered with honey bees noses into a log. Bird and animal life is captured so realistically, the scenes seem more like stop-action 3-D photography. But don't worry—all the creatures died of natural causes. It's an impressive blend of taxidermy, design, and curriculum.

"We've had some amazing students who are incredibly talented," said Swann, noting that graduates have gone on to work in some of the nation's foremost museums, including the Smithsonian.

A touch tank is home to muscles, starfish, crabs, and other creatures from nearby Frenchman Bay. Visitors can also hold, smell, or see up close skulls, baleen, fur pelts, jaw bones, and wings. All this in an airy space splashed with sunlight, dappled with shade, in the remodeled original headquarters of Acadia National Park.

The museum was founded in 1980 by Stanley Grierson, a retired taxidermist who spent thousands of hours teaching COA students, and Butch Rummel, COA professor of anatomy and physiology. The two men were intellectual kindred spirits and crazy people, said Swann. Exhibits reflect the college's interdisciplinary approach to learning and the close working relationship between faculty members and students at the college, which has an undergraduate enrollment of just 350. Graduates receive a Bachelor of Arts in human ecology after completing individualized programs designed to suit their interests in environmental science, marine studies, landscape, and building design, visual and performing arts, natural-history museum studies, public policy, international and regional studies, sustainable agriculture and community development, teacher certification, and humanities. What fires their interests on campus or field work at a college-owned, 86-acre organic farm and two lighthouse field stations sometimes takes shape in the Dorr Museum.

USEFUL INFORMATION: Interpretive programs for school groups and families explore the natural history of the Mount Desert Island region.

Bob Mendelsohn

Diorama of fox and its prey at the Dorr Museum of Natural History.

Time to allow: 30 minutes.
Admission: Free
When it's open: Tues.–Sat., 10 am–5 pm but may vary. Call ahead to confirm hours.
Directions: On Route 3 between downtown Bar Harbor and the Ferry Terminal.

FUN FACTS:

• The eyes of a snowy owl seem to follow you no matter where you stand near the glass-enclosed diorama. "It's really eerie, especially when I'm in the museum at night," says Swann, the curator.

• In a behind-the-scenes workroom where damaged dioramas are repaired, there are trays of meticulously pinned and labeled insects created by Neva Rockefeller Goodwin, of the prominent Rockefeller family. She's now a Tufts University economics professor, but she organized this extensive collection when she was about nine years old. Among rows of bugs are some insects barely larger than the head of the pin that anchors them to the tray. As a child, she catalogued and labeled specimens in minute handwriting on slivers of paper with exacting scientific accuracy.

• Gardeners who visit in the summer will want to walk across campus to a series of stone-walled garden rooms, remnants of a former estate. The gardens were created by the renowned landscape designer Beatrix Farrand in 1928, at the height of Mount Desert Island's Golden Era. The gardens are located behind Kaelber Hall. Look for the original roses and a perennial border of original plantings.

Wendell Gilley Museum
4 Herrick Road
Southwest Harbor, Mount Desert Island
www.wendellgilleymuseum.org
207-244-7555

WHAT YOU'LL FIND HERE: More than 100 wooden birds by master carver Wendell Gilley. Miniature waterfowl by master carver A. Elmer Crowell. Works by carver-in-residence and museum members. Prints and paintings of nature. Temporary exhibits by contemporary artists. Natural history programs. Carving demonstrations and workshops. Gift shop.

WHY GO: Wendell Gilley's carvings are graceful, lifelike birds perched on driftwood or caught in the moment, standing in marsh grass or meadow. Birds of prey grasp fish or small game in their talons. Herons are deceptively peaceful while on alert in shallow water. Northern bobwhites, American woodcocks, tree sparrows, and ring-necked pheasants rest watchfully in their natural habitat. His favorite subjects were black-capped chickadees, the state bird of Maine.

Gilley (1904–1983) was a plumber, fixing oil burners and making tanks for boats, long before he earned recognition as one of the nation's finest bird carvers. An avid hunter, he greatly admired the beauty of the game birds he pursued. While preparing to cook them, he felt it was wrong not to "stuff and save them," so he took a correspondence course to learn taxidermy. In 1930, at age 26, he went to a taxidermy exhibit in Boston where he was more intrigued by a nearby collection of miniature birds carved by the renowned maker of decoys A. Elmer Crowell. Gilley had whittled since boyhood and with those rudimentary skills he was inspired to carve a miniature mallard duck.

"After I made five or six, I didn't know what to do with them," said Gilley in a video documentary portrait made in 1981. "One of the summer people suggested I contact Abercrombie & Fitch to see if they wanted to buy them," referring to what was perhaps the largest sporting goods outfitter in the world at that time. For the next 13 years, the New York store took every bird he could make, paying Gilley $3.75 apiece and marking them up to $7.50. As his reputation grew, admirers and would-be customers found their way to the Gilleys' home. Reportedly, during the 1970s on some days more than 100 people showed up. He was still working full-time as a plumber, carving birds in the evening, and he couldn't keep up with demand. "We never advertised. Word traveled through the grapevine and people came from all over the United States," said Gilley, who put his son through college by carving birds. At 52, he decided two full-time jobs was too much and sold the plumbing business after 27 years. "I thought I'd go fishing, make a few birds now and then. But I ended up busier than before."

In the introduction to his book, *The Art of Bird Carving,* Gilley wrote, "I believe that every human being has what I like to call creative power. The secret is to learn how to release it. Wood carving is an excellent way to set that power in ourselves free."

Everything Gilley learned in plumbing he applied to his new profession, says Nina

Gormley, curator and executive director. "The joinery is art in itself." He worked with metal to craft talons and attach mounts, and used molds to cast feet and fish. He pioneered the technique of wood burning to create delicate feathers and fish scales, initially rigging up an old soldering iron, then refining it with tips. Using taxidermy models, he improved his art until colors, texture, wing structure, and body position exactly duplicated nature. Artists showed him how to mix and use paints. A local naturalist guided him on realistic habitat, but primarily Gilley relied on the knowledge he gained over decades of bird hunting.

In his home garage-workshop, a few blocks from the future museum, Wendell Gilley carved more than 10,000 birds. Most were bought by collectors and retailers but fortunately his wife, Addie, kept more than 100 of their favorites, and these are what you'll see at the museum.

Wendell and Addie Gilley wanted to establish a museum to preserve the collection but realized the task was beyond their scope. Instead, Stephen Rockefeller, a Middlebury College professor and environmentalist whose family summered in nearby Seal Harbor, launched the project in 1979 by setting up a nonprofit board to ensure preservation of the artist's work. A local architect was hired to design an energy-efficient building in the rugged style of Mount Desert Island. Many on the construction crew knew and respected Gilley from his years as a plumber in their community.

The museum opened in 1981. Its signature piece is the majestic bald eagle Steven Rockefeller commissioned as a gift to his father, Nelson, to mark the occasion when the latter left office as vice president of the United States.

Gormley said the value of Gilley's carvings today depends on where you find them and what condition they're in, but prices might range from $2,500 for a pair

Jack Ledbetter, courtesy of Wendell Gilley Museum

A miniature group of bobwhite quail carved by Wendell Gilley in 1960, inspired by a Currier and Ives print of the A. F. Tait painting, The Cares of a Family.

of chickadees to tens of thousands of dollars for a great horned owl. Gormley, who knew the late artist well, said Gilley preferred game birds over song birds because he understood their behavior and how they moved. Even an untrained eye can sense that familiarity in his work. "He was very warm and generous," she said, "the kind of man who if you did him a favor would kill himself to do something for you in return. And he was droll. He enjoyed walking into the museum anonymously to listen to visitors' comments. He'd go into our book shop, sidle up to someone flipping through his book, and quietly say, 'Would you like me to autograph that?' He used to say he was born with a jackknife in his hand but didn't get serious about carving until he was in his 50s. Still, he carved for 53 years and always had more orders than he could fulfill."

Steve Valleau, the museum's resident artist for more than 25 years, teaches carving classes for children and adults. Summer sessions are geared for vacationers. Valleau also pre-cuts rough forms of puffins and loons for starter kits sold in the shop. Exhibits of work by sculptors, painters, and other contemporary nature artists are featured in annual shows. A resource library lends books to members and is available for browsing at the museum.

USEFUL INFORMATION

- Demonstrations by an expert carver are given on most days during visitor hours.
- A wheelchair is available at the front desk for visitor use.
- From late June to Columbus Day, Island Explorer bus Route 7 stops at the museum on request. Free. See www.exploreacadia.com.
- Workshops, from 90-minute lessons to 10-week classes, are offered year-round.
- From January through April, there are no gallery hours. Year-round, Valleau's workshops and a Friday afternoon carving club welcome men and women seeking camaraderie as they sharpen their skills. The Carving Club meets Fridays from 1–4 pm.

Time to allow: 45 minutes
Admission: $5 Adult
  $2 Ages 5–12
  Free Age 4 and younger
When it's open: Last admission to galleries 30 minutes before closing.
  June, Sept., Oct.
  Tues.–Sun., 10 am–4 pm
  July and Aug.
  Tues.–Sun., 10 am–5 pm
  Free (in 2010) Sat., 10 am–1 pm and all day Aug. 21, Wendell Gilley's birthday.
  Closed Mon. and July 4.
  May, Nov., Dec.
  Fri.–Sun., 10 am–4 pm
Directions: From Bar Harbor: Mount Desert Street to Route 233 (Eagle Lake Road). Turn left to continue on Route 233 to the stop sign and turn right onto Route 198 (Sound Drive), then left at the light in Somesville onto ME Route 102 South. Continue into Southwest Harbor where Route 102 becomes Main Street. Turn left onto Herrick Road. Or a short walk from Great Harbor Marina in Southwest Harbor.

Seal Cove Auto Museum
1414 Tremont Road
(Pretty Marsh Road), Tremont
Mount Desert Island
www.sealcoveautomuseum.org
207-244-9242

WHAT YOU'LL FIND HERE: Antique automobiles and vintage motorcycles built 1895–1924, with an emphasis on the Brass Era. Classics and limited-edition vehicles owned by the late Richard C. Paine, Jr. Gift shop.

WHY GO: Several of the cars here are literally one of a kind. These automotive gems were built in an era when the wealthy bought a chassis (the mechanical parts of the car), then paid to have a body designed and built to their specifications, like commissioning a piece of art. Sculpture with power under the hood. Whether impressive in size and detail or surprising in their simplicity, these cars and early motorcycles beg to be photographed. They inspire daydreams of slipping behind the wheel and out onto the road, past the purple and pink lupines blooming in spring, to a picnic with wine and fine china beside one of Mount Desert Island's many coves.

Specializing in the Brass Era, when automotive elegance was accented by gleaming golden yellow ornaments, the museum is located in a nondescript warehouse off a country road and across Seal Cove Pond from Acadia National Park. The bland building seems an unlikely home for such rare, often elegant, cars.

Among the custom designs is a knockout for those who admire wooden boats—a beguiling 1913 Peugeot crafted of deep brown, polished tulip wood in the form of a small boat with rich black leather seats. The Peugeot Skiff is trimmed out like a yacht, with nautical gauges on the dash. The exterior is adorned with an eight-pipe brass horn that was sounded by squeezing a big rubber bulb that looks hefty enough to blast through the densest Down East fog. When acquired by the museum, the Peugeot was a relic. Before it was fully restored, the automobile actually looked like one of the decrepit boats often abandoned near the shore.

In the early 1900s, steam, electric, and gas competed for dominance in powering automobiles and the outcome was uncertain. All three types of vehicles are on display, including a Stanley Steamer and an imposing Pierce Arrow. There's an electric-powered Kimball with only 34 hours on the engine, reportedly because it was driven until the power ran out, then put in the garage and never driven again. Among those built by companies long gone, with no connection to today's manufacturers, is a 1910 Stoddard-Dayton with a programmable horn reminiscent of brass organ pipes. A driver could sound the horn by playing a piano-style keyboard attached to the exterior above the running board. A 1915 FRP is one of only nine built. Here, too, are automobiles built by Maxwell and Stevens-Duryea, and a magnificent French-made 1899 De Dion Bouton, painted burgundy with black fenders. Staggering in height and length, these handsome

Courtesy Seal Cover Auto Museum

1905 Pierce Great Arrow. Passengers could use a key pad to tell the chauffeur to stop, turn right or left, follow car ahead, etc. Pierce motorcycles are also seen.

automobiles tower over visitors. They are commanding by any standard. Unconfirmed reports allege a celebrated four-star World War I general once owned the Simplex Crane Model S, built in 1916. It is painted Army khaki and weighs 11,800 pounds.

"We're off the beaten track on the far side of Mount Desert Island," said Roberto Rodriguez, executive director. "People come up the driveway, see this nondescript building, walk inside and find an incredible collection." At Seal Cove, you won't see '50s and '60s muscle cars, the lightning-fast GTOs and souped-up Mustangs made famous in the lyrics of early rock 'n' roll. "The trend in collecting these days is muscle cars, yet these beautiful brass automobiles were the genesis for everything, the whole evolution of cars. They epitomize ingenuity but you don't often see them in museums or car shows." He motioned toward steam- and electric-powered cars built a century ago. "It's interesting to ponder what would have happened if either of those power supplies had won instead of gasoline. Here we are again today, looking at those same energy sources."

Amassed by Richard Cushing Paine Jr. (1928–2007), a successful banker born into a prominent Boston family, this is the core of his collection, which included 120 vehicles he stored here in his adopted home state. Paine's passion was cars and everything related to them, especially early-20th-century Edwardian Age of Brass models, but he collected all kinds, as well as early motorcycles that are little more than standard bicycles with small motors attached to the frame, plus tools and mechanical paraphernalia, automotive memorabilia, and dozens of license plates that hang on one wall. Everything was jammed so tightly into several buildings on the island that it was nearly impossible to walk around the cars, even after the museum was founded and opened to the public in 1964. Upon Paine's death, and following his instructions, in 2008 dozens of his vehicles were sold at auction to relieve the overcrowded conditions and raise funds to maintain the collection. From that point on, the museum's focus has been on American cars and those with connections to residents of Down East Maine.

"One of the changes we'll be making here now will be to tell the story from making buggies to cars, from carriage to wheels, how bicycles came along and evolved into motorcycles," said Rodriguez. "Gradually we're improving signage, with background histories of individual cars and the details that make their stories come alive." Increasingly, not every vehicle will be exhibited in like-new condition. Rodriguez explained that the art of automobile restoration has been refined to the point where classic vehicles are becoming better than new. Expert restorers today have at their fingertips technology, and especially paint, that far surpasses the best available when these cars were built. In collections worldwide, accuracy is forfeited in the name of polish and pizzazz, he said.

"Paine bought most of his automobiles restored or semi-restored," said Rodriguez. "It is no longer considered proper to make them perfect, because they lose character that comes from road wear and things like words someone etched on the dash." At Seal Cove Auto Museum and elsewhere, new acquisitions now are being restored mechanically but the bodies will be left the way time and use have treated them.

Time to allow: 1 hour
Admission: $5 Adults
$4.50 Seniors (65 and older)
$2 Ages 12 and younger
$4 per person for groups of 6 or more
10 percent discount for AAA members and members of other automotive museums
Free Members of museum professional associations
When it's open: Memorial Day–Columbus Day
Daily, 10 am–5 pm
Directions: Take ME-3 to Mount Desert Island. Just after the bridge, bear right at the light onto Route 102 toward Southwest Harbor. Past the town of Somesville, turn right just after the fire department onto Pretty Marsh Road. Follow that for 5.8 miles to the museum. It's on the right side of the road, set back and opposite the pond.

FUN FACT: In 1900, a public-opinion poll at the New York National Automobile Show found that most people preferred electric-powered cars, with steam the runner-up. The least-favored power source was gasoline. According to the Seal Cove Auto Museum, the nearly 4,200 motorcars built that year were split equally among the three energy sources. Women preferred electric vehicles because they were deemed safe, cool-running, and quiet, with a maximum speed of 12 mph that was apparently fast enough to be exciting. Men reportedly preferred gasoline-powered cars for their speed, range, and hill-climbing ability, as well as mechanics. But gas engines were less reliable, had to be cranked to start, required a clutch, and carried volatile, flammable gas, which frightened people. Steam-powered cars were considered dependable but slower to get up to speed and their limited boiler size meant they couldn't travel as far as the others. A 1908 Stanley Steamer in the museum's collection could cover 50 miles.

IF YOU'RE ON MOUNT DESERT ISLAND . . . MOUNT DESERT ISLAND HISTORICAL SOCIETY MUSEUMS & GARDENS

Close to Somes Harbor, beside a mill pond, the Somesville Historical Museum is surrounded by woodland gardens and beds of 19th- and 20th-century heirloom flowering plants and herbs. Across the pond by way of a little arched bridge is the Selectmen's Building (circa 1780); nearby is the Old School House & Museum, which served the community as a one-room schoolhouse from 1892–1926. At the three locations, the MDI Historical Society Museum tells the stories of life in an earlier era on this exceptional Maine island.

Mount Desert Island Historical Society Museum & Gardens
2 Oak Hill Road, Somesville
373 Sound Drive (ME-198)
Mount Desert Island
www.mdihistory.org
207-276-9323

The Telephone Museum
166 Winkumpaugh Road, Ellsworth
www.thetelephonemuseum.org
207-667-9491

WHAT YOU'LL FIND HERE Early telephone switching systems, antique phones, and memorabilia. Complete former central office switching system of the Island Telephone Co. of Frenchboro, Maine. Gift shop.

WHY GO In just about every town in America, there's a big, windowless, brick building that used to belong to the telephone company. Here's a chance to find out what was inside. You probably remember when cell phones and even mobile phones didn't exist. Maybe you even remember the days before push-button dialing, when you had to pick up a receiver attached to a base unit with a real dial. You stuck a finger in a numbered hole, pulled it partway around a circle, then repeated dialing until the sequence of numbers was complete. Decades earlier, when phones were boxes on the wall, to place a call you had to turn a crank to reach a live operator, tell her the number you wanted, and wait while she moved a cable from one slot to another, connecting it manually to ring on the other end. How all these systems worked and how they led directly to development of computers makes for an interesting, if technically focused, visit.

Bob Mendelsohn

A manually operated telephone switchboard at the Telephone Museum.

Whether you worked on those old systems or you've seen telephone operators working switchboards in old movies, you'll get a kick out of hearing the *click click click, buzz buzz, brrrrrring! brrrrrrrring!* sounds of the past. You can even try out the equipment, setting relays in motion to connect one caller to another inside the museum. It quickly becomes obvious how someone could eavesdrop on private conversations when a "party line" was used. Similarly, you gain new appreciation for the role of the local telephone operators in the days before communities had 9-1-1 emergency systems. For anyone interested in the social or technical aspects of telephony, this is a good place to learn about the field's more than 125-year history, from Alexander Graham Bell's patent in 1876 to the end of the electro-mechanical era of telephone switching.

To some extent, what you learn depends on who leads the tour that day and the questions you ask. The all-volunteer staff is manned by an active corps of former linemen, operators, and knowledgeable history buffs who will shape their talk to your interests.

Much of the equipment was donated by Charles Galley, who collected telephone equipment in his basement until he ran out of room and decided to build a barn next to his home to store it all. One of the museum's active volunteers, Galley said he has been fascinated with networking systems since he was a child. Independently, around 1983, another group of enthusiasts incorporated as the New England Museum of Telephony to preserve a historically significant switching system, called "Panel," that was used only in large cities between 1925 and 1975. When they heard about Galley's collection and his plans for the barn, they contacted him and combined efforts.

The Telephone Museum in Galley's barn opened in 1997. Half of the people involved—and half of those who visit—are former phone company employees who are as attached to the antique equipment as writers are to old typewriters and fountain pens.

Several switching stations that previously served towns in New England have been moved here. Most were used in Maine, including Belfast and Branford, and you'll find the entire stand-alone, central office of the little company that provided service for all 20 homes in the island community of Frenchboro. After the breakup of the Bell System and its successors, the "Baby Bells," those companies, several independent ones and individual collectors donated telephone sets, historical photos and documents, switchboards, and other operating pieces of equipment to make them available to demonstrate the technical innovations that came before digital technology. All of the working systems are interconnected to show how a mid-20th-century regional system might have worked.

You'll also hear how early telephones created their own social circles and initiated entrepreneurial solutions to common problems. One story is that of an undertaker named Almon Strowger, who discovered he was losing business because one of the local telephone operators was the wife of his competitor and she was intercepting and re-directing his business calls to her husband. He decided to find a way to eliminate the operator's role. In 1890, he invented, and later patented, the Strowger Switch, an automatic exchange system that revolutionized the telephone business. His early electromagnetic switching system introduced the device that enabled customers to create pulses corresponding to the numbers zero through nine using telegraph keys. Later it evolved to use a dial, and was widely used until the invention of the more reliable crossbar system. You can learn about Strowger's crossbar and all-relay systems at this Down East side-trip one summer afternoon.

Time to allow: 1 hour if you have a serious interest in the topic;
30 minutes otherwise
Admission: $5 Adults
$2.50 Children
When it's open:
July, Aug., and Sept.
Thurs.–Sun., 1–4 pm
May, June, and Oct. by appointment only.
Directions: Between Bangor/Brewer and Ellsworth, on US Route 1A (Bangor Road), about 10 miles from downtown Ellsworth. Opposite Annie's Pride Farm Stand, turn onto Winkumpaugh Road, a two-lane road that's easy to miss. About 1 mile from Route 1A, past Hanson's Landing Road, the museum is the second building on the left.

ELSEWHERE IN WASHINGTON COUNTY

Maine Coast Sardine History Museum
34 Mason Bay Road, Jonesport
www.mainesardinemuseum.org
207-497-2961

WHAT YOU'LL FIND HERE: History of the sardine industry in Maine from fishing to canning, with equipment and tools donated by former factories and artifacts from towns in which they were major employers. Archival photos. Colorful labels and signs from dozens of canneries. Self-led or guided tours. Passamaquoddy baskets for fish scales. Factory gauges, whistles, and clocks. Special section honoring Down East women, including champion packer Rita Willey, who spent decades packing fish into cans. Gift shop.

WHY GO: Near the tip of a peninsula known for its working waterfront and not many tourists, museum co-founder Ronnie Peabody offers every visitor a personal tour of the museum he and his wife built. Peabody is passionate about preserving an accurate record of what once was one of the state's key industries, employing generations of coastal residents. His guided tour brings to life the story of Maine's sardine canning industry and how its rise and demise affected local families. The last sardine cannery in Maine closed in 2010.

Inside a plain, gray building are shelves of colorful and distinctive inch-high sardine cans whose labels bear bold graphics depicting fish, fishermen, boats, and lighthouses, fine examples of commercial art. Elaborating on the story are black and white historical photos and weathered fishing gear, tools, and machinery, from seining nets to cooking racks, sauce ladles, a labeling machine, and crates. Exhibits show the steps from ocean to finished product. A tribute wall of open scissors, each labeled with a name and home town, honors women throughout Maine who worked as packers up to 12 hours a day, often for decades, cutting heads and tails off fresh-caught herring, fitting the raw fish into cans in neat lines and ladling mustard sauce over the rows before the fish were cooked. As one 90-year-old visitor, a former cannery worker, reportedly said, everything's here except the "aroma" of the stinking fish.

"The last cannery closed in April 2010, in Prospect Harbor, but at one time there were about 420 companies that made this one of the biggest industries in the state," said Peabody, who with his wife, Mary, spent more than eight years developing the exhibits. The museum opened in 2008 in a building adjacent to their home. The Peabodys' warmth and enthusiasm elevate this exhibit beyond what you might expect. To call the place "quirky" or its items "artifacts" doesn't do justice to the collection that they've organized by coastal communities where the canneries operated, from Kittery to Robbinston.

"I grew up hearing the cannery whistles blowing, calling workers to their jobs as the sardine carriers went in and out," said Peabody, who worked at L. Ray Packing Co. during the 1970s. "They used steamboat whistles. A call code announced when the seine boats were coming in or going out. The combination of blasts indicated who should to report to unload and process the fish." One long and three short whistle blasts meant packers had to drop what they were doing at home and return to the line. "It was a good job for people like me who weren't highly educated," he said. But it also was cold and exhausting work, whether on the water or in the cannery. "Before you have sardines, you need herring," he said, citing the boat *Gary Allen's* carrying capacity as an example of one haul in 1950. Fishing for the L. Ray Packing Co., the *Gary Allen* could haul of 59.21 hogsheads (roughly 3,300 gallons) of fish that had to be unloaded, transported to the cannery, and processed—cleaned, cut, cooked, and packed by hand into those little cans. "Packers had the hardest part of the job and the packers were all women," said Mary Peabody. "They worked up to 12 hours a day handling cold fish, putting them in the cans in tight little rows of four, eight, or 16 fish." At first, packers individually ladled mustard sauce into each can. Later machines, including one displayed at the museum, automatically poured oil which had replaced the sauce.

Over time, other machines also speeded up the process, including labeling. Around 1913, women were still hand-feeding cans into a wrapping machine that slid paper labels over the cans, wrapped the sides with the paper's glued edges and hand-stacked

Bob Mendelsohn

Maine Coast Sardine History Museum.

the cans into boxes. In 1926, a lithograph machine was invented, eliminating the old paper labels, printing directly on the lids. Another advance, in 1937, was the introduction of machines capable of sealing 150 cans a minute.

Despite lacking previous experience or formal museum training, the Peabodys have put together a well-conceived and attractive exhibit that gives visitors a feel for the people who worked in every stage of the sardine industry as well as how dependent these people were on jobs at both big corporations and small, family-owned businesses.

In the 1800s, sardines were imported from Norway, Spain, France, Italy, and Portugal, becoming hugely popular delicacy on this side of the Atlantic. By 1871, when the Franco-Prussian War cut off supply, Americans had a big appetite for the fish tidbits that were suddenly unavailable. To meet the demand, in 1876 the Eagle Preserved Fish Co. opened in Eastport, becoming the first sardine cannery in this country. Maine's industry peaked around 1952 when, according to Ronnie Peabody's estimate, there were 15 factories around Jonesport and about 50 in the region.

What happened? Some point to offshore foreign "factory ships" netting vast quantities beyond the range of local fishermen. Or maybe there was a decline in herring population due to changes in water temperature. Draw your own conclusions from what you learn at the museum. Regardless, you'll rarely see sardines on American tables any more.

USEFUL INFORMATION

• Call ahead to be sure the museum will be open or to schedule a visit.

• The Maine Coast Sardine History Museum to date is only staffed by Ronnie and Mary Peabody. During posted hours, if they're not inside the museum, cross the parking area and knock on the door to their home. Group tours welcome with advance notice. But it is always better to call ahead.

Time to allow: 1 hour with guided tour
Admission: $4 Adults
   $2 Students
   Free Preschool age
When it's open: Call ahead to verify hours.
   Memorial Day and roughly from the third Sun. in June to late-Sept.
   or Columbus Day
   Tues.–Fri., and Sun., noon–4 pm
   or by chance or appointment.
Directions: Take US-Route 1 North past Columbia Falls and turn right onto Route 187 into Jonesport.

FUN FACT

Rita Willey of Rockland, Maine, was a five-time champion of the World's Fastest Sardine Packer competition. At her peak, she packed more 400 cans an hour, an astounding speed. Willey began packing sardines in 1956 and won her first competition in 1970. After victory number five, she appeared on TV's *The Tonight Show with Johnny Carson, To Tell the Truth, Truth or Consequences,* and *What's My Line,* and was featured in *Sports Illustrated, Down East Magazine,* the *Boston Globe,* and the *New York Daily News.* Following the 1983 contest, the host of *Real People* came to Rockland to pack sardines by her side. In 2009 and 2010, the museum celebrated her achievements with an exhibit on "The Muhammad Ali of All Sardine Packers," highlighted by a visit from Willey, who signed autographs and talked about her career.

WHILE YOU'RE IN EASTPORT . . .

Down East sardines traditionally were packed in mustard sauce. Raye's Mustard Mill claims to be the last traditional stone-ground mustard mill in North America. At one time, there were more than 20 sardine factories in Eastport alone. The mill was founded in 1900 by J. Wesley Raye, the 20-year-old son of a sea captain, who decided to try making mustard sauce for the canneries instead of the oil used for canning sardines elsewhere. Raye's recipe called for a 50–50 mix of seeds from Aroostook County and Saskatchewan, all of which went through steel rollers, were mixed with a vinegar-turmeric brew, soaked overnight, and churned into a runny sauce that was a hit. Four generations later, the family still runs the whole process by hand, using the original equipment to produce a full line of mustards. The mill, a working museum, is located behind the store. When the mill schedule allows, tours are given on the hour, from 10 am–3 pm weekdays and some Saturdays.

Mustard Mill Museum
83 Washington Street, Eastport
www.rayesmustard.com
800-853-1903

The Quoddy Dam Model Museum contains a 14-foot-by-15-foot model of a proposed 1930s hydroelectric development project. At the time, the project won support from President Franklin D. Roosevelt, whose summer home was nearby on Campobello Island in New Brunswick, Canada. The project was initiated in 1935 but suspended one year later when Congress refused further funding. The model looks amateurish now, but the idea remains intriguing. Envisioned by a hydroelectric engineer named Dexter Cooper, the Quoddy Project would have built a series of dams to harness the power of the extreme tides where water passes between Cobscook and Passamaquoddy bays. Electric turbines were planned at the isthmus on Moose Island, but tidal power generation remains an untapped resource.

Quoddy Dam Model Museum
72 Water Street, Eastport
Open seasonally.

Tides Institute & Museum of Art
43 Water Street, Eastport
www.tidesinstitute.org
207-853-4047

WHAT YOU'LL FIND HERE: Paintings, photographs, and crafts by American and Canadian artists of the Passamaquoddy Bay region. Cross-border perspectives and cultural exchanges.

WHY GO: Eastport's 2,000 residents live on a series of islands linked to each other by causeways and by water to New Brunswick, Canada. To the east and south is Passamaquoddy Bay, an inlet of the Bay of Fundy, where extreme tides vary more than 25 feet and the rushing water causes a "reversing falls" phenomenon that made the list of finalists for the "New Seven Wonders of the World." This is where the North Woods bump up against the serpentine coast and the morning sun first hits the United States. It is a captivating landscape to paint or photograph, but living here is often challenging. People's livelihoods frequently depend on their ability to rake wild blueberries, make Christmas wreaths, clam, and fish. Eastport has the deepest port on the U.S. East Coast, but shipping has declined since its heyday as one of the nation's leading ports. Nonetheless, this is still among the region's working harbors, home to an active lobster fleet. While Americans and Canadians of British, French, and other European ancestries, First Nation peoples, and Native Americans retain their individual traditions, as neighbors on the coast, their lives are interwoven.

In 2002, the Tides Institute & Museum of Art was founded to bridge these many worlds. The young arts institution is now building both an art collection that reflects the region's character and a cultural network that stimulates collaboration.

"On both sides of the border, people felt there was a need for something to bring us together around the arts, exploring who those artists are and where they came from," said Hugh French, TIMA's director. "Things used to stop at the border. But artists have always flowed through here from New York, Nova Scotia, New Brunswick, and elsewhere." The small museum's eclectic collection began with several hundred paintings and several thousand photographs. Works by renowned

Tides Institute and Museum of Art

Janet Mendelsohn

photographers Berenice Abbott and Paul Caponigro might hang near Impressionist oils, handmade quilts, antique maps, mixed media sculpture, or watercolors and drawings by George Pearse Ennis. Passamaquoddy sweetgrass baskets might be displayed near a five-piece sterling silver tea service. TIMA emphasizes history and architecture, and fosters new work through residency programs and printmaking. Recent renovations to the historic brick building, a former bank built in 1887, created printmaking, letterpress, and digital imaging facilities on the third floor.

While building renovations are underway, TIMA is simultaneously expanding its online presence. Resources on the museum's website include thumbnails of "One Hundred Works from the Art Collection" and "Passamaquoddy Suite: A Collaborative Geography," a cross-border art project by printmaking students and faculty from the Maine College of Art and the Nova Scotia College of Art and Design. For the latter, real nautical maps and works in the Tides collections were used as the genesis for reimagining history and culture. Also online are selections from TIMA's library of 4,000 volumes focusing on the Passamaquoddy region, New England, and the Atlantic Provinces.

In its effort to build collections with cross-border perspectives and cross-cultural ties, TIMA collaborates on exhibits with the New Brunswick Museum in St. John, New Brunswick, Canada. There's also an annual "Two Countries, One Bay" art studio tour, and an alliance with Down East Maine's other Historic Bold Coast museums and historic sites, including the Abbe Museum; Ruggles House; Burnham Tavern;

Woodlawn Museum (Black House); Waponahki Museum at Sipayik (Pleasant Point), which is currently closed; Fundy culture sites in New Brunswick and Nova Scotia, Canada; and Roosevelt Campobello International Park, the summer home of Eleanor and Franklin D. Roosevelt.

USEFUL INFORMATION: CulturePass is a free, online network of collaborating museums, organizations, businesses, and individuals in the greater Passamaquoddy region on both sides of the international border. Project participants post events related to culture; history; crafts; or folk, traditional, or fine arts. To subscribe to a weekly e-mail or check upcoming events, click on "CulturePass Cultural Guide" at the bottom of the Tides Institute and Museum website.

Time to allow: 30 minutes
Admission: Free
When it's open: June–Sept.
   Tues.–Sun., 10 am–4 pm
Directions: From US Route 1-North to ME-190 into Eastport. Turn left at Washington Street, then right onto Water Street. The museum is in the heart of town, near the big statue of a fisherman.

FUN FACT: On December 31, neighbors in two countries bid farewell to the old year and welcome the new with celebrations that include cheering a giant red maple leaf at 12 midnight Atlantic time (11 pm Eastern) and an 8-foot sardine at midnight Eastern time drop from the third story of the Tides Institute & Museum of Art building to Bank Square in downtown Eastport.

WESTERN MOUNTAINS & LAKES
REGION
CHAPTER 5

Bates College Museum of Art
Olin Arts Center
75 Russell Street, Lewiston
www.bates.edu/museum.xml
207-786-6158

WHAT YOU'LL FIND HERE: Permanent collection of nearly 5,000 works emphasizing nationally and internationally prominent artists with connections to Maine. Visual art and collaborative programs that break from traditional roles for academic museums. Marsden Hartley Memorial Collection. Works on paper. Three major original exhibitions a year plus annual senior thesis exhibition by Bates art majors. Annual student-curated series called "Students in the Vault."

WHY GO: A refreshing blend of youthful interests and academic studies drives this academic museum. While the collection emphasizes works by major artists with connections to Maine, the museum is also known for its fine collection of works on paper, from Old Masters to Asian and contemporary art. Exhibitions often develop from interdisciplinary subjects of broad interest to the Bates campus. An illustration of this was a recent show, "Our Positive Bodies: Mapping Our Treatment, Sharing Our Choices," that connected public health, African cultures, gender studies, and art. Created in Kenya, the exhibit involved "body mapping," a technique that helps HIV-positive women, often mothers, face the reality that they will die prematurely. The women painted their thoughts and memories on life-sized silhouettes of their own bodies, commenting on their options and how others influence their ability to stay healthy. Their art challenged viewers to consider their own life experiences and, however briefly, enter another person's world. The museum's student-driven projects can offer interesting perspectives and after graduating, several interns have gone on to careers in museums across the country.

The core is the Marsden Hartley Memorial Collection. Bates College Museum of Art was founded in 1955 as the Treat Gallery when Norma Berger, a niece of Marsden Hartley, fulfilled her late uncle's wish by donating his collection of drawings, oil sketches, works by other artists, personal photographs, autographed editions of his published books, his writings on art and life, and objects from his home and studio in Corea, Maine. The gallery expanded when the Olin Arts Center opened in 1986.

Hartley (1877–1943) is considered one of Maine's most important artists. The collection includes 99 drawings and several oils by the modernist painter, who was born in Lewiston and died in Ellsworth. During his career, he moved from Impressionism to Abstractionism to Expressionism. Hartley left the state at a young age, lived in many places and was inspired by poets, writers, artists, and the shifting cultural and political climate, yet he remained spiritually close to Maine's people and landscape. Near the end of his life, he reportedly declared himself "the painter from Maine." What's often striking is how he veered away from traditional depictions of its beautiful land- and seascapes, focusing instead on what Mainers refer to as "the real Maine."

"The Hartley Memorial Collection is becoming increasingly interesting to scholars who are beginning to look at how his personal effects may have worked their way into his imagery," said Anthony Shostack, the museum's education curator. Selections from Hartley's work are always on view. The museum owns a series of Cezanne-style graphite drawings on paper (circa 1927) from his time living in France; his New Hampshire series (circa 1930) in graphite, litho crayons, and scratch techniques on paper; a German alps series (1933); and the "Dogtown and Gloucester series" (1933–1936), black ink on paper.

Another fine collection is 12 etchings by Mary Cassatt including several counterproofs of typical Cassatt subjects, little girls and mothers in feminine dresses and bonnets. Work by faculty in the Bates College art department, which has a strong history of printmaking, is often featured. The museum is also a repository for prints by Charlie Hewitt, a Lewiston native, and graphics by Claire Van Vliet and Sigmund Abeles. If you specifically want to see these works, call in advance.

Mirroring the increasing influence of China in global economic and political arenas, Bates has a growing body of contemporary Chinese art, including photography, by participants in a show held here some years ago. Like other examples of Chinese culture, the photographs are used extensively by Bates and Bowdoin faculty in their courses.

USEFUL INFORMATION:

• A weekly figure drawing group open to all meets Wednesdays from 6–9 pm throughout the year. Sessions are not art classes. Students, faculty, and the general public, at all levels of experience, are welcome. Contact the museum for information.

• An online database includes slide shows of selected works from past exhibitions.

• "Hartley at Home: The Marsden Hartley Memorial Collection" is an online introduction to the artist that includes links to his works in the collection, a brief biography, a list of some 250 personal items in the museum archive, and resources for further study, at http://abacus.bates.edu/acad/museum/hartley/collection/collection.html.

Time to allow: 45 minutes
When it's open: Tues.–Sat., 10 am–5 pm
Wed., 10 am–6 pm during the academic year.
Admission: Free
Directions: Bates College is approximately three miles from I-95/**Maine Turnpike, Exit 80**. Follow Plourde Parkway until it ends at Webster Street (second traffic light). Turn left onto Webster and follow for 1 mile to the first traffic light, Farwell Street. Turn right onto Farwell and follow 0.6 mile to a light; continue across the intersection onto Russell Street. Follow Russell through two lights. Turn left onto Bardwell Street (across from the Russell Street Variety) into the museum parking lot.

Museum L-A
35 Canal Street, Lewiston
www.museumla.org
207-333-3881

WHAT YOU'LL FIND HERE: Industry and labor in the Lewiston-Auburn area. Real stories and photographs of former textile mill-, brick-, and shoe-workers, and the production processes for which they were hired. Exhibits in historic textile mill. Gift shop.

WHY GO: The twin cities of Lewiston and Auburn since the 1880s have been home to people from many cultures who moved here to find work. As waves of immigrants settled in, they changed the social, economic, and civic fabric of the community, a pattern that continues to this day. Similarly, Museum L-A is still evolving, much like its home town.

At Museum L-A, you're witnessing the birth of a museum as well as learning about local mill operations and the people whose lives were entwined with their labor, said executive director Rachel Desgrosseilliers. In 2004, the museum opened in temporary quarters in a huge old Bates fabrics mill. Five years later, its future home was acquired along the Androscoggin River. The new museum is tentatively slated to open in its permanent location, the former Camden Yarns Mill, in 2014. Established in 1864, the building was one of the first cotton mills in Lewiston and one of two mills devastated by fire in 1945. When restoration is completed, not only will the new location lend itself to exhibits on water power, the canal system, and the mills, it also will be near several traditional immigrant communities, including Little Canada, Irish Patch, and New Auburn.

Permanent exhibits describe the local textile, shoe-, and brick-making industries, once among the most important in New England. You'll learn the steps in production and hear about the lives of millworkers in- and outside the factories. Temporary exhibits develop themes such as the role of women in the factories, child labor, technology, organized labor, and the hard existence faced by those who worked long days far from home.

What sets Museum L-A apart, and keeps it from dwelling on what could be depressing or dull, is its emphasis on preserving and sharing the stories of real people. Many millworkers had deep roots in Maine but many others immigrated here, initially from Ireland and French-speaking Canada, later from Lithuania, Germany, Greece, Italy, and most recently, Somalia. The museum's oral history project documents their experiences by taping interviews and photographing workers still willing and able to share their memories. Archives developed through the project are also being translated into new exhibits that go beyond the mills. They show co-workers who formed bowling teams or played in bands with fellow musicians. They played hockey together and went snowshoeing, influenced by the French Canadians' love of winter sports. Students, faculty, and staff from nearby Bates College are actively engaged as partners in the museum's projects and exhibits.

"Just showing the mill equipment was not enough," said Desgrosseilliers. "It's the

Courtesy of Museum L-A, Lewiston, Maine

Crompton & Knowles C-4 Jacquard loom with head, at Museum L-A.

people who did the work that are the heart of the industry. Our oral history project evolved out of a reunion of mill workers who met here. We expected 100 people and 556 showed up. One man donated his old loom fixer's tools to us that day. When he was thanked, he replied—with tears in his eyes—'Now I can die in peace. Somebody cares about the work I did in my life.'"

That powerful sense of connection also drives visitors to look for their grandparents, or themselves, in the old photographs. One show had so many recognizable faces that its panels were duplicated on paper and displayed in the same gallery so visitors could write notes on it, identifying people by name and occupation. Their notes are now part of the archive. Former mill-, shoe-, and brickworkers are involved in planning exhibits, assuring their accuracy. Currently, sewing machines and leather-working tools are laid out ready for use; the brick-making process is told through photographs, videos, and personal histories; and a textile room presents a simplified version of how bedspreads were made, from carding cotton to twisting and spinning yarn and designing and weaving the fabric.

"In the 1940s in Maine and beyond, you didn't get married without the bride ordering a bedspread from Bates in one of its popular patterns named for George Washington, or Abigail Adams, or Queen Elizabeth, and perhaps matching drapes and accessories," said Desgrosselliers. "People still order them today." Spreads inspired by these designs are woven by former Bates employees nearby at Maine Heritage Weavers and sold in the museum gift shop.

USEFUL INFORMATION: Museum L-A anticipates moving to 1 Beech Street, Lewiston, in 2014. Check the website or call for an update.

Time to allow: 1–1½ hours
Admission: $5 Adults
    $4 Seniors (62 and older)
    $4 Students
    Free Ages 5 and under
    Groups by arrangement
When it's open: Mon.–Sat., 10 am–4 pm
    Closed Thanksgiving, Christmas, and New Year's Day.

Directions: From I-95/Maine Turnpike, Exit 80 /Lewiston to the Alfred A. Plourde Parkway. Take the second right onto Route 196/Lisbon Street heading west for 2 miles to downtown Lewiston where Lisbon Street becomes one-way. Shortly thereafter, turn left onto Chestnut Street. Go over a small cement bridge spanning the canal, and take an immediate right into the parking lot of the Bates Mill Complex. Park at the far end of the lot in front of Museum L-A.

Sabbathday Lake Shaker Village
707 Shaker Road (Route 26), New Gloucester
www.shaker.lib.me.us
207-926-4597

WHAT YOU'LL FIND HERE: The 200-year history of Shaker community life in Maine. An 1,800-acre working farm with orchards, herb and vegetable gardens, Scottish Highland cattle, sheep, and pigs. Guided tours of six buildings open to the public. Exhibits of traditional Shaker art and crafts. Research library. Store selling Shaker products and dried herbs.

WHY GO: This is the last active Shaker community in the world. The last three members (as of this writing) live at this peaceful place where cattle graze in a rocky pasture, curiously eyeing strangers before they—and we—wander off to absorb the surroundings. Other former Shaker communities now exist only as museums or have been converted to other uses, but Sabbathday Lake is still their home and working farm.

No one is born a Shaker. All members are converts drawn to a communal way of life in which all property is owned by the group, everyone is both celibate and a pacifist, and every day combines work with prayer, following the teachings of the New Testament. A meeting house for prayer, and neat, simple, white shingle or brick farm buildings and dwellings without shutters or ornament are shaded by old maples and brightened by a summer patch or two of orange lilies. Nothing is showy. The rushing of our ever-connected world is irrelevant. Time spent here quiets the soul and follows the rhythms of nature, daily prayer, and patiently accomplished chores.

But at the same time, these practical-minded souls look forward. They welcome visitors for crafts demonstrations and workshops taught by Maine artisans. The community participates in Maine Farm Days and hosts a festival of traditional American music. A research library welcomes scholars and, in 2008, the village redesigned the former spin house to replace an existing museum, creating a modern, spacious gallery for exhibitions that change every two years. The museum highlights selections from an extensive collection of arts and crafts made by Shakers at this community and others that no longer exist.

The Shaker religion was founded more than 260 years ago in Manchester, England, as the United Society of Believers, a loosely organized group of dissenters who broke from the Church of England to pursue a freer, more personal expression of Christian faith. They became known as "Shaking Quakers," or Shakers, because their worship practices involved exuberant singing, shouting, and violent bodily movements. They came to America in 1774, settling first in rural Niskayuna, New York, near Albany. During the American Revolution, their religious practices, pacifism, and British origins attracted both ridicule and converts. They were persecuted and driven out of town. Eventually, members established 18 Shaker communities in New York, Connecticut, Massachusetts, Maine, New Hampshire, Kentucky, Ohio, Indiana, Georgia, and Florida.

At its peak in the decade prior to the Civil War, there were 5,000 members in this country. As woodworkers, artisans, and farmers, they earned a reputation for craftsmanship and innovation, particularly for the sturdy wooden furniture and cabinetry for which they are widely known. Beginning in the early 1900s, for both their own enjoyment and income, members were encouraged to learn painting, photography, and poetry writing, and study voice and musical instruments. Arts lessons became part of the children's schooling. Even their handmade everyday objects came to reflect the skillful attention to proportion and good design that remains a hallmark of Shaker style.

Sabbathday Lake, founded in 1783, was among the smallest and poorest of these villages. Within one year, close to 200 people living and working together formally organized here as a Shaker community. Today their 1,800-acre property includes vegetable gardens, hay fields, and pastures for livestock and sheep that supply wool for yarn. In keeping with a commitment to self-sufficiency, the Shakers now lease some farm operations and hire workers to help with other tasks related to their tree farm, apple orchard, quarries, and commercial herb garden.

It is not true, as generally believed, that the Shakers cut themselves off from the outside world, said Leonard Brooks, community director. The men became skilled woodworkers whose oval boxes, spinning wheels, butter churns, ladles, bowls, and furniture provided important income. Early on, the women learned to grow and process flax, which they processed and spun into wool that they wove and knitted into blankets and garments. Their herb gardens evolved into profitable businesses. They became printers, basket makers and seamstresses. Later they began making trinkets and "fancy goods" that they sold to tourists in the region's emerging resorts.

"All of their activities were, and still are, rooted in pragmatism," said Brooks. "They needed food, clothing, and shelter, and wanted to provide for their own needs. That meant doing those tasks well so repairs and replacement would not be required. Underlying all was faith and religion. Shakers were certainly aware of worldly styles but what they produced was essentially designed for their community. They felt no need to spend time on unnecessary work when the sheer responsibility of maintaining their property was demanding." According to Brooks, Shakers, unlike the Amish, have always kept up with the times. They had electricity here by 1926 and telephones were installed even before they were in the nearby town of New Gloucester.

As our tour group walked past the kitchen, an enticing aroma heralded the noon meal but it wasn't for us. (There's no public café.) Through the kitchen screen door we couldn't see Sister Francis, now in her 80s, but Brooks said she still does all the cooking for the resident Shakers and staff, and sometimes makes fudge that is sold in the store. She is continuing a long tradition of making candy, preserves, jellies, and pickles. Following the Great Depression, food items were among the community's most successful enterprises.

The Shaker communities' needs inspired numerous innovations and inventions that we've all come to know. They built peg boards for every room to hold anything from coats to cooking utensils. They designed woven wood seating to last longer and be more comfortable than solid wooden chairs. They introduced packages of garden seeds for retail sale and invented the first circular saw, the first mechanical washing machine, and flat brooms constructed from corn plants. They came up with "tilta-buttons" for the bottom of chair legs, an idea still used in schools.

None of their products were patented because they believed in sharing with the world. As membership in the communities declined after World War II, the Shakers streamlined work methods to enable individuals to handle labor previously accomplished by teams, and they adapted to use modern materials.

The museum was established in 1926. For many years it was a room on the second floor of the meeting house where in summer the public is welcome to join the believers in prayer. As other Shaker communities in Maine closed, many of their furnishings and handmade goods were brought here. Some antiques were sold but the museum and library collections now form the largest repository of Maine Shaker culture.

The collection includes needlework samplers, oil paintings, knitting, hooked rugs, painted typewriter ribbon tins and pin cushions, intricately woven baskets, photography, letterpress-printed holiday cards, and woodworking. You might see oval boxes made from sycamore, cherry, or mahogany wood; buckets; cherry and maple tables or bird carvings. Some exhibits include hand-written and -bound books of Shaker songs or dolls in Shaker clothing. "Fancy work," the name given to items intended for retail sale, veered away from the simple designs for which Shakers are known. Ornate Victorian taste is reflected in decorated wooden objects, elaborate paper boxes, and frilly pin cushions created to please customers in the outside world.

Not everything is great art. Some are simply cherished personal possessions and mementos. But many are wonderful examples of classic folk art, regardless of how that is defined. As curator Michael S. Graham wrote for the catalogue of a recent museum exhibition, "The Human & The Eternal: Shaker Art in its Many Forms," many Shaker objects on display are offered "as 'Americana,' reflecting the eras in which they were created in addition to the creativity of their makers."

USEFUL INFORMATION:

• Pets are not permitted anywhere, not even in vehicles, because this is a working farm. The only exceptions are service dogs.

• Access is restricted to visitors on guided tours because this is also the Shakers' home and workplace. The only exceptions are the Museum Reception Center and Store.

• Photography is only permitted outdoors.

• The Museum Reception Center contains exhibits on the children's schooling and other subjects, as well as items for sale.

• The library and museum are open to researchers all year by appointment. Catalogues of the collections are available.

• Culinary herbs and herbal teas are sold by mail and in the Shaker Store. For a catalogue, call the main number.

• Workshops and demonstrations are held on selected dates from late May through early October. Pre-registration is required. Topics range from woodworking and carving to growing and using herbs, making Shaker oval boxes, chair-caning, basket making, knitting and crocheting. Children and their families can create fairy houses or tin punch candle holders. Herb garden internships run June–July providing instruction in herb gardening, herb lore, and creative uses of herbs.

• Special events include guided nature hikes (reservations required) throughout the season and cider pressing on Apple Saturdays in the fall. A Shaker Christmas Fair in December features homemade holiday baked goods.

Time to allow: 1 hour and 15 minutes for the guided tour
  15 minutes for self-guided visit to the museum
Admission: $6.50 Adults
  $2 Ages 6–12
  Free Ages 5 and younger
  Tour tickets include admission to the museum.
When it's open: Memorial Day weekend–Columbus Day
  Mon.–Sat., 10 am–4:30 pm
  Closed Sun.
  Guided tours begin hourly on the half hour (except the last one) from 10:30 am–3:15 pm.
Directions: Eight miles north of I-95/Maine Turnpike, Exit 63 to ME-26 North towards Gray or 8 miles west of I-95/Maine Turnpike, Exit 75 (Auburn).

Maine State Building
37 Preservation Way, Poland Spring
www.polandspringps.org
207-998-4142

WHAT YOU'LL FIND HERE: Maine State pavilion from the 1893 Chicago World's Fair with its original exhibits on Maine. History of the building's move from Illinois to Maine. Vintage golf equipment. Architectural models from the Big Hotel Era. All Souls Chapel. Art Gallery. Gift shop.

WHY GO: Looking at this massive octagonal granite building, it is nearly impossible to imagine how something so substantial could have been moved half way across the country. But that's exactly what happened, twice. This was the State of Maine pavilion in Chicago at the 1893 World's Columbian Exposition, popularly called the World's Fair, which marked the 400th anniversary of Columbus's arrival in the Americas. A train left Maine carrying skilled tradesmen and granite from 10 quarries for the exterior, 40 tons of black slate for the roof, and other construction materials to erect the turreted building on a prime location on the shore of Lake Michigan. The pavilion, designed by architect and Lewiston native Charles Sumner Frost, promoted the best of Maine craftsmanship, products, and cultural resources, including books and paintings by the state's leading authors and artists. Among Frost's later projects was Chicago's Navy Pier.

After the exposition, the building was sold by the State of Maine to the Ricker family of Poland Spring for $30,000. The Rickers were given three weeks to disassemble the building or it would be demolished by the state. Within 19 days, they had the granite, timber, and slate loaded on a special 16-car freight train for the return trip from Chicago to Danville Junction, near Auburn, Maine. From there, it was hauled by horse-drawn wagons over country roads to their resort hotel, where it was reassembled.

In 1894, the Maine State Building reopened as a library and art gallery in time to celebrate the Town of Poland's Centennial, as well as the 100th anniversary of the Ricker family settling here and opening their first inn in 1797.

The Maine State Building originally was the state pavilion at the 1893 Columbian Exposition in Chicago.

The building's lovely hilltop setting is on the grounds of the Poland Spring hotel close to where, in 1793, Joseph Ricker, while working outdoors, drank from a nearby spring whose medicinal qualities supposedly cured his dyspepsia. As the story spread, his small inn flourished. In 1844, the Ricker family which now operated a larger inn, began selling the natural spring water. Another generation of Rickers in 1907 opened a water-bottling plant and distribution company. At its peak, between 1876 and 1935, Poland Spring House was one of the most famous health spas and resorts in the country. The Rickers welcomed visiting presidents, sportsmen, movie stars, and business leaders, many of whom undoubtedly came to play on the first golf course in the United States built for a resort, as well as for the beautiful rural setting. Poland Spring Water partially owes its reputation to the "Medal of Excellence" it was awarded at the Columbian Exposition, when it was featured in the State of Maine pavilion.

Of 200 buildings that represented 44 states, dozens of countries, and numerous companies at the Columbian Exposition, the Maine State Building reportedly is one of only five still in existence. Among others are the Art Institute of Chicago and that city's Museum of Science and Industry. Frost designed the building in the Queen Anne style popular during the Victorian era. The base and first floor are octagonal, the second floor is square, and a third floor, added in 1895 (without changing the height of the building), is circular. At the World's Fair, it had four porches where visitors could enjoy views of Lake Michigan. The central hall, or Great Room, is a rotunda with a massive oak fireplace and a glass ceiling that now is more elaborate than the original. At one time, the rooms surrounding the rotunda were reading rooms for resort guests; today they contain World's Fair exhibits on Bath Iron Works and B & M Baked Beans (two companies founded during the 1800s in Maine), as well as hotel models from the state's Big Hotel Era. One room contains vintage golf equipment and photographs that describe changes to the course and the game made over time. On the third floor is the Nettie Ricker Art Gallery featuring work by local and regional artists.

Across the road is All Souls Chapel, built in 1912 as a place of worship for hotel guests and staff. No expense was spared. The chapel has nine hand-painted windows that look like stained glass, a paneled oak ceiling, mosaic tile floor, and a 1926 Skinner Pipe Organ. Both buildings are maintained by the Poland Spring Preservation Society and are on the National Register of Historic Places.

USEFUL INFORMATION:

• A short walk from the Maine State Building, through gates of Poland Spring Preservation Park, are the spring house and Poland Spring Museum with historical exhibits on the water business.

• A summer concert series on Monday evenings from June through August is held in All Souls Chapel. Season tickets are less than $10 per person.

• Preservation Park has scenic hiking trails and groomed cross-country skiing and snowshoe trails in winter.

Time to allow: 30 minutes
When it's open: Memorial Day–Columbus Day
   Tues.–Sat., 9 am–4 pm
   Guided tours available.
Directions: From the south, take I-95/Maine Turnpike to Exit 63-Gray-New Gloucester. After the toll plaza, turn right, then take the next two left turns to ME-26 and follow ME-26 through Gray and New Gloucester, past Sabbathday Lake Shaker Village, through the intersection with ME-122. Preservation Park and the Poland Spring Resort are one mile ahead, on the right.

Poland Spring Museum
115 Preservation Way, Poland Spring
www.polandspring.com/wecare/preservationpark.aspx
207-998-7143

WHAT YOU'LL FIND HERE: Elaborate Victorian marble and bronze spring house. Former water bottling facility now used as a museum and environmental education center. Vintage and educational exhibits on the bottled water industry. Conference center. Picnic tables.

WHY GO: "The Source" in the spring house is no longer the all-natural spot where around 1793 Joseph Ricker allegedly was cured of his ills after drinking pure water bubbling up from the grounds of his family's small Wayside Inn. In 1845, his descendant Hiram Ricker began bottling the spring's water, selling it commercially, and touting its purity and healing powers. As word spread, the inn's reputation grew, becoming a favorite of Victorian-era celebrities from the worlds of politics, sports, and the silver screen. They came here to unwind, play croquet, and drink complimentary glasses of spring water.

By 1895, the inn had evolved into a resort and health spa. An elegant spring house was designed for hotel guests who wanted to take healthful country walks to the source. Beside the charming structure, the Ricker family built a state-of-the-art bottling facility, their second business. The exterior of both buildings pays tribute to Spanish architecture. Together the two are known as Preservation Park and listed on the National Register of Historic Places.

The spring house interior is Italian Povanazzo marble. Its mosaic floor bears the Ricker family crest with the phrase "Sapientia Donum Dei" ("Wisdom is a gift from God"). The precise spot where the spring bubbles up, the "source," is enclosed by a bronze grill and glass to keep the water free of dust and impurities. As water flows from the spring, it is diverted through silver and glass pipes into granite tanks sealed with plate glass. Today, the spring house has the aura of a wealthy person's memorial shrine surrounded by deep woods and quiet country walking trails.

Water from Poland Spring earned the Medal of Excellence at the Columbian Exposition in 1894 and was honored as "the best spring water in the country" at the St. Louis World's Fair in 1904. Informative exhibits in the former bottling plant focus on environmental issues involving the aquifer and the history of the mineral spring and bottling company, with photos of Babe Ruth, presidents, and other recognizable visitors who came here to play golf and drink the water. The story of the Poland Spring water company is not chronicled in the Maine State Building elsewhere on the hotel grounds; the two historic sites are respectfully separate.

USEFUL INFORMATION:
• Even when the museum is closed, it is possible to see through glass doors into the spring house to admire the marble and glass interior.

• Picnic tables are next to the parking lot.

Time to allow: 15 minutes

Admission: Free

When it's open: Memorial Day–Columbus Day

Thurs.–Sat., 9 am–4 pm (but vary—best to call ahead and ask)

Tours are available off-season, on request.

Directions: Follow directions to Maine State Building, continuing on Preservation Way to the parking lot at the end.

Rufus Porter Museum
67 North High Street
260 Main Street (annex), Bridgton
www.rufusportermuseum.org
207-647-2828

WHAT YOU'LL FIND HERE: Original folk art murals and decorative objects painted by the early American artist Rufus Porter. Temporary exhibitions of work by other artists and illustrators. Drawings of inventions patented by Porter. Archive of *Scientific American,* the magazine Porter founded. Annual summer series of intensive workshops on traditional folk arts and crafts. Gift shop. Porter's Westwood Murals, in nearby annex.

WHY GO: A self-taught artist, musician, teacher, inventor, and publisher, Rufus Porter (1792–1884) was an early American creative spirit. His formal portraits and rural landscape murals may lack refinement, but their naïve style epitomizes what many of us picture when we think of folk art paintings.

Porter was something of a Renaissance man whose extensive travels in New England inspired countless ideas for useful and time-saving inventions. After 20 years as an itinerant artist and art teacher, and while continuing to paint, he began to focus his attention on a second career. He eventually patented more than 100 inventions and founded the magazine *Scientific American,* in part to promote them. His range is astounding. In 1844, Porter sold his design for a revolving rifle to Colonel Samuel Colt for $100. He received patents for boat improvements, a floating dry dock, a distance measuring device, a butter churn, a corn sheller, a life preserver, a fire alarm, and a cheese press. He published plans for an elevated railroad, a rotary plow, and a hot-air ventilation system. Although he himself traveled on foot, he designed a hot-air balloon and built a working model of an airship. When he was unable to raise funds to build the airship, he petitioned the U.S. Senate to take the project further; at first the Senate supported the idea but it died in committee.

But before all that, Porter painted houses and commercial signs and he played the fiddle. In 1812, as the nation went to war, he joined the militia, which sent him to Munjoy Hill in Portland where he was assigned to a fife and drum corps. When his military service ended, he became a music teacher and opened a dancing school.

Through it all, he continued to paint.

Although Porter was a devoted family man and the father of 10 children, his work as a muralist and portrait painter required him to travel throughout New England throughout his adult life. His frescoes and decorative objects are devoted to the scenes he knew best—the lakes and mountains of western Maine, drummers in marching units, patriotic eagles, sailing ships in Portland Harbor, gristmills, and farms.

This is the only museum devoted to Rufus Porter's work. The house was built in 1800. In the front parlor are wonderful original frescoes he was hired to paint here in 1828. One room is devoted to his inventions and publishing career, with a collection of early editions of *Scientific American,* which is still published today.

A short drive from the museum is an annex that contains murals removed from the home of Francis Howe in Westwood, Massachusetts, before it was demolished in 1965. Painted by Rufus Porter and his son and protégé, Stephen Twombly Porter, in 1838, the Westwood Murals are considered to be his best. They are richer in detail, perhaps because he used the project to instruct his son in techniques for creating depth of field and perspective. Porter rarely signed his work, but these murals are signed and dated by both men.

The museum continues Porter's interest in teaching through a series of folk art workshops held each year in July. Students come from all over for classes in traditional arts, from Rufus Porter–style murals to rug hooking, stenciling, chair-caning, painting floor cloths, paper-making, building dry stack stone walls, and creating fresh milk cheese. Future plans include building an education center adjacent to the house that will be devoted to 19th- and 20th-century creative arts and sciences.

USEFUL INFORMATION:

• Call ahead if you are traveling from a distance to be sure it is open. The museum is staffed by volunteers. Occasionally there are unexpected closings.

• School group tours are free; call to arrange in advance.

• Contact the museum to arrange special tours in the spring and fall.

Time to allow: 30 minutes plus 15 minutes at the annex
Admission: $8 Adults
　　$4 Seniors and groups of more than 15
　　Free Ages 15 and younger
When it's open: Late June–Labor Day
　　Wed.–Sat., noon–4 pm
　　Early Sept.–early Oct.
　　Thurs.–Sat., noon–4 pm
　　Or by appointment
Directions: From I-95/Maine Turnpike, Exit 48, turn right after the tollbooth. At the third light, turn left onto ME-302. Take this to Bridgton. At the second light in Bridgton, turn left to continue on ME-302 through town and up a hill. At the monument, bear right. The museum will be 0.3 mile on the right.

A "MUSEUM" WITH MOXIE

This is a museum in name only, but proprietor Frank Annicetti is a master of the art of storytelling. Moxie is the official beverage of the state of Maine. If you're in the neighborhood, stop by the small dusty corner store to spend five minutes admiring his Moxie memorabilia and an hour listening to his entertaining history of the first mass-produced soft drink. He'll deliver his narration word-for-word in the same cadence he has done over the years on *Good Morning America,* the Discovery Channel, and for countless publications. Ask about Moxie Day, the second Saturday in July, and he'll launch into tales of how efforts to keep the Moxie brand alive gave birth to an annual one-mile parade that the police reportedly estimate brought 30,000 people to little Lisbon Falls from all over the United States. Sign his guest book and you'll notice previous visitors hailed from foreign countries as well.

Janet Mendelsohn

Frank Annicetti, Moxie's No. 1 fan and a master of the art of storytelling.

Moxie is the oldest carbonated beverage continuously on the market today. It was first sold as a nerve tonic by Dr. Augustin Thompson of Union, Maine, in 1876. In 1884, it was reformulated so you could take it from a glass instead of a spoon.

"As Dr. Thompson would say in his apothecary shop, Moxie is guaranteed to cure everything from dyslexia to dyspepsia, locomotion to ataxia, but it's mainly for the nerves," recites the collection's "curator," whose dry wit and classic Maine accent suit the salesman's spiel of days long ago. A smile of delight fills his round face, eyes twinkling behind big brown glasses, as once again he gets to recite the benefits of his favorite drink. Dispelling the rumor that Moxie originally contained cocaine, he said it was always formulated only of healthy ingredients, mainly roots and herbs. Annicetti's white-bearded friend, Gilbert, who stopped by to say hello, declared, "Moxie's good for heartburn. I've taken it all my life."

As you pop open the bright orange can for your first taste of the bittersweet beverage, Annicetti points his forefinger at you in the same way the actors did in old Moxie ads, and recites:

"On the first taste, you may want to spit it out and throw it away. Don't.

"On the second taste, you may want to do the same. Don't.

"Wait for that third taste to allow the true flavor of Moxie to tickle the taste buds and you'll know why we call it the beverage of gourmets."

The old store has seen better days. Behind its well-worn lunch counter are piles of mail, crossword puzzles, and old phone books, but not much to eat. Annicetti only sells candy, several brands of sodas ("I don't discriminate"), and ice cream. Try a scoop of Moxie. He makes it himself and it's actually quite good. Also for sale (surprise!) are hunter orange Moxie T-shirts, sweatshirts, and Frisbees, a collection of prize-winning Moxie recipes ("Moxie and ham—oh, that's good"), and reproductions of tin advertising signs that featured Moxie's longtime spokesman, Red Sox slugger Ted Williams.

Annicetti's personal collection of Moxie items is mostly along the back wall of the long, narrow store. It's a motley assortment of cans and bottles, more advertising signs, metal trays, and thermometers embellished with the beverage's logo; *Smithsonian* and *MAD* magazine covers; an airplane model or two made from Moxie cans. At one time, the soda was sold in 38 states and three Canadian provinces, he said. Now it's hard to find outside of Maine.

According to Annicetti, the flavor has been modified over the years. It's not as bitter or as carbonated as the original beverage, but allegedly Diet Moxie is close to the original taste. Everything reminds him of a story about documentary film and TV crews that have chronicled the man and his Moxie museum, how it captured the state's official designation and favorite authors including some who wrote books on the history of the brew. "I'm just a retailer having fun," he said.

Moxie Museum
Kennebec Fruit Co.
2 Main Street
Lisbon Falls
207-353-8173
Open daily 9 am to 5 pm unless Frank Annicetti is away.

Fans of Moxie may also want to visit the Moxie section of the **Matthews Museum of Maine Heritage** in the Union Fairgrounds. Open July and August, Wednesday to Saturday, from noon–4 except holidays; and during the Union Fair, or by appointment June through September.

Nordica Homestead Museum
116 Nordica Lane, Farmington
www.lilliannordica.com
207-778-2042

WHAT YOU'LL FIND HERE. Childhood home of an international opera star. Costumes, stage jewelry, and memorabilia from her Victorian-era performances before royalty and at major opera houses around the globe.

WHY GO. Who knew that more than a century ago an internationally acclaimed opera singer was born in a farmhouse just off State Route 4 in Farmington, Maine? Madame Lillian Nordica (1857–1914) made her debut in *La Traviata* at Brescia, Italy, in April 1879. In swift succession, she performed at the Paris Grand Opera house, the Academy of Music in New York, and in London. She gave private concerts for Queen Victoria and for Czar Alexander II in St. Petersburg a week before his assassination. And she was chosen by Cosima Wagner, widow of composer Richard Wagner and his successor as director of the Bayreuth Festival, to create the role of Elsa in *Lohengrin* at the Bayreuth Festival in 1894, becoming the first American singer to perform there. Some considered the diva's performance to be the high point of the Golden Age of Opera.

Nordica's performances are said to have elevated the stature of the Metropolitan Opera House. At the Met, where she achieved international prominence for her Wagnerian roles, in 1898 she sang Brunnhilde of *Die Walkure* for the first time on any stage, and appeared with Enrico Caruso in a 1904 revival of *La Gioconda,* in which she performed again for both the opening of the Met's 1905–1906 season and the grand opening of the Boston Opera House in 1909.

But before the great soprano thrilled heads of state and opera audiences in all the principal cities of Europe, she was Lilly Norton, born in this traditional white frame house built by her father in 1840. Lilly lived here until she was six, when her parents moved the family to Boston. Following the death of her older sister, a promising vocalist studying at the New England Conservatory of Music, Lilly became a voice student at the conservatory. She graduated in 1876. And although she enchanted royalty and high society around the globe, she never abandoned her rural Maine roots. She returned often to Farmington and performed here several times at the peak of her career.

The stage name Giglio Nordica, "Lily of the North," was given to her by San Giovanni, her Italian voice coach, who sensed it would smooth the way for her acceptance in Europe. Indeed, she was celebrated for the purity and power of her voice, exceptional range, and dramatic talent.

Inside the house, you're struck by the incongruity of those ordinary early years and her eventual stardom. The family's bibles, quilts, and tools are typical of their time and place. Letters written by Amanda Norton, her mother, who often accompanied the diva on tour, describe embassy concerts with barons and baronesses in elegant gowns and her daughter, the star of the evening. Lilly's wide-spool bed and small chairs are still in her childhood bedroom. Scattered about are photographs and daguerreotypes of the family and famous composers and musicians.

In portraits, Nordica has a large presence but in reality she was petite, as is evident from several elegant gowns she wore on stage in the 1880s. The original forest green velvet dress with gold thread crochet work that she wore in *La Gioconda* is lovely. Equally feminine is a reproduction of the spring-green gown she wore in *Aida,* adorned with the original sequin trim. Her vanilla silk costume for *La Traviata* is embellished with delicate beaded lace. Even those unfamiliar with the opera will recognize a beige dress with red cape and armor she wore as Brunnhilde. Valued at thousands of dollars at the time, the collection of Nordica's gowns is too big to fit in the small house. Most are in storage at the Maine State Museum.

Janet Mendelsohn

In 1898, Lillian Nordica sang Brunnhilde of Die Walkure *for the first time on any stage.*

Costume jewelry made by Tiffany for Nordica is dramatically large for the stage, yet elegant. Cabinets contain bone china collections from her country home in New Jersey and another of her estates, which later became a golf clubhouse. Portraits, porcelain busts, and gifts from her fans are throughout. A black ostrich-feather fan was a prop she held in photos for posters and trays advertising Coca-Cola, looking much like another legend of the day, actress Lillian Russell. A rare Tiffany clock has ebony figures from Greek myths. An 11th-century, black carved teak chest protected her gowns while traveling. Here, too, is her entire collection of opera scores, with personal notations.

In the parlor is a heavy wooden throne, elaborately gilded and carved with cherubs and leaves, that was a gift from Diamond Jim Brady. What appears to be a tapestry is actually a round swivel table given to her by the empress of China. Photographs show Nordica's last performance in New York, in 1913, with the New York Philharmonic Orchestra, an appearance at the Waldorf Astoria, and the christening of the SS *Lillian Nordica* at the South Portland shipyard in 1944.

Nordica's sisters restored their childhood home and gave it to the diva as a birthday present. Later, in 1920, ten Farmington residents donated funds and took out a $500 mortgage to buy the 115-acre property and buildings. It opened as a museum in 1928. Two life-size oil paintings were acquired by the museum. One hangs inside; the other is too large for the house. It hangs in Nordica Hall at the University of Maine at Farmington, where she performed on her last visit to her hometown on August 17, 1911.

Lillian Nordica was an early supporter of women's suffrage. She planned to build a school for women singers at Harmon on the Hudson, New York, but her plans never came to fruition. It was one of numerous disappointments in a life full of professional success but personal pain, including three unhappy marriages. On a 1914 concert tour of the Pacific, she developed pneumonia and died in Java at the age of 57.

Guided tours are given by a resident caretaker. Because the house is not large enough to contain everything, much of the Nordica collection is stored in a large fireproof vault in the barn.

Time to allow: 30 minutes
Admission: $2 Adults
$1 Children
Free Ages 4 and younger
Half price Groups, arranged in advance
When it's open: June 1–Sept. 15
Tues.–Sat., 10 am–noon and 1–5 pm
Sun. 1–5 pm
Closed Mon.
Sept. 16–Oct. 15 by appointment.
Directions: From I-95/Maine Turnpike, Exit 112B to Augusta, take ME-27 North for about 35 miles. In Farmington, turn right onto Main Street, then left to stay on Main Street. Turn right at Holley Road, then left at Nordica Lane.

IF YOU'RE IN THE FARMINGTON AREA . . .

Wilton Farm & Home Museum, like many others in Maine, tells stories of a very local nature that really are chapters in the encyclopedic history of New England. In the early 1900s, this was a boarding house for workers at the G. H. Bass Shoe Factory next door. In the parlor is a piano where the girls gathered after supper. Rooms are furnished as they would have been in a variety of eras, with items donated by area residents. There are period wedding dresses and special-occasion attire trimmed with cream lace and embroidery, bonnets and men's hats, and Bass family memorabilia. Upstairs is a room devoted to the former Wilton Academy and to Sylvia Hardy (1823–1888), Wilton's most famous citizen. Hardy finally stopped growing at age 40 when she was 7 feet, 10½ inches tall, and weighed 400 lbs. She was known as "The Maine Giantess, the tallest lady in the world" when she joined Barnum's circus after becoming good friends with Tom Thumb and his wife, whom she met when they visited her cousin. Hardy said her years with the circus were the happiest of her life.

Wilton Farm & Home Museum
Canal Street
Wilton
207-645-2261
www.wiltonmaine.org
Open July and Aug., Sat., 1–4 pm or by appointment and during the annual blueberry festival

Nowetah's American Indian Museum
2 Colegrove Road (Route 27), New Portland
www.nowetahs.webs.com
207-628-4981

WHAT YOU'LL FIND HERE: Family-owned museum of American Indian crafts. More than 600 handmade baskets and bark containers, most made by Maine Indians. Crafts and art by Indians of the Americas from Canada to Mexico and Peru. Gift shop with wide variety of crafts and clothing, including items made by curator and proprietor Nowetah Cyr and her daughter Wahleyah Black.

Maine Indian-made baskets at
Nowetah's American Indian Museum.

WHY GO:

This is another of those wonderful surprises that await if you go out of your way to see what's there. Nowetah Cyr, a descendant of the St. Francis and Paugussett Indians, began collecting Indian-made baskets and other crafts more than 40 years ago when she was a volunteer for the Audubon Society, said her husband, Tom Cyr. When traveling for Audubon in rural and tribal areas, during her free time she noticed local tribes tended to exhibit only their own arts and crafts. "Nowetah began visiting and trading with tribes throughout New England, building her collection. Instead of being tribe-specific, she wanted people to see what all Indians are capable of making," Cyr said. Since 1969, she has owned and operated the museum and store which he said is on ancestral ceremonial sacred ground. Nowetah and Tom married about 11 years ago. He's the one you're likely to meet; allow him to guide you through the collections.

Everything is carefully tagged by Nowetah, who researches the place and year of origin of each artifact, as well as how it was used. "Nowetah is most proud of her basket collection," said Cyr. There are more than 600 made by Indians in New England, but primarily Maine, over the past 200 years. Cyr showed us intricately woven baskets that were often made for the tourist trade. Handsome sewing baskets on tall stands. Large containers for drying apples. Fishing baskets and Abenaki birch-bark baskets illustrated with leaf or fish designs. Micmac-made curlicue ash baskets that dazzle the eye, and sturdy utility baskets for many tasks.

The next-largest collections are probably those from Indians of the Pacific Northwest and Alaska, southwestern United States, and Canada. A 12-foot dugout racing canoe was carved by Maliseet Indians from a single maple tree in the St. John River

Valley during the late 1800s. Porcupine quill boxes with intricately woven designs, sometimes incorporating birch bark, are the work of Micmac and Ojibway artists, usually women. Seal boots are among practical items made by Eskimo, Cree, and Ojibway Indians in the northwest. Decorative arts include Mexican painted ponies, gourd instruments accented with beads and branches, and straw dolls from Peru. There are cases of prehistoric stone implements, embroidered moccasins and belts, hunting decoys, bows and arrows, rain sticks, rugs, drums, Sioux shields, crooked knives, bone games, carved bear-claw and antler necklaces, clothing made of pelts and furs—the list seems endless and everything is neatly organized by region.

Nowetah and one of her seven daughters make many of the traditional crafts sold in the adjacent store, which supports the museum. They also sell a wide array of other Indian-made and related items, from leather moccasins to T-shirts, American Indian flute music CDs, and musical instruments, books, baskets, jewelry, dream catchers, toys, and more.

USEFUL INFORMATION: No credit cards for store purchases.

Time to allow: 30 minutes to 1 hour
Admission: Free
When it's open: Daily, 10 am–5 pm
Directions: On ME-27 midway between Farmington and Kingfield.

Ski Museum of Maine
256 Main Street, Kingfield
www.skimuseumofmaine.org
207-265-2023

WHAT YOU'LL FIND HERE: Vintage ski equipment, clothing, and patches. Archival photographs and memorabilia. Tributes to Maine's legendary manufacturers of ski equipment. History of the state's slopes. Maine Ski Hall of Fame.

WHY GO: "People come in here all the time, point to a pair of skis, and say, 'Wow! I had these back in the '60s,'" said Bruce Miles, executive director. "Or they say, 'I remember having to wrap the strap around the boot like that.' They go down memory lane."

Founded in 1995 to preserve the 140-year history and heritage of the downhill and cross-country ski industry in Maine, the place feels like a ski shop with its long row of vintage skis and poles chronicling the evolution of materials, bindings, and styles. It's a place for skiers devoted to their sport. Racks hold boots with seemingly antique bindings, bulky parkas, team uniforms from the Lake Placid Olympics, a raccoon coat worn on the slopes in the 1950s. A scattering of snowboards is the start of a growing collection. Fading pamphlets, likely dusted off in attics and pulled from musty drawers, relate the sport's increasing popularity since 1905, when Theo Johnsen of Portland wrote one of the first books on "skeeing."

Colorful patches recall lost ski areas such as Bald Mountain in Dedham; Big A, on Mount Agamenticus in York; Enchanted Mountain in Jackman; and Evergreen Valley in Lovell-Stoneham. Active slopes are represented, too, like Titcomb Mountain, which was created in 1939 by the Farmington Ski club and is still the oldest continuously operating ski area in the state. From local areas served by just one rope tow to the growth of the big Sunday River and Sugarloaf resorts, the history of skiing in Maine is duly noted.

Vintage skis at the Ski Museum of Maine.

"Everyone knows about Bass Shoes but not everyone knows that the company outfitted the 10th Mountain Division during World War II," said Miles, pointing to photos of the elite alpine combat arm of the U.S. military. "Made in Maine," another exhibit, recognizes the state's leading manufacturers of ski equipment. In addition to Bass, there was Paris Manufacturing Co., which made skis from 1900 to 1965, longer than any competitor. Maine's woodworking industry in the early 1900s also gave birth to W. F. Tubbs, makers of skis and snowshoes in neighboring Norway. Tubbs reportedly produced 60,000 pairs of skis in 1922 alone.

The Maine Ski Hall recognizes competitors, teachers, and others whose achievements helped build the sport in the state.

USEFUL INFORMATION: The museum is located above the Sugarloaf Sports Outlet in downtown Kingfield. Its hours match those of the store. Extended winter hours begin when the slopes open for the season at Sugarloaf Mountain Resort, generally around Thanksgiving.

Time to allow: 15 minutes

Admission: Free

When it's open: Summer–Thanksgiving
    Thurs.–Mon., 9 am–5 pm
    Winter
    Mon.–Thurs., 8 am–5 pm
    Fri., Sat., Sun., 8 am–6 am
Directions: I-95/Maine Turnpike to ME-27 North into Kingfield and across from the intersection of ME-16 and ME-27.

FUN FACT: Maine's first ski tow, Jockey Cap in Fryeburg, opened in 1936. Ten businessmen had formed a corporation and put in $25 each for construction. During the '30s, local farmers often met the ski trains that brought skiers from Portland to Fryeburg and then brought them back to the station at the end of their vacation. Jockey Cap closed in 1938. The rope tow was sold to Cornish, Maine, and the corporation members who originally invested in Jockey Cap each received $17 back.

Stanley Museum
40 School Street, Kingfield
www.stanleymuseum.org
207-265-2729

WHAT YOU'LL FIND HERE: Three models of Stanley Steamer cars representing progressive stages of design. Automotive memorabilia. Chronology of the Stanley Dry Plate Photography Co. Portraits drawn by F. E. Stanley. Fine art photographs by Chansonetta Stanley Emmons. Family mementos and furniture from their home, circa 1900. Gift shop.

WHY GO: Car enthusiasts often treat Stanley Steamers as a footnote in automotive history. Perhaps an odd footnote, at that. Steam was used to power all kinds of machinery at the start of the Industrial Revolution. The Stanley brothers didn't invent steam-powered automobiles, but they perfected them. In the early 1900s, close to 100 small companies manufactured steam cars in the United States but the Stanleys came out on top. In their day, their cars were clean-running and more reliable than gas-powered vehicles, but a tad scary to start. Ironically, today as we search for alternative energy sources, there is some renewed interest in steam-powered cars.

It was the identical twins Freelan Oscar (F. O.) Stanley and his brother Francis Edgar (F. E.) who made the technology famous. Stanley Steamers are beautiful machines, elegantly designed. But they were also well engineered. In 1899, F. O. built the first car to climb New Hampshire's Mount Washington. A few years later, F. E. built the Stanley Racer, called the "Rocket," which broke the world speed record in 1906 when its driver, Fred Marriott, achieved 127.659 mph, the first automobile to exceed 2 miles in one minute.

However, the museum is devoted to a wider legacy because the Stanleys of Kingfield, Maine, were an innovative and artistic family. F. E. was an accomplished artist.

Years before manufacturing cars, he patented the airbrush which he developed by using an atomizer to improve the quality of his "crayon portraits," or charcoal pigment. Renowned for his talent at portraiture—several fine examples of his work hang in the museum—he switched to the faster process offered by the emerging art of photography. As was typical, he tried coating his own plates, developing an emulsion formula for wet plate photography. But like others around 1881, he switched to a dry-plate technique. F. E. soon persuaded his brother to join him in what became their first business partnership, the Stanley Dry Plate Co. With F. O.'s knowledge of the paper-making industry, the twins in 1886 patented the first machine that could make dry photographic plates better than the job could be done by hand. They revolutionized the manufacturing process, increasing production from 60 plates an hour to 60 plates a minute, and they built a manufacturing facility in Watertown, Massachusetts. By 1900, they were grossing $1 million a year. In 1902, they sold the company to George Eastman of Eastman Kodak. That is how F. O. and F. E. made their fortune, before they began building cars.

The cars also were made in Massachusetts. The story goes that F. E.'s wife had trouble learning to ride a bicycle when that was the craze in the 1880s, so Stanley told her he would invent something they could ride in together. Familiar with how steam power worked, he first built a car for himself, the Locomobile in which he and his wife made their momentous Mount Washington climb. Then he built a car for his brother. In 1898, the promoters of the first automobile show in Boston invited the Stanley twins to demonstrate their car's speed and hill-climbing ability in trials at the Charles River Park Velodrome in Cambridge, Massachusetts. When their unofficial entry broke an unofficial world speed record, their car was a hit with the crowd.

What F. O. later said was intended as "an interesting hobby, not a trade," soon became a car manufacturing company. The Stanleys' vehicles were champions in straight-ahead, short-distance racing until 1908 when Daytona racing officials changed the rules, effectively excluding steam- and electric-powered cars by requiring qualifiers to average 60 mph or more for 100 miles in at least one distance race. Steam-powered cars have a fairly short distance range while gas-fueled cars are able to travel farther, one reason they became more popular. But there was another problem.

"Firing up a steamer is a bit complicated," said Jim Merrick, museum director. "The cars have no gears so you don't need to shift, just keep your eye on the valves, watching the oil and water levels. Drivers generally had siphon hoses to refill the engine when they reached a stream or horse trough. In the early days, they used white gasoline until the gas tax shot up and the cars were redesigned to burn kerosene to light the pilot, which was done with a torch."

The Stanleys manufactured just under 11,000 steam cars. About 600 of them are still functional today, including three displayed at the museum in Kingfield: a 1905 Model CX with folding front seat, and two five-passenger touring cars, a 1916 Model 725 and a 20-horsepower 1910 Model 70. (A fourth is at the Stanley Museum in Colorado.) Surrounding the latter two in the "car room" are vintage photographs and automotive memorabilia.

The museum building was a schoolhouse from 1903–1980. It was designed by the Stanley brothers, who also paid for its construction. A former classroom is now largely

Bob Mendelsohn

Driver's view of a Stanley Steamer.

devoted to the history of their dry-plate photography business as well as a gallery of portraits by F. E. and violins made by the twins, a family tradition. There is also a collection of 20 fine art photographs taken by their sister, Chansonetta Stanley Emmons. Her work is well-composed, using glass plate negatives and hand-colored glass lantern slides to capture scenes of rural life in New England and the South in the early 1900s. They are worthy of a visit on their own.

USEFUL INFORMATION: Another, smaller Stanley Museum is in the Stanley Hotel in Estes Park, Colorado. F. O. Stanley spent every summer there after he was diagnosed with a severe recurrence of tuberculosis in 1903. He was critically ill and weighed 100 pounds when he was sent to Colorado under a doctor's care. While recuperating, in 1909 he built the first grand hotel based on service by the automobile, and went on to develop other properties in the area. F. O. Stanley died in 1940 at the age of 91.

Time to allow: 45 minutes
Admission: Free
When it's open:
   June–Oct. Tues.–Sun., 1–4 pm
   Nov.–May Tues.–Fri., 10 am–4 pm
Directions: From I-95/Maine Turnpike, Exit 12/Auburn, take ME-4 to ME-27 to Kingfield. Or take I-95 to the Belgrade exit to ME-27 to Kingfield.

Wilhelm Reich Museum
Orgonon
Dodge Pond Road, Rangeley
www.wilhelmreichmuseum.org
207-864-3443

WHAT YOU'LL FIND HERE: Physician Wilhelm Reich's laboratory, inventions, library, study, and personal memorabilia in the mountainside retreat and observatory he helped design. Video biography of Reich's life and theories. Children's nature-study Discovery Room. Seminars, conferences, and nature programs. Walking trails. Gift shop.

WHY GO: For the controversial psychoanalyst Wilhelm Reich, M.D., this isolated laboratory surrounded by serene western mountains and lakes must have been an escape zone. Here, where the most immediate challenges tend to be moose and deep snow, in the place he called "Orgonon," the Austrian-born Reich (1897–1957) could pursue research he began as a medical student at the University of Vienna, where he was trained by Sigmund Freud. Reich was drawn to Freud's idea that libido is central to human functioning. But he took Freud's concept of sexuality farther, believing there is a deeper level of functioning than the unconscious submersion of libido. Reich devoted his career to demonstrating that sexual energy, which he called "orgone," is a powerful force within the human body that must be allowed to develop freely in children and adults and that if it is discouraged, pent-up sexual energy leads to anxiety and neurotic disorders.

With the assistance of colleagues at the Oslo Physiological Institute, during the 1930s Reich built laboratory equipment designed to study the exact nature of sexual excitation by positioning electrodes on the human body. Using his students, friends, and himself as subjects, he conducted experiments measuring the electricity that he said surfaces in different parts of the body when aroused. Reich claimed that erogenous zones can exhibit different, higher levels of energy than ordinary skin. Furthermore, he conducted experiments to determine whether orgone energy can be harnessed for a variety of purposes, from treatment of cancer to mechanical power and weather experimentation.

One of the missions of the museum is to correct public understanding and published information about Reich's work. His supporters say that despite easy access to his scientific writing, including his five published books, Reich's work has long been oversimplified, misunderstood, and misconstrued by both the medical community and the media. According to the museum, Reich never claimed the invention he called an "orgone energy accumulator" could cure cancer, he never charged terminally ill cancer patients fees when they volunteered for his studies, and he never promised to help patients achieve "orgiastic potency." Nonetheless, published accounts attributed all these claims to Reich. Increasingly his radical theories attracted widespread attention and charges that he and his inventions were fraudulent.

In 1940, he began building his "accumulators," boxes that were large enough for patients to sit in to harness the alleged therapeutic effects of orgone energy. Reich's experiments also increasingly violated cultural taboos against touching during psychotherapy. As a result, Freud distanced himself from Reich and his work and Norwegian physicians and scientists ridiculed his experiments.

Reich moved to New York, where he taught his theories at the New School for Social Research, continued writing, and captivated interest among leading intellectuals of the day. References to his theories appeared in lyrics by Bob Dylan and Jack Kerouac's novel *On the Road,* among other works of popular culture.

In 1941, days after the attack on Pearl Harbor, Reich was arrested by the FBI and jailed for three weeks before being cleared of charges that he was a former communist sympathizer and a potential threat to national security.

The following year, he bought this 160-acre property near Rangeley, where he helped design and had built Orgonon as his home and laboratory. The spacious, modern, multilevel building is constructed of native fieldstone and local timbers, with walls of windows that maximize the view of its mountaintop wilderness location, an enviable retreat and ideal for another of his interests: cloud-busting.

The observatory, with its tiers of outdoor terraces and clear access to the skies, was perfect for his meteorological experiments. Reich's alleged discovery of orgone energy in the atmosphere led him to seek a way to alter its concentration in the environment, thereby causing the clouds to make rain. He conducted dozens of experiments with an accumulator made from a series of hollow tubes connected to water and aimed at the sky. When a severe drought in 1953 threatened Maine's blueberry crop, he was credited with successfully making it rain around Ellsworth.

Along with his scientific equipment, the museum presents explanations of how the cloud-buster worked, as well as how he captured orgone energy to power a motor.

Reich's psychotherapy practice flourished along with considerable interest in his research. But much of that changed in 1947, when an article in *The New Republic* claimed Reich's orgone accumulators were being falsely promoted to cure cancer and sexual disorders. The U.S. Federal Trade Commission, which regulates medical devices, contacted the Food and Drug Administration, which launched a 10-year investigation that concluded Reich was guilty of medical fraud. A federal injunction was issued requiring him to destroy the 250 accumulators he had built. When he violated the injunction by traveling to Arizona to conduct weather experiments, the FDA went to Orgonon to supervise the destruction of the few devices that remained there, as well as several boxes of his books and promotional materials. Soon after, the FDA oversaw burning of literally tons of Reich's books and publications. In 1957, Reich was sent to prison, where he died of an apparent heart attack. His tomb is in the woods at Orgonon.

USEFUL INFORMATION

• Visitors are given a guided tour that begins with a half-hour video biography of Wilhelm Reich and describes his work. After the video, there is a guided tour of the building, which is on the National Register of Historic Places.

• Handicapped access is limited to the first floor of the multilevel building.

• Hiking trails on the property range from a 0.25-mile "Trail of Thoughts," marked by quotations on nature to an easy, 0.1-mile looped hike for children and a 2.2-mile brook trail that has steep inclines.

• Sunday nature programs are free and cover topics such as geocaching, campfire cooking, and mushrooming.

Time to allow: 1½ hours
Admission: $6 Adults
  Free Ages 12 and younger
  When it's open:
  July and Aug.: Wed.-Sun., 1–5 pm
  Sept.: Sun. only, 1–5 pm
  Private tours available by appointment year-round.
Directions: From the intersection of ME-4 and ME-16 in Rangeley, follow Route 4 North/Route 16 South for 3.6 miles. Look for the museum sign on the right. Turn right onto Dodge Pond Road. The museum is 0.25 miles on the left.

KENNEBEC

CHAPTER 6

VALLEY

Children's Discovery Museum
171 Capitol Street, Augusta
www.childrensdiscoverymuseum.org
207-622-2209

WHAT YOU'LL FIND HERE: Storefront play space for ages 2 to 8. Let's Pretend areas: restaurant, bank, construction zone, campground, veterinary office, supermarket. Touch tank with marine life. Small stage for readings by children's book authors and other programs. Gift shop.

WHY GO: Although not a museum to go out of your way for, local families and others with young children will enjoy the range of activities that allow youngsters to play at being adults, imagining they work in jobs just like those they see around town. All play areas are on one floor and visible from anywhere in the room so parents, grand-parents, and caregivers can let the kids wander and make friends on their own in this safe, hands-on learning environment.

On a summer afternoon, at first there didn't seem to be much happening here, but about a dozen children were scattered about, happily dancing on a stage, treating stuffed animals in a mini-clinic and otherwise engaged. A four-year-old girl looked quite serious as she tapped computer keys, helping her grandmother in the bank. Three young girls waited on teen "customers" seated at the restaurant counter. A boy played a drum in the music corner while others relaxed in the campground where there's a tent, kayak, and tree house to climb.

Perhaps most popular is the construction zone with a real front-end loader to climb on, a Lego table, a mock office, and, for adults, information on civil engineering proj-ects in Maine.

USEFUL INFORMATION:
• Appropriate for children up to about eight years old.
• The Association of Children's Museums offers an ACM Reciprocal Membership at more than 165 participating children's museums in the United States and Canada. Ben-efits vary from place to place but generally include free admission for a minimum of four members of the same household. Ask about the ACM Reciprocal Membership at this or any participating museum, or see: www.childrensmuseums.org/visit/reciprocal.htm.

Time to allow: 30 minutes or more
Admission: $5 Ages 1–12
    $4 Ages 13 to adult
    Free Ages 12 months and under
When it's open: Tues.–Thurs., 10 am–4 pm
    Fri. and Sat., 10 am–5 pm; Sun., 11 am–4 pm
Directions: In Shaw's Plaza, lower level, less than a five-minute drive from the Maine State House.

Old Fort Western
16 Cony Street, Augusta
www.oldfortwestern.org
207-626-2385

WHAT YOU'LL FIND HERE: New England's oldest surviving wooden fort (1754), a National Historic Landmark. Restored 17th-century trading post/18th-century store. Furnished colonial house. Guided tours led by costumed interpreters. History camp for high school students. Summer apprentice program for ages 8–12. Gift shop.

Janet Mendelsohn

Stories of hard times emerge at Old Fort Western.

WHY GO: For a real sense of what citizens and soldiers experienced in the 1700s, little compares to walking where they walked, surrounded by their cannons and guns, boats, household furniture, tools, and supplies while listening to stories of their actions during the American Revolution and the French and Indian War. Visiting Old Fort Western reminds us that Maine and its capital, Augusta, and this nation itself exist because centuries ago, real people settled in a place that was still the frontier and fought in armed political battles that shaped this country's culture and its future.

From 1628–1661, an offshoot of the Plymouth Colony called Plymouth Proprietors operated a trading post on this site. A century later, the post was resurrected by their successors, Kennebec Proprietors, a Boston-based company attempting to settle lands granted to the Pilgrims along the Kennebec River and help England and her colonies strengthen their hold on the territory. It's a choice location across the river from present-day Augusta. At this point, the Kennebec becomes too shallow for heavy boats to travel farther north but it's still navigable by lightweight boats from both directions and easily reached by land.

At the start of the French and Indian War (a seven-year conflict in which England and her colonies battled with France and her Indian allies for control of North America), when the English needed supplies 17 miles upriver at Fort Halifax, Fort Western was built in 1754 by a Massachusetts Provincial Unit (Maine was still part of Massachusetts). The purpose of the fort was to defend navigation on the river as well as operate and protect the storehouse. Somewhere between 300 and 500 soldiers constructed Fort Western in three to five days; their work in large part still stands.

The garrison was commanded by James Howard and first manned by his sons and 15 other men who had been stationed at Fort Richmond, about 15 miles away. Soon after construction was completed, sloops and schooners from Boston Harbor began arriving four times a year loaded with barrels of candles, musket balls, pork, beans, and other supplies. When the ships reached Fort Western, 20 soldiers would off-load the cargo and store it in the garrison until it was time to transfer the supplies to flat-bottom, wooden boats, called bateaux, that were designed for shallow water. Each 30-foot-by-6-foot bateau also held four swivel cannons for defense, making the boats so heavy that seven soldiers were needed to row one upriver to Fort Halifax, often against strong river currents, an exceedingly difficult task. The military supply operation continued year-round until 1766.

The fort was never attacked but a 4-pound cannon, positioned above the Kennebec, is still in place in the block house, along with other armament, and the cannon is still functional.

When the war ended and the garrison was no longer needed by the military, Captain Howard took ownership of the post, which he and his sons ran as a store. No money was exchanged for the goods they sold. Instead, customers traded animal pelts—fisher, mink, bear, and moose hide—for sugar, molasses, alewives, mackerel, tool parts, and other necessities. Two of his sons formed S & W Howard, a successful storekeeping company, and one of them, Samuel, regularly sailed one of the family's sloops between here and Boston. Shelves and cabinets hold samples of goods they stocked—everyday dishes made of red clay, farming tools, knives used by midwives, cast-iron kettles, indigo-blue dye, rolls of homespun and mill-made fabric to be made into clothing, fishhooks, iron heads for hoes and other farm tools, and other items documented among hundreds listed in the Howards' account books. The store was also a busy center of commerce and news-sharing for settlers who came from throughout the growing Kennebec region, from Boston to Newfoundland, and traders and seamen with connections to the West Indies.

Attached to the former store is the Howard family's 16-room house. For its time, their home was stylish and the rooms look much as they would have then, with authentic chairs, tables, dishware, and beds from the late 1700s and early 1800s. It is furnished based on the actual probate inventory taken when Samuel Howard died in 1799.

The buildings are only open if you join a guided tour, but don't hesitate to do that.

You'll learn about the fort's multiple lives, as well as American history that occurred here before and after it was used by the military. After 1850, among various uses by different owners, the house was a tenement house for laborers in the Augusta area. Its occupants apparently were a rowdy bunch who caused problems for the community. The building fell into serious disrepair. A local nonprofit group restored the structure for historical purposes.

Tours are led by interpreters steeped in historical information and outfitted in correct military clothing for the period 1754–1766, the French and Indian War. You'll also hear about the role the Howard family and their store played in the founding of Augusta.

The fort is surrounded by a high stockade fence with two "block" houses and two "watch boxes," buildings at the corners with clear views of the river and surrounding land. Records show that at one time there was a second, outer fence beyond this one, perhaps as much to block drifting snow as for military defense.

USEFUL INFORMATION:

• Not all buildings are fully handicapped accessible, but they're working on it. If you need special accommodations, call two weeks in advance.

• Special events range from fort-to-fort canoe and kayak expeditions to French and Indian War encampments.

• Pre-scheduled history programs are designed for kindergarten through grade 12 and meet selected Maine Learning Results social studies standards or homeschoolers. Additional programs are offered for adults.

Time to allow: 1 hour with tour (required to enter buildings)
Admission: $6 Adults
$4 Ages 6–16
Free Ages 5 and younger, and all Augusta residents
When it's open: Memorial Day–Labor Day
Daily, 1–4 pm
Labor Day–Columbus Day
Weekends only, 1–4 pm
Nov., Dec., Jan.: First Sun. of the month, 1–3 pm
March: Maple Syrup Day, fourth Sun., 1–3 pm
Group tours by pre-arrangement (and at group rates) Memorial Day–Columbus Day.
Directions: From I-95/Maine Turnpike, Exit 113, merge onto Route 3 East Augusta/Belfast. Turn right at West River Road onto Northern Avenue. Continue onto Water Street. Turn left at Bridge Street to Cony Street.

FUN FACT: In 1755, Benedict Arnold used Fort Western as his staging point on the way to Quebec during the American Revolution. Several of his officers were lodged in the main house.

Maine State Museum
State House Complex
230 State Street, Augusta
www.mainestatemuseum.org
207-287-2301

WHAT YOU'LL FIND HERE People and industries that shaped Maine. Three-story water-powered woodworking mill and reproductions of workshops and rooms where Maine products were made in years past. Archeological artifacts dating back 12,000 years. Natural science specimens, from minerals to woodland settings with live trout and taxidermied animals. Military flags and artifacts predating the American Revolution through the struggle for Maine statehood (1820). Educational programs for school groups, families, and adults. Gift shop.

WHY GO: Imagine stepping inside a children's pop-up book about the history of Maine. Following a ramp that guides you through the museum is like turning the pages as still-life scenes from the past appear. Here's a logging camp, there's a granite quarry, and over there, ice harvesting is underway. There's a gunsmith shop on one floor and a classy parlor like elderly Aunt Martha's on another. The Maine State Museum is a favorite of our friend and neighbor, Charle Tobey, a native of the Pine Tree State, and it's easy to see why. Exhibits are reminiscent of the Smithsonian Museum of American History, in Washington, D.C., but on a smaller scale and all about Maine. Plus they remind us of school field trips—"Hey, there was a picture of that in my social studies book!"—with tons of stuff to spark kids' curiosity.

Just past the front door you come face to face with "The Lion," a massive green and black railroad steam engine built in 1846. For 50 years, this workhorse pulled cars loaded with logs from Whitneyville to the wharf in Machiasport. The logging exhibit is one of those seemingly pop-up scenes, with real tools and heavy equipment, a saw mill, and a black-and-white film clip of lumbermen running across logs as they floated down a river. Along the ramp, the series of room-sized scenes are snapshots of agricultural production, sardine canning, lobstering, and fishing. They are static, without humans in action, but nonetheless they make a good introduction to industries that were historically important to the state's economy; some still are.

"Back to Nature" is a more sensory exhibit, like a walk in the woods but indoors. The sounds of chirping birds and a real trickling stream, with live fish, are wonderful touches in settings that show native woodland creatures poised in their natural habitat. It's a fun break from all the serious learning that happens elsewhere in these halls.

Downstairs the ramp winds through "Made in Maine," circling a working three-story water-powered woodworking mill and past what might be called a tour of 19th-century workrooms. Full-sized scenes depict shops where rifles, shoes, furniture, dresses, and fishing rods were made; only the craftsmen are absent. Here, too, it's like the pages of a history textbook come alive.

Among the reasons Mainers can be justifiably proud of the Maine State Museum is that, whether they know it or not, they own the collections. The museum holds title on behalf of the people of Maine to natural science specimens and artifacts found on or below state-owned land, including navigable waterways and coastal waters. And that makes for diverse collections of good stuff that some 20,000 students come to see with their classmates each year. One of their stops is the "Struggle for Identity," about the fight for Maine statehood and battles from 1640 through the 1840s among the French, English, and Native Americans who all sought control of the land and its bountiful resources. There are maps and rifles from the American Revolution, the War of 1812, and later boundary disputes. In "12,000 Years in Maine," another longtime favorite, children especially seem to enjoy walking past a primitive riverside campsite representing a Paleo-Indian settlement as it might have been built by the first humans to live in what is now Maine. Archeologists affiliated with the museum continue to search for clues to what life was like for the people who lived here thousands of years before Europeans arrived. Their digs have unearthed more than 2,000 stone tools, pottery fragments, animal bones, birch bark canoes, and baskets, and they're all on display, along with historical documents that record the experiences of the Popham Colony (1607–08), the first English settlers in New England.

Courtesy of the Maine State Museum

The shoe shop where boots and shoes were "Made in Maine" at the Maine State Museum.

The "Cabinet of Curiosities" gallery is filled with natural science specimens that were the first exhibits when the museum opened around 1830. Children and families can borrow clipboards to "explore like a scientist" using activity sheets that guide their discoveries with such tips as what we can learn about bones.

The newest and perhaps most engaging exhibit, "At Home in Maine," occupies most of the fourth floor. These are the stories of immigrants from many countries who settled in the state, bringing treasured possessions and traditions to their new home, gradually weaving their foods, languages, and customs into the fabric of Maine. Reproductions of rooms in their homes reveal similarities and differences among ethnic groups over time. An 1880s Acadian kitchen, 1940s Midcoast summer kitchen, 1938 upscale Bangor dining room, 1960s ranch-style living room, and an old attic speak to family life and what home and family mean to all of us. There's even a bathroom (circa 1910) that reveals the benefits of indoor plumbing.

Temporary exhibits run the gamut of arts, crafts, and history, from Wabanaki textiles to Civil War flags and life in the Popham Colony.

USEFUL INFORMATION:

• You enter on the third floor of the museum. Most exhibits are well marked as you follow the ramp through display areas to lower floors. But it's easy to miss some. One of these is Maine's fight for statehood, "Struggle for Identity," on the first floor; another is "Back to Nature," at the rear of the third (entrance lobby) floor. Maps are available at the front desk. To reach the fourth floor, return to the entrance, pass the Museum Store, and turn left for an elevator or go farther down the hall to the stairs.

• Touch Stations, small kiosks identified by a bold letter "T," invite visitors to handle objects representative of a particular exhibit. Put your hand inside a lobster trap, rub a woolen cloth used to make clothing, or grasp the handle of a tool to see how it felt in a workman's hand.

• An online database of selections from the extensive collections allows students and researchers to see and read about everything in advance, from military flags to pocket watches, duck decoys and glassware. See www.mainestatemuseum.org/collections/explore_the_collections/.

• Many exhibits are designed with informative signs and cases at appropriate height for children and people in wheelchairs.

Time to allow: 2 hours
Admission: $2 Adults
    $1 Ages 6–18
    $1 Seniors (62 and older)
    $6 Maximum per family
    $5 Special programs or tour
    No fee for school groups
When it's open: Tues.–Fri., 9 am–5 pm
    Sat., 10 am–4 pm
    Closed Sun., Mon., all state holidays and state government closure days.
Directions: I-95/Maine Turnpike to Exit 112 (Augusta) to ME-11 (East). At the rotary, take the first exit and follow State Street south. Immediately after the Capitol Building, turn right into the parking lot. The museum shares a building with the Maine State Archives and Maine State Library.

FUN FACT: Most objects in the archives of the Maine State Museum were donated by individuals seeking a good home for their personal collections and items of historical importance. Not every item offered is accepted because space is limited. Those items of special interest to researchers or with stories attached about how or where they were used are most likely to become part of the museum.

SPOTLIGHT

A Conversation with Earle Shettleworth, Jr., Maine State Historian and Director of the Maine Historic Preservation Commission

Earle Shettleworth's name came up often while I was researching this book. Museum directors, curators, and collectors all seem to rely on his expertise. When it comes to Maine history and architecture, he's the "go-to" guy. A frequent guest speaker and author, he can tell you all about legendary figures like architect John Calvin Stevens and "Fly Rod Crosby: The woman who marketed Maine." Online you'll likely find a long list of Civil War monuments he photographed statewide for the war's sesquicentennial. Who is this fellow whose depth and breadth of knowledge about Maine is so highly respected? And what exactly does a State Historian do?

As it turns out, the Maine State Historian is a voluntary position with a budget of only $500 a year. Shettleworth said it's probably the only state appropriation that hasn't changed since it was created in 1907. Fortunately, he also has a "day job" as director of the Maine Historic Preservation Commission, a post he has held since 1976.

We met in Augusta at the brick house (1845) that is the Commission's office, across the street from the Capitol and Blaine House (1833), home of Maine's governors and their families. En route to a former dining room that now serves meetings, we wound our way through hallways lined with stacks of bulging manila folders and boxes of old photographs, journals, and letters, passing desks piled with reports. Engraved prints and maps hang on the walls. Small models of vernacular architecture decorate a mantle in the foyer where wooden bookcases hold leather-bound ledgers and piles of broadsheets. It is just what you'd imagine, and Shettleworth probably resembles your image of a historian. His slim frame is slightly bent, perhaps from decades poring over those cartons of artifacts and old books. His blue Oxford shirt and khaki pants ignore the latest fashion and his straight blond hair, approaching the color of dust, occasionally spills across his eyes. A delightful man with a warm smile and sparkling eyes, he often speaks of the past in the present tense.

What first sparked your interest in history?

ES: It goes back to when I was four years old. My father was a businessman with a small chain of stores in the Portland area. He could sell anything. He acquired a block of remaindered books and brought home a set of little illustrated paperbacks about the history of Britain that had been published before World War II. This was about 1952. I sat down and became fascinated. That's when it began. By the time I was in junior high, I was very interested in local and Maine history. It was at that point that I met Elizabeth

Ring, the vice president of the Maine Historical Society, who brought me there and later became my high school history teacher. She opened up all kinds of doors for me. But even before then, when I was six, I went into my first antique shop, in Bingham, Maine. My family was on a trip to Quebec City. On the way back, I begged my parents to stop at a shop where in the window I'd seen a framed picture of the Gilbert Stuart portrait of [George] Washington. That year, when my parents asked what I wanted for my birthday, I said, "Take me back. If it's still there, that's all I want." And they did. It cost all of $2 and I still have it.

My parents were wonderful. They understood they had this strange child and encouraged me at every turn. They were both the children of immigrants and believed strongly in the importance of education.

Why do people from away find Maine so intriguing?

ES: Maine has had an historical mystique for a long time. From an economic standpoint and even today, we have not been as extensively impacted by development as have other parts of the country, particularly the Atlantic corridor. That's not to say those pockets haven't appeared, but for people outside of Maine, the state still has this aura that it is a beautiful, unspoiled place, that it is removed from the rest of the northeast. Part of that is its size, approximately as large as the rest of New England put together and magnified by three areas that have long been attractive to people—the rugged coast with its beaches and incredible multiplicity of islands; the northern woods; and Aroostook County, which is another whole world. Plus it is a decentralized state, with 1.3 million people living here but scattered over 450 to 500 municipalities. Wrapped around all these physical attributes is the fact that there are still many communities still intact from the 19th century. They give Maine its character-defining features as far as buildings are concerned. One can go to Wiscasset on the coast or Paris Hill, or wherever, and feel like you're in the 19th century.

Somebody once pointed out to me that Mainers and Texans are more loyal to their home states than people anywhere else. I wonder, is their connection to the past part of that?

ES: Oh, I think so. If you go back into Maine history, people were integrally tied to the land and the sea in the 17th, 18th, and well into the 19th century. They chose to be here and assumed a series of challenges brought on by the geography. Beginning in the 1840s and 1850s, you could take steamboats, railroads and so on to travel. People began to leave Maine, particularly after the Civil War, in which a very high percentage of our men participated. Those who returned after the war often decided to seek broader horizons. In this period, you find many families going west and south, with surprisingly strong connections to New Orleans and Galveston, Texas. You have the phenomenon of the abandoned farm, except for Aroostook, which is opening up. But the ties back home are never really broken. You see this in writings of the period, how strongly people feel about coming back.

A classic example is that of the Washburn [or Washburne—subsequent generations changed the spelling] family of Norlands in Livermore which had seven sons and three daughters. Six of the sons had national and international careers as congressmen, governors, and senators. Elihu Washburne lives in Galena, Illinois, where he introduces

Ulysses S. Grant to his close friend, Abraham Lincoln, and after the Civil War becomes U.S. Ambassador to France. But all of them come back to their home, Norlands, and give money to build a family library and rebuild the family house when it burned in 1867. There is this tie that brings people back.

What are your responsibilities as Maine State Historian?

ES: They are defined by a law that goes back to 1907, modified a little over the last century. But essentially, the State Historian is an honorary position here to inform the governor, the legislature, and the people of Maine on historical questions. And I do receive questions from them all. The State Historian is expected to write, publish, and speak to the public in his areas of expertise, and to encourage the teaching of Maine history. I'm the sixth person to hold the post. The $500 budget is strictly for expenses and originally probably paid for publishing a book but now barely covers Xeroxing.

By nature of my day job as director of the Maine Historical Preservation Commission, I also serve in an unpaid dual position as the State Historic Preservation Officer, which is the liaison from the State of Maine to the federal government for matters of historic preservation. Every state has one and I'm the longest actively serving State Historic Preservation Officer in the United States.

What are you working on now?

ES: In addition to lectures that I enjoy giving very much, and photographing more of the Civil War monuments, I'm chairing a committee that the governor created for the 150th anniversary of the Civil War. We're doing that for no money. I've authored or co-authored six books in the Arcadia historical series and now I'm writing another, on postcards of Bar Harbor, which is sheer fun. With the Cushing Island Association, I'm working on a book about the island's architectural history. Most of the cottages were designed by the great Portland architect John Calvin Stevens and many of them are still there.

Down the road, I have many projects. Some years ago, I worked with the Osher Map Library, a fantastic facility, on an exhibition called "The Changing Peninsula," seeing the history of Portland through maps and prints. We didn't do a catalogue and I want to do that. Also, at one time I gave the Maine Historical Society a major collection called the Vickery-Shettleworth Collection of Early Maine Photography. It consists of the earliest photographs taken of Maine, from 1840–1865, a fascinating view of people and places. Vickery refers to another of my mentors, a great collector and friend, James Vickery, who left me his collection when he passed away in 1997. One of the agreements with MHS is that the gift, which combines Vickery's photographs with my own, is that I will write a catalogue of the collection.

Is it true that every town in Maine has a historical society and museum?

ES: I wouldn't go that far but it seems that way! In the 1960s, there were between 250 and 300 local historical societies in Maine and I suspect it has grown since then.

By 1900, the first museum was housed in an historic building. That, of course, is the Old York Gaol which was presented as a museum of curiosities, full of Colonial artifacts. Within a year, Anne Longfellow Pierce [the poet's sister] leaves the Wadsworth-Longfellow House to the Maine Historical Society, which opened it in 1902. One of the first visitors was Teddy

Roosevelt. And so on. The preservation of the physical remains of history in collections, and the presentation of that to the public, is integrally related to its historic buildings.

Is interest in our past or the arts on the decline?

ES: Oh, no! If anything, it's blossoming. I've worked for 37 years with the Maine Historic Preservation Commission and there's hardly a day that goes by when someone doesn't call us wanting to know the answer to a question. Is there a photograph of this building or that town? How do I find out about my ancestor? It's an endless stream of interest. I think you'd find that's also true if you talk to the folks at the Maine State Archives, the State Library, or Maine Historical Society.

I realize part of it is economic and part is our changing entertainment culture, but you read that visitation levels at some of our broader historical sites may be off, like Old Sturbridge Village [in Massachusetts] or Williamsburg [Virginia] or Mystic Seaport [Connecticut], and people try to puzzle that out. I don't know the answer. Certainly whatever is happening affects how museums and historical societies are patronized and supported in Maine, but my general impression is that in Maine interest has remained strong.

I'm on the board of the Portland Museum of Art. In 2009, we had the second-best attendance figures in its history, the best being in 2000. At the Maine Historical Society, where in 2009 they opened a $9.5 million research facility, they're getting increased interest and visitation. Other museums have been at least able to maintain their figures. Sometimes the problems arise from other factors. You need to find ways to let people know you're there, have convenient hours, and hold special events that draw visitors in.

Why is all this important?

ES: Probably the most important underlying reason is something I learned many years ago from my great mentor, Elizabeth Ring, who was a noted Maine historian in her own right. Just as Tip O'Neill said "All politics is local," Elizabeth Ring would say to her classes, "All history is local." To understand state and national history, you need to start at the local level. What's happening in American society—which is open, democratic, decentralized in that towns and states have certain powers and the federal government has other powers—is that power rises from the bottom up. If you want deep insight into the Civil War, for example, you can read broad, encompassing works by Bruce Catton or Carl Sandburg to understand the trends of the war, but you can learn just as much by reading the letters exchanged between a man and wife from the battlefield to the home front and back again. I once came upon a letter from a woman describing in great detail her trials trying to run a farm and the modest support she is receiving from the town because her husband is serving in the war.

History is broad, with epic events and trends, but men and women and children shaped and participated in those events. Local history gives us immediate insights into how people lived and worked at the time. And it's the local history museum that is responsible for gathering up those remains. It might be that series of letters or a poignant group of toys that belonged to a little girl who died of scarlet fever. Because the local museum captured and documented these things from the past, they haven't been tossed onto the antiques market where they lose their provenance, their meaning, the collective memory that comes with these objects or writing.

Another of my mentors was Abbott Lowell Cummings, a notable architectural historian. When I was in high school, he was the head of the Society for the Preservation of New England Antiquities, now Historic New England, which owns several wonderful properties in Maine. He's now in his 80s but early on Abbott said to me, "When I was at the very beginning of my career, I worked at the Metropolitan Museum of Art in the American Wing. It was a marvelous experience. I was working with great paintings, great pieces of furniture, great objects. But, you know, I would happily trade it all for what's in the local historical society museum because it is in those historic houses and museums that we have the true treasures of our past, the truly interesting things that allow us to understand how the great number of people lived, as opposed to the upper five percent."

Janet Mendelsohn

A Civil War monument in York.

Yes, of course we should preserve a Copley painting or a Federal desk by John Seymour. They are the greatest expressions of what our culture can attain. But at the same time, a chair made by an Acadian French farmer in the St. John Valley may tell us just as much, and you're not going to find that chair at the Metropolitan. You're going to find it at the Acadian Village in Van Buren.

I believe very strongly that our ability to connect with our history, if we open ourselves to it, is really everywhere. It's very accessible through postcards, photographs, newspapers, documents, objects. And where do you find them? Historical societies are the keepers of the light, so to speak. Which brings me to the core of your book project. Maine is the museum. All the things we've been saying fit into the concept that you need to journey throughout the state and visit all these destinations with a purpose, such as visiting museums. Then you will not just arrive at a place but will experience the overall environment as well.

I can attest to that concept. Beginning in 2006, I gave myself, as State Historian, the assignment of locating all the Civil War monuments. I've traveled in Maine extensively but having that purpose gave me the opportunity to re-travel the state with fresh eyes, determining anew what is meaningful.

MID-MAINE

L. C. Bates Museum
Good Will–Hinckley School
Route 201, Hinckley
www.gwh.org
207-238-4250

WHAT YOU'LL FIND HERE Cultural and natural history exhibits
that haven't changed in 100 years. Taxidermied animals and birds in 32 dioramas of
Maine. Exotic species, fossils, and bugs, Native American crafts and tools, shells, fish,
and art. Antique farm equipment and printing presses. History of the Good Will–
Hinckley Homes and School. Gift shop. Miles of walking trails. Indoor and outdoor
nature programs for children and adults. Gift shop.

WHY GO: This place is weird. Nothing but the lighting has changed since the
1920s. Surrounded by extinct animals, wood and leaf specimens, beetles and fossils by

the score, you'll likely feel transported to another time. Or a movie set. It's easy to imagine a wise owl flying in to offer sage advice, speaking in a human voice. And the strange dislocation begins when you first see the stark, rural Good Will–Hinckley campus.

In 1889, the Reverend George Walter Hinckley (1853–1950) founded the Good Will Home for disadvantaged boys and built a manual training school to prepare them for productive employment. An avid naturalist and progressive educator who believed in the educational theories of Horace Mann, Hinckley gradually acquired a quirky natural history collection that reflected his varied interests. During the Victorian era, when developing a "cabinet of curiosities" like this was popular, his collections grew larger than most.

Courtesy of LC Bates Museum

The Good Will–Hinckley School was founded to give orphans a new home and an education.

Hinckley decided to turn this rich material into a museum for the students. He sought donations from other collectors and received hundreds of taxidermied birds, including many exotics. A gigantic, flightless cassowary, among the largest birds in the world, was sent from Australia. The huge fellow is mighty intimidating atop a tall, old-fashioned display case of dark wood and glass. There are toucans, owls, and kookaburras; trays of insects, row after row of rocks, gemstones, minerals; and some 100,000 archeological samples alone. Rooms are inhabited by calico deer, now extinct, caribou no longer native to Maine, coyotes and cottontail rabbits, still rare in the region. A trophy-size blue marlin landed by Ernest Hemingway hangs on the wall.

If a museum itself can be an exhibit of how museums used to be, this is it.

Hinckley established a school based on a concept he called Good Will, blending education, spiritual connection, counseling, and recreation into a supportive residential environment. A home for girls was added by 1896. During his lifetime, the community expanded to include residential cottages, faculty homes, a Carnegie library, nondenominational chapel, indoor and outdoor athletic facilities, and the museum, as well as the farm. The first training school closed in 1914 but was soon replaced by the Good Will–Hinckley Homes for Boys & Girls. Since 1889, the nonprofit organization has served more than 6,000 students and families on its 2,450-acre campus. Today it is home to about 300 youths, ages 11 to 21. The community remains committed to his Good Will philosophy.

Lewis C. Bates, president of a manufacturing company in West Paris, Maine, answered Hinckley's prayers by donating enough money to improve the museum building and exhibits. The museum was named for L. C. Bates in honor of his gift.

Hinckley then turned to his friend Charles David Hubbard, an artist who shared his dual passions for the outdoors and religion. Perhaps inspired by the new bird habitat dioramas at the Museum of Natural History in New York, the two men decided to create similar exhibits here. Hubbard was hired as consultant, exhibit designer, muralist, sign painter, and handyman. The 28 bird and mammal settings he created were installed between 1922 and 1924. They are not only the second-oldest existing dioramas in New England (the oldest are at the Fairbanks Museum in St. Johnsbury, Vermont), they may be the only dioramas done in an Impressionist style by one artist. Hubbard spent part of the summer searching for locales where specific specimens had lived or died. He would paint on location on a flexible board that could be curved to serve as authentic backdrops for the mounted creatures, rocks, and dried vegetation. Hubbard's dioramas closely capture distinct locations in Maine from the mountains to the coast and still are wonderful habitats for all that taxidermy.

The three-story Romanesque Revival building originally contained classrooms, workshops, and the campus laundry. Within its walls, boys learned drafting, carpentry, printing, and metal working. The basement is jam-packed with much of the machinery they were taught to operate. There's an Otis Acorn printing press (circa 1839) with movable type, farm wagons, and a plow (circa 1780) that was owned by Quakers who previously owned the land.

An exhibit and a 17-minute, black-and-white video documentary tell the story of Hinckley and his philosophy, the history of the home and school, and the Industrial Age origins and traditional values of faith, hard work, self-discipline, and recreation that remain the cornerstones of the Good Will community.

USEFUL INFORMATION

• Miles of easy, self-guided walking trails cover hundreds of acres of forest habitat. They begin behind the museum. Trails are free and open to the public. Naturalists are available through the museum, by appointment, to lead guided tours all year, as well as for regularly scheduled programs on ferns, spring wildflowers, tree identification, forest birds, and pond study.

• Trail maps, Children's Outdoor Discovery Packs, and Museum Animal Discovery Boxes are available inside the museum. Picnic tables are located in the arboretum.

Time to allow: 1 hour in the museum.
Additional time for self-guided nature trails or programs.
Admission: $2.50 Adults
$1 Ages 17 and younger
When it's open: April to mid-Nov.
Wed.–Sat., 10 am–4:30 pm
Sun., 1–4:30 pm
or by appointment
Mid-Nov. to March
Wed.—Sat., 9 am–4:30 pm
or by appointment
In winter, call ahead to be sure the museum is open; it's closed when roads

are snowy. And dress warmly. The building is not heated.

Directions: From I-95/Maine Turnpike, take Exit 133 to ME-201 North and follow that for 5 miles. The campus is midway between Skowhegan and Fairfield.

FUN FACTS:

• Three interesting rocks given to Hinckley when he was eight years old sparked his interest in collecting specimens of natural history. Although the three rocks were later lost in a fire, there's now an entire room devoted to gems, rocks, and minerals.

• Hinckley purchased the farm from the Chase family, grandparents of former Maine Senator Margaret Chase Smith. Today it is a Maine Organic Farmers and Gardeners Association–certified organic farm and still a central part of the Good Will–Hinckley Homes for Boys and Girls.

• In 1902, Hinckley and Dr. A. L. Lane, both of Fairfield, initiated an effort to create the first statewide Maine Audubon Society that would go beyond bird watching to both discourage the killing of birds for their feathers (popular on Victorian hats) and encourage the study of natural history, establishing a dual commitment to education and advocacy that MAS continues today.

Margaret Chase Smith Library
56 Norridgewock Avenue, Skowhegan
www.mcslibrary.org
207-474-7133

WHAT YOU'LL FIND HERE: Official library of U.S. Senator Margaret Chase Smith (Republican, Maine). Timeline of her career with photographs, honors and awards, gifts from world leaders, and memorabilia. Guided tours of Smith's home, adjacent to the library.

WHY GO: Margaret Chase Smith (1897–1995) was the first woman elected to serve in both houses of the U.S. Congress, the first woman elected a U.S. senator in her own right, and the first woman nominated (1964) by a major political party to run for president of the United States. She was also the first woman to chair a U.S. Senate subcommittee, the first woman to hold a ranking position on the Senate Armed Services and Appropriations committees, and the first person to chair a televised senate committee hearing.

Born before women had the right to vote (the 19th amendment changed that in 1920), Margaret Chase Smith personified "the new woman." She was a basketball player and coach who planned to study physical education and business, but family finances prevented her from going to college. Instead, she worked as a school teacher, telephone operator, newspaper reporter, and secretary before age 33, when she married Clyde H. Smith, 54, a local and state politician.

Six years after their wedding, Clyde Smith was elected to Congress. His wife served as his political secretary until 1940, when he died unexpectedly. In the special election to fill his unexpired term, she ran for and won his seat in the U.S. House of Representatives. Later that year, she was elected in her own right for a full term. She served eight years in the House before being elected to the Senate. Throughout eight successive terms, she was known for maintaining a perfect attendance record in Congress, making a record 2,941 consecutive roll-call votes, a record she held until 1981. She also rigorously rejected campaign contributions and spent little to get elected, a philosophy of frugality that was appreciated by Maine voters.

Margaret Chase Smith was known as a trailblazer. She had a keen interest in medical research and military affairs, and is credited with ensuring women permanent status in the armed services. An outspoken defender of individual rights and free speech, she consistently stood against bigotry and injustice, and condemned the tactics of Senator Joseph McCarthy when others still feared him. A strong supporter of the nation's space exploration program, Smith served 15 years on the Senate Committee on Aeronautics and Space Science. Her interest grew out of her concerns regarding U.S.-Soviet relations during the Cold War and the launch of Sputnik in 1957, with its implications for national security, national pride, and international prestige.

Courtesy of the Margaret Chase Smith Library

In the Margaret Chase Library, keepsakes and newsclippings record Senator Smith's distinguished career.

Smith received 95 honorary doctoral degrees and more than 270 other awards and honors, including the nation's highest civilian honor, the Presidential Medal of Freedom, in 1989. After her 32-year career in politics, she was a visiting professor and lecturer with the Woodrow Wilson National Fellowship Foundation at many colleges and universities, and worked with Northwood University to establish her library.

The library's visitor lobby contains attractive exhibits for a self-guided tour along a visual timeline displaying memorabilia from her life and career. Photographs, documents, newspaper clippings, gifts she received, and tributes from everyone from national and foreign leaders to local girls' sports teams tell the story of the woman from Skowhegan whose signature accessory was a single red rose.

Time to allow: 1 hour for a self-guided tour of exhibits and a 20-minute video
15 minutes to tour her home

Admission: Free
When it's open: Mon.–Fri., 10 am–4 pm
     Closed major holidays and Christmas week.
Directions: From I-95/Maine Turnpike, Exit 133, go to Route 201 North to Skowhegan. In town, turn right at the first light, go over the two Margaret Chase Smith bridges and circle clockwise by continuing to follow Route 201 North (Madison Avenue) and left at the first light heading out of town. The library is ahead, at the top of a hill, on the left.

Or take Route 2 to Skowhegan, follow signs to either Pleasant or Elm street, opposite a Chevrolet dealership. The roads merge into Norridgewock Avenue. The library is at the top of a hill, on the left, one half mile west of either junction.

Colby College Museum of Art
5600 Mayflower Hill, Waterville
www.colby.edu/museum
207-859-5600

WHAT YOU'LL FIND HERE: Permanent collection of more than 6,000 works, focusing on American and contemporary art. A wing devoted to the work of Alex Katz. Special collections of early Chinese art and European prints, drawings, and paintings. Archive of art lectures given since 1952 at the Skowhegan School of Painting and Sculpture. Temporary installations include works by emerging artists on the national scene.

WHY GO: In 2007, the museum received as a promised gift what is reportedly the largest collection of American art ever given to an American college or university. Peter and Paula Lunder's promise of more than 500 works, and still growing, is a comprehensive teaching collection that includes masterworks in still life, portraits, and landscapes from the 19th, 20th, and early 21st centuries, with more than 200 prints by James McNeil Whistler. But the Lunder collection is not the only one of note. In 1992, the contemporary painter Alex Katz (b. 1927) donated 414 of his own works. Over the years, he and others have added to the collection which now totals more than 700 of Katz's drawings, collages, sculpture, prints, and paintings. In an entire wing devoted to Katz, they are shown on a rotating basis. The wide-open, industrial space with high ceilings, exposed ironwork rafters, soft gray walls, and skylights focuses attention on his distinctively bold figures and objects against solid backdrops. It's the perfect setting for his many large-scale canvases.

Richard Serra (b. 1939), another prominent contemporary American artist, is represented by a site-specific steel sculpture outside the museum entrance and, soon, 150 works on paper covering 30 years of Serra's creative output, a promised gift from Paul J. Schupf. The collection includes a lithograph from Serra's first year as a printmaker, as well as drawings, print hybrids, and a 2005 etching, *HBS.*

The John Marin Collection is considered by some to equal the scope of the artist's work at the National Gallery of Art. A gift from members of his family, it is a 65-year retrospective of the American Modernist's paintings, watercolors, drawings, etchings, and photographs. Created between 1888 and 1953, it reportedly forms the largest Marin survey in any academic museum. Marin (1870–1953) is known for his urban New York scenes and watercolors of coastal Maine. He was a member of the artistic circle associated with the influential photographer Alfred Stieglitz. Seven photographs of Marin, including a platinum print by Stieglitz and prints by Paul Strand and Arnold Newman, accompany the collection. Norma Marin, the artist's daughter-in-law, donated the print along with others in her superb collection by photographers Berenice Abbott, Edward Weston, Imogen Cunningham, Ben Shahn, Ansel Adams, and others. Another special collection is that of more than 250 prints by Terry Winters (b. 1949) whose prints of cellular clusters, spirals, and grids are closely tied to his paintings and drawings.

Beyond all this are works by such major artists as Mary Cassatt, John Singleton Copley, Marsden Hartley, Winslow Homer, Sol LeWitt, and Georgia O'Keeffe.

The origins of the permanent collection go back to the 1930s and 1940s, but Colby's museum didn't open until 1959. "The real question may be, 'Why American art?'" said Lauren Lessing, Mirken Curator of Education. "The answer is that at that time in American history, especially in New England, there was real interest in finding what Van Wyck Brooks, the great historian, called 'a usable past.' People were looking to American history as a source for something unique, something different from what was going on in Europe that would speak to us about what makes us special. Maine lumber heiresses Adeline F. and Caroline R. Wing gave a number of 19th-century American masterpieces to the college. Edith and Ellerton Jetté, who owned the Hathaway Shirt Factory here in town, were very interested in collecting folk art. They had a large collection of American folk portraits, paintings, and sculpture they called the American Heritage Collection that they donated in 1956. These became two of the core collections of the museum and we've continued to build on their strength, most recently with the Lunders' fabulous collection."

The Whistler collection is one of the three largest in the world, said Lessing, who referred to it as "extraordinary." Of the hundreds of Whistlers in the Lunder collection, the majority are works on paper, including drawings. "Whistler was a printmaker whose every print is unique," said Lessing. "He didn't make editions in which each print was the same. We're working with the Freer Gallery of Art and Arthur M. Sackler Gallery at the Smithsonian Institution in Washington, D.C., another major holder of Whistler's work; and the Centre for Whistler Studies in Glasgow, Scotland; on a symposium that will be held every three years, rotating between Colby and Washington, and sharing a full-time position endowed by the Lunder family. The symposium will bring scholars from all over the world to speak about Whistler and his influence." The first is tentatively scheduled for 2013.

Visitors to the museum often ask to see Robert Henri's painting *La Reina Morra* (1906), a beautiful portrait that is usually available. They look for Alex Katz's iconic painting *Pas De Deux* (1983), and a Joseph Mozier sculpture, *Undine* (circa 1866), as well as the Marin collection and a series of Copley portraits, one of which is shared with the Bowdoin College Museum of Art.

Construction of a new wing will soon increase the museum's current 28,000 square feet of exhibition space to 38,000. The new glassed-in galleries will extend off the lobby, which itself will be nearly doubled in size, for events. A new sculpture court and an education center for school groups are planned and there will be two entrances, one facing campus, the other facing the road from town.

Colby College courses are often linked to the museum's rich collections and exhibitions. During the 2009–2010 academic year, for example, about 85 courses took advantage of what's here. An online database, accessible through the museum's website, includes nearly all of more than 6,000 works in the permanent collection, although only about 30 percent include images; photographing them for this purpose is a slow process.

"Eventually everything will have a photograph in the database," said Lessing. "I'm hoping that it will become useful not only for faculty and students at the college but for the public as well so that it makes this stellar collection accessible to an audience worldwide. Scholars working anywhere will know what we have and be able to make use of our collection, and the general public, when planning a vacation in Maine, will be able to get a sense of our collection in advance."

USEFUL INFORMATION:

• The museum will be closed for 18 months beginning October 2011 for construction of a new wing. Some galleries will close prior to that date so call ahead or check the website to confirm what is showing. The museum will reopen for Colby College's bicentennial in 2013.

• Prior to the planned construction, the building is wheelchair accessible through the rear entrance to the Bixler Art and Music Center.

• Upon reopening, the museum will host a major exhibition of the Lunder Collection in 2013. An exhibition of Maine Indian baskets will follow in 2014. Historical as well as contemporary, it will span across time, from before contact with Europeans to the present day, with photographs, films, cultural programs, and tools. An environmental aspect will look at the destruction of ash trees by the emerald ash borer beetle and other threats to the traditional basket-making material.

Time to allow: 1 hour
Admission: Free
When it's open: Tues.–Sat., 10 am–4:30 pm
  Sun., noon–4:30 pm
  Closed Mon. and major holidays.
Directions: I-95/Maine Turnpike to Exit 127 (Waterville/Oakland). Turn right (east) into Waterville on Route 137 (Kennedy Memorial Drive) for 0.9 mile, following the blue signs to Colby College. Turn left onto First Rangeway (opposite Inland Hospital). Go 1.1 miles and turn left onto Mayflower Hill Drive. Follow this for 0.5 mile to campus. The museum will be another 0.5 mile, on the left.

FUN FACT: The first bronze sculpture ever cast in the United States is in the
Colby collection. *The Choosing of the Arrow,* cast by Henry Kirke Brown in 1849, is about 2 feet high. Lauren Lessing said Brown was part of a generation of sculptors who went to Italy to learn to carve marble but while there, he recognized they were usu-

ally done life-size in white Carrara marble for very wealthy patrons. Brown wanted to cast small bronzes that would be affordable on middle-class salaries and fit inside their homes. He went to France, where he studied bronze casting technique, then set up a foundry in his Brooklyn, New York, studio, where he did sand casting. One in an edition of 20, this little figure was cast in several parts.

"It is an Indian youth, completely nude, which caused quite a stir in 1849," said Lessing. "He's reaching over his shoulder to take an arrow from his quiver and he's holding a bow. It's Neoclassical in style. He's like a young Apollo. At that time, nude females were very generalized, sanitized; the idea was to not show any genitalia, which were concealed by a leaf or loin cloth. But Brown didn't do that. When the figure was exhibited at the American Art Union Galleries, he was asked to cover it. He made a little fig leaf belt but made it gold so it would intentionally stand out."

Washburn Norlands Living History Center
290 Norlands Road, Livermore
www.norlands.org
207-897-4366

WHAT YOU'LL FIND HERE: A distinguished Maine family's 19th-century home and working farm. Storytellers in period costumes. Rural 445-acre property with one-room schoolhouse, library, carriage house, meeting house, barn, and 1880s working farm. Guided tours, programs, and events.

WHY GO: Living history museums, as the name implies, are settlements, factories, homes, and other historic places where interpreters take on the roles of historical figures, speaking and acting as they would have in the past. At Norlands, we met Mercy Lovejoy, a pauper and "the homeliest woman in town," portrayed by Willi Irish, who, like the characters she brings back to life, was born in Livermore.

"Someone tells me I'm like an old iron pot, sturdy and useful," stated "Mercy" as she mended socks in the mansion's big country kitchen. "We can't all be beautiful." A large woman with short gray hair and wire-rim glasses, she wore a plain black cap tied beneath her plump cheeks, a floral blouse coordinated with the violet stripes of a long apron that, like her navy blue skirt, covered her feet. As she sewed, seated beside a large, black, cast-iron stove, Mercy told visitors what it was like growing up the youngest of six, far from town, before Maine achieved statehood in 1820. Her father ran the first ferry bringing settlers across the river to establish farms, she said, and when she married, her life was one of hardships.

"It was 1816, the year of no summah," said Mercy, whose Maine accent was thick. "Times wah hard. People either pull togethah or they don't and here they didn't. Azel, my husband, didn't help. He left town in the dark of night, left me with five children. I was 'bid off' at $3.95 a week—that was high, I'm proud to say—to someone who would take care of my children, for which the town of Livermore paid them."

Mercy was a real woman who actually lived at the town's poor farm, and our guide explained that the saga we were hearing described how they really handled folks who had nothing. On other days, the same interpreter portrayed her own great-great aunt, Clara Howard, a school marm and widow; or Eunice Merrill, an early settler; and occasionally Caroline Washburn Holmes, youngest child in the family that once owned this land.

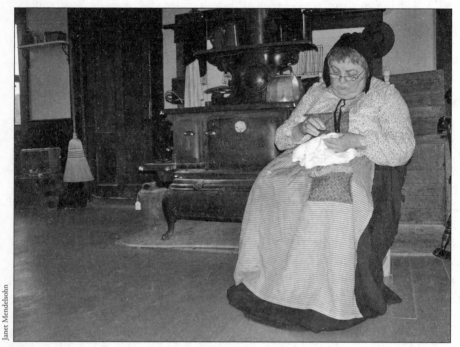

Janet Mendelsohn

"Mercy Lovejoy," the self-proclaimed ugliest woman in town, at Norlands.

Norlands is a historic home built by Israel and Martha Washburn, who gave birth to 11 children between 1813 and 1833 and raised them all here. The Washburns had little money but Israel and Martha instilled in their children a love of learning, a reverence for the church, a passion for politics, and the belief that hard work has its own rewards. One child died, their three daughters became wives and mothers, and seven sons went on to national and state prominence. Altogether, the Washburns produced two state governors, two congressmen, a U.S. senator, two foreign ministers, a Civil War general, a captain in the U.S. Navy, a Secretary of State, the founder of Washburn-Crosby Gold Medal Flour, the inventor of a typewriter, a railroad president, and three authors.

First-person role-playing is Norland's way of teaching about the past. When this living history center was founded in 1974, its methods were considered innovative. And as the nation's bicentennial approached, Americans hungered to learn about their nation's history as well as traditional crafts. Open-air museums like this became favorites for school field trips and family vacations. Gradually the popularity of this type of experience waned, perhaps because new technology presented more immediate diversions. Nowadays it takes a shift in expectations, an altered attitude, for children and adults to appreciate the slower pace and hard lives of the people they "meet" in historic homes and farms like this. On the plus side, Kathleen Beauregard, Norlands' executive director, observed that among adults interest in living history museums seems to be rebounding, apparently as an offshoot of the eat local/grow local movement.

Tours of Norlands introduce visitors not necessarily to how the Washburns lived but to what was typical in the region at the time the house was built. Visits generally begin in the house kitchen, where there might be a fire in the cookstove, cookies baking, an iron heating on the stovetop, and a costumed interpreter ready to demonstrate spinning wool on a wheel or how to play dominos, as well as tell stories that bring the residents back to life. A "Washburn daughter" might lead the tour through her father's house, then send you off to the one-room school to do an arithmetic problem. Students attended classes there in summer and winter but not spring and fall, when their help was most needed by the family. Often boys only attended in winter, when there was even less work to be done on the farm.

The fully furnished house, referred to as the mansion, is surprisingly elegant for its agricultural setting. In truth, it is the third house on the site. The others were more modest but destroyed by fires, a fairly common event. In 2008, fire ravaged the farm again, destroying the barn and a summer kitchen attached to the house. Smoke and water damage to the house has been cleaned up. The farm's agricultural program was put on hold until a new barn can be raised, slated for 2011; call ahead or check the website to learn its status and that of related activities.

Special events are the liveliest days here, with maple sugaring in March, a Civil War reenactment, crafts workshops, and Christmas among the busiest times.

USEFUL INFORMATION:

• Live-in programs on summer weekends welcome guests to stay overnight and become part of the family in rural 19th-century Maine. Guests help with farm chores, cook, clean, play games, and attend school. They tend to the cows, collect eggs, bring in water, and sleep on cots in a rustic bunk house. Restroom facilities are chamber pots and outdoor privies. Minors must be accompanied by an adult. The popular programs were suspended after the 2008 fire but are expected to resume when the new barn is up.

• History programs can be arranged for school groups on-site or off-site in school classrooms. Programs offered to other groups include tea parties paired with a special tour geared to the group's interests, such as women's roles on 19th-century farms or holiday celebrations. Meal, Laugh & Learn includes lunch and two interactive programs. Fees vary and reservations are required. Contact by phone or e-mail norlands@norlands.org.

• Picnic tables are available.

Time to allow: 1–1½ hours
Admission: $10 per person
    $25 per family
When it's open: July and Aug.
    Tues. and Thurs., 11 am–4 pm

All year for special events and guided tours by appointment.
Annual events:
Winter: Ice harvesting
March: Maple sugaring–pancake breakfast
June: Civil War reenactment
Fall: Agricultural celebration
December: Christmas at Norlands with sleigh rides
Directions: I-95, Exit 75 toward US-202/ME-4/ME-100/Auburn. Left on Washington Street, which becomes Minot Avenue. Right on Court Street. Take the third left onto Turner Street and continue onto Center Street to ME-4 North/Turner Road. Follow ME-4 to ME-108-Boothbay Road and then left onto Norlands Road. Washburn-Norlands will be about 1.7 miles farther, on your right.

NORTHERN
MAINE

CHAPTER 7

Acadian Village
Route 1, Van Buren
www.connectmaine.com/acadianvillage/
207-868-5042

WHAT YOU'LL FIND HERE: Seventeen buildings re-creating a late-1880s Acadian community in the St. John River Valley. Original furnishings and equipment. Reproduction chapel containing authentic bells, Stations of the Cross, pump organ, font, and furnishings from churches throughout the region. Period clothing, dolls, medical and dental equipment, church vestments and musical instruments. Art gallery. Gift shop.

WHY GO: It's not unusual to hear French spoken in Maine today but rarely is it the Acadian patois once common throughout the St. John River Valley. Not long ago, growing up in Aroostook County meant you were probably bilingual and had relatives across the river in Canada. The County, as it's called, is known as a potato-growing region that's by far the largest county in Maine (nearly the size of Connecticut and Rhode Island combined) but with the smallest population, and not much else. Its northernmost portion, the St. John valley, is actually a beautiful rural landscape of working forests, clear lakes, and rolling farmland under big skies. It was settled by Acadians whose history and rich culture are preserved in this recreated settlement. You might know their story from Henry Wadsworth Longfellow's epic poem *Evangeline: A Tale of Acadie.*

Acadians are descendants of French settlers who first arrived in Acadie (now Nova Scotia) in 1604. For 150 years, they farmed, lived harmoniously with the neighboring Micmac Indians, and remained neutral in the regional fighting between the English and French. Although they were British subjects, in 1755 the Acadians refused to sign a loyalty oath or fight against the French. As a result, the British government forcibly expelled them from their homeland. During "The Expulsion" or "Deportation," Acadians were exiled to the British colonies and beyond, families were separated, couples split apart. Many settled in Louisiana, giving birth to Cajun culture, while others landed in Quebec, where some married French Canadians. After the Treaty of Paris ended the war, they were allowed to return home. Many resettled in Sainte-Anne-des-Pays-Bas (now Fredericton, Quebec). After the American Revolution, they moved up the St. John River to the Madawaska Territory and in 1785 settled in St. David, about 20 miles from here, in northernmost Maine.

"When the deported Acadians didn't want to talk about their past, they would always refer to Longfellow's poem, *Evangeline,*" said Anne Roy, director of Acadian Village. A work of fiction, the poem is nonetheless based in enough truth that it inspired Acadians to recognize their heritage and the story's heroine became a mythic figure, particularly among Acadians in the two regions where the poem is set, Louisiana and Nova Scotia. At Acadian Village, a marble statue of Evangeline stands in a place of honor, outside the art gallery. It was a gift from the Roman Catholic Diocese of Boston, which originally commissioned the Italian marble statue in memory of all displaced Acadians, enshrining it at a church in Chelsea, Massachusetts. Years ago, the statue was severely burned in a fire in Chelsea and painted white to cover smoke damage.

Evangeline at Acadian Village.

Thirteen of the museum village's 17 buildings are original Acadian structures moved here from elsewhere in Aroostook County. None have electricity or heat, which means visits are limited to daylight hours in summer. The one-room Roy House (circa 1790) is constructed of hand-hewn logs held together with wooden pegs, with a dirt floor and interior fieldstone fireplace. The children slept on straw mattresses in the loft or on the floor. During extremely cold winter nights, the farm animals were stabled inside with the family to help heat the house. Morneault House (circa 1857) from Grand Isle was once the home of a prosperous lumberman; it is one of the oldest in the valley. Typical of Acadian architecture, the structure incorporates nautical features, such as "ship's knees" to support the roof. Walls are caulked with a mixture of flax and lime, and insulated with birch bark. During the early 1900s, the house also served as the post office. The Levasseur/Ouellette House (1859) was home to subsequent families that had 12, 10, and 19 children, respectively. Every house had a pump organ or piano for entertainment and the newest and wealthiest families also had a record player and radio, as this house does. The second floor, where the children slept three or four to a bed, has walls covered with newspapers to discourage spider webs and bugs, and patchwork quilts made from discarded clothing. It was the oldest child's job to empty and clean the chamber pot daily.

Bob Mendelsohn

An early grist mill and carding mill are inside a new building constructed on site. Both mills performed vital roles in the community. At its peak, the grist mill ran 24 hours a day and processed eight barrels of buckwheat per hour. Nothing was wasted; some parts of the grain became buckwheat flour for "ployes" (Acadian pancakes), while others became animal feed; hulls and other parts were used to insulate the walls of homes. The carding mill (1803) came from Fort Kent by way of Frenchville, where it was used to comb (or card) wool, straighten fibers, and remove impurities prior to spinning it into yarn.

Notre Dame de L'Assumption Chapel replicates a log church built during the early 18th century. It is filled with artifacts from churches throughout the region. Today, weddings and, on special occasions, Mass are celebrated inside the chapel.

A barber shop and general store with the telephone switchboard (1891–1894) and a collection of antique telephones; shoe repair, carpentry, and blacksmith shops; the one-room schoolhouse (circa 1880–1952) from Hamlin, Maine; a Bangor and Aroostook Railroad Station; and a barn full of potato farm machinery are among the buildings that round out the village. Collections include antique dolls and church vestments prior to Vatican II in 1962.

In 1976, Acadian Village was selected as the "Best Bicentennial Project" by the State of Maine. It was built by La Societe Historique-Heritage Vivant/Historical Society of Living Heritage, with help from numerous area residents and Acadian descendants, and now is supported in part by the Maine Acadian Heritage Council, a branch of the National Park Service.

Janet Mendelsohn

Sirois House parlor.

USEFUL INFORMATION: Enthusiastic local teenagers are available to guide your tour, or you may enter the buildings on your own. The best way to get the most from your visit and learn about Acadian history, however, is to speak with Anne Roy, the director, if she's available.

Time to allow: 1–2 hours
Admission: $6 Adults
　　$3 Ages 12 and younger
When it's open: June 14–Sept. 15
　　Daily, noon–5 pm
　　Memorial Day–June 14, Sept. 15–Oct. 1
　　Open by appointment.
　　Group tours for 10 or more can be arranged from May 31–Oct. 31.
Directions: I-95 North to Houlton, then ME-Route 1 North to Van Buren.
　　From Canada, travel the Trans-Canada Highway to St. Leonard, New Brunswick, to the border entry at Van Buren, Maine.

FUN FACT: Northern Maine, New Brunswick, and Quebec will host the 2014 World Acadian Congress. The three-week event, held every five years, is expected to bring 50,000 visitors to the region. Always the largest gathering of Acadians in the world, it combines cultural and sporting events with conferences and discussions of what it means to be Acadian in terms of history, geography, language, culture, and society.

WHILE YOU'RE IN NORTHERN AROOSTOOK COUNTY . . .

The New Sweden Historical Society Museum chronicles the history and heritage of Maine's Swedish colony since 1870.
116 Station Road
New Sweden
207-316-7306
Open late May–Labor Day, afternoons only.

Nylander Museum of Natural History
has a seasonal botanical garden and fossils, rocks, minerals, native plants, and animals mostly collected by Swedish-born naturalist Olof Nylander.
393 Main Street
Caribou
www.nylandermuseum.org
207-493-4209

Patten Lumbermen's Museum
61 Shin Pond Road, Patten
www.lumbermensmuseum.org
207-528-2650

WHAT YOU'LL FIND HERE: Replica of an early logging camp with woodsmen's work and living quarters in different eras. One-room camp (1820) for 12 men. "Double camp" (1850) divided for sleeping, cooking, and meals. Saw mill, blacksmith shop, and work sheds. More than 1,000 historical photos and 5,000 artifacts from hand tools to portable saws and heavy equipment used over the past 175 years. Two Lombard log haulers. Picnic pavilion. Dioramas of early logging camps and riverways. Reception center with art gallery, small library, logging videos, and gift shop.

WHY GO: On a three-day trip, we counted 17 fully loaded logging trucks, and six empty ones, passing us on roads in northern Maine. Only one was on Shin Pond Road, but if you drive past the museum, eventually you come to the northern gate of heavily forested Baxter State Park. If you've been there, to camp or hike Mount Katahdin, you know the terrain.

Logging trucks rush and rumble throughout Maine, hauling heavy loads of timber from the backcountry in the Northern Forest and along I-95 to a nation still heavily dependent on wood and wood products. Most of us have never seen a logging operation up close, and have no idea of the conditions lumbermen traditionally endured through long winters deep in the forest. We just know they provide the timber we rely on for everything from cartons and menus to bridges, furniture, and schools, and that people have relied on the logging industry that way for generations. At the Patten Lumbermen's Museum, you begin to appreciate what it takes. It's obvious how hard the work is, how the industry has changed many times over the past 175 years, and how logging has long been essential to the economy of the Pine Tree State.

"So many people don't recognize the forest economy but they live in wooden houses and write letters to the *New York Times* complaining about all the trees being cut without realizing the paper it's printed on comes from a mill the Times Co. owns up here," said Bud Blumenstock, a museum volunteer. Before retiring, Blumenstock assembled a logging operation and ran a saw mill for major companies, then taught forestry at the University of Maine. He knows the industry inside out and is among those who help ensure the story told here is accurate.

Logging in Maine began on Monhegan Island in the early 1600s when English settlers needed wood for houses and ships. The first sawmill powered by water was built in South Berwick in 1634. Between 1832 and 1888, when as many as 3,000 ships were anchored between Bangor and Brewer, Bangor was the world's largest shipping port for lumber. In those days, Patten was at the center of industry activity. Trees harvested in the vast surrounding forest during winter were floated downstream in huge log drives in the spring. The last drive of long logs on the Machias River took place in 1966; the last in Maine was on the Kennebec River in 1976.

A "stink pole" to dry clothes hangs above the cook fire in a cabin (1820) that housed 12 loggers all winter.

I met Blumenstock and his wife, Helen, in the reception center, one of nine buildings that together give a full picture of woodsmen's work and living quarters over more than a century of logging operations. We walked out back to a clearing in the woods surrounded by camps and sheds representative of various eras. There's also a large picnic pavilion for groups. Most visitors explore here on their own. Whether or not yours is a guided tour, you get a sense of how hard a woodsman's life was. We began at an exact replica of a camp used in 1820. The rough, small cabin housed the men, mostly farmers who became lumbermen when their farms were not producing.

"Think of a group of loggers, axes on their shoulders, in the woods," said Bud. "They had to build with logs and pegs. There were no nails and no nearby hardware stores like today. A camp like this housed 12 men in one small room all winter." Inside is an all-purpose wooden sink, rough-hewn from a log, that they filled by bucket from a nearby stream. The men slept side-by-side on straw or branches on the dirt floor under the sloping roof. Cooking pots, the only metal in the cabin, hang over an open fire pit in the center beneath an opening in the roof for smoke. Helen and I exchanged grimaces when she pointed to a wooden pole suspended near the fire and told me, "They called that a 'stink pole.' It's where the men hung their wet clothes to dry. Working in the woods all winter, there was no place to bathe or wash clothes. It's been said you could smell a logging camp before you saw it."

The 1850s "Double Camp" is more spacious and better equipped. Two log cabins are connected by a "dingle," or breezeway, where provisions for meals were stored in barrels. One side of the building is the sleeping quarters with separate bunks for a dozen men, pegs to hang possessions on the wall and, yes, a "stink pole." On the other side of the dingle are the cooking quarters, equipped with a cast-iron stove, pots, barrels of supplies, and a long table with benches for meals that were served in shifts. A "No Talking" sign, in English and French, set the rule. The men were only there to eat four meals a day in shifts. They had to leave quickly so the next group could sit down. The cook slept in one corner of the room. A small measure of nighttime quiet was not the only benefit for his all-important job. A "labor schedule" dated September 1, 1919, posted by the Great Northern Paper Co., Spruce Wood Department, indicates cooks earned the highest salary in the camp—ranging from $3.15 to $4 per day. Blacksmiths and saw filers were next, earning $3 to $3.65 per day. Low men on the pay scale were the "team swamper" and "main road swamper," who made $2.30, slightly less than the cook's helper, teamsters, sawyers, sled tender, wagon sled loader, and landing man.

In the mechanized equipment shed, there's a huge Lombard steam log hauler (circa 1910) and a smaller Lombard gas hauler from a few years later. Each revolutionized jobs that previously relied on horses and oxen. You'll see early snow plows, tractors, water carts, bateaux, chainsaws, saw mills from various eras, primitive snowmobiles, boom boats, and birch-bark canoes, all speaking to the wide scope of the work. Many were developed as logical solutions to common problems. A road icing cart carried barrels of water from the river to spray on dirt roads because icy, frozen roads make it easier to move cumbersome, heavy logs. A wall-mounted oxen sling enabled the monstrously heavy beasts to balance on three legs while the blacksmith shoed the fourth.

The museum was founded in 1962. Inside its original building, built with hand-hewn logs from a cabin on Mount Chase, are several dioramas of logging camps. They were created by Dr. Lore Rogers, a bacteriologist who co-founded the museum with Caleb Scribner, a retired game warden. Rogers's large tabletop model of the Telos Cut shows how the lumbermen moved logs from the north-flowing St. John River to the south-flowing Penobscot River.

USEFUL INFORMATION: Tours are self-guided with an informational packet presented at registration unless a guided tour is requested in advance of your visit.

Time to allow: 1 hour
Admission: $8 Adults
  $7 Seniors (65 and older)
  $3 Ages 6–11
  Group rates and tours available by advance request.
When it's open: Memorial Day weekend–June 30
  Fri.–Sun., 10 am–4 pm
  July–Columbus Day
  Tues.–Sun., 10 am–4 pm
  Closed Mondays except holidays.
Directions: From the south: I-95 to Exit 264 (Patten, North entrance to Baxter State Park). North on ME-11 for 9 miles to Patten. Take ME-159 West (Shin Pond Road) for 0.5 mile to the museum.
  From the north: I-95 to Exit 276. West on ME-159 for 10 miles to Patten. Continue as above.

According to the 2005 report "Maine's Future Forest Economy,"* "today Maine's forest economy is in the midst of significant changes, some of which are painful to both the state and the industry. . . . Many opinion leaders in the state, both within and outside the forest industry, believe incorrectly that the forest industry is dying. While clearly there are a series of challenges—and the industry is in the midst of what will be continued and rapid evolution—forestry remains a pillar of Maine's rural economy, and steps are being taken to retain or improve competitive position. Paper and lumber production remain at or near record levels when measured by volume, although employment in both of these sectors has decreased. Between 1997 and 2002, employment in Maine's forest industry went from 23,430 employees to 18,130 . . . and total value of shipments declined." There are fewer jobs for workers in pulp and paper mills, saw mills and wood products manufacturing, forestry and logging, although average wages are growing. But the biggest change is the increasingly global economy.

The report continues, "While a decade ago a mill may have considered its competitors to be other mills in Maine, New England, and the Maritimes, today mills face competition from every corner of the globe. As global shipping infrastructure improves and more nations move to turn their forest resources into economic engines, this situation is only expected to continue."

Paul Bunyan, standing tall on Main Street in downtown Bangor for more than fifty years.

Source:
*"Maine's Future Forest Economy," March 2005, for the Department of Conservation–Maine Forestry Service and Maine Technology Institute by Innovative Natural Resource Solutions LLC
www.maine.gov/doc/mfs/fpm/ffe/

Hudson Museum
The University of Maine
5746 Collins Center for the Arts, Orono
www.umaine.edu/hudsonmuseum
207-581-1901

WHAT YOU'LL FIND HERE: Anthropology and archeology artifacts from diverse world cultures, from Maine to Micronesia. Maine Indian baskets, clothing, tools, transportation, cooking implements, ceremonial masks and crafts, and the history and native culture of Alaska, the American Southwest, and Arctic regions. Pre-Columbian art. Environmental studies on the impact of climate change. Gallery programs for groups, by arrangement.

WHY GO: If you visited before October 2009, you haven't seen the Hudson Museum. Before moving to its new home on the second floor of UMaine's Collins Center for the Arts, the collections were scattered over three levels of the building. It had nothing like the handsome, large-scale, glass-enclosed galleries that now showcase traditional crafts and practices of the Maine Indians, introduce us to cultures around the globe, and open a window to ongoing geological and ethnographic research. Even now, technology is being installed to expand the ways we can learn from the Hudson's internationally recognized collections. This is a new museum, evolving year to year.

Courtesy of the Hudson Museum, University of Maine

Iglulingmuit Dolls, circa 1951, at the Hudson Museum, University of Maine.

New technology is gradually being added to improve your self-guided tour. Interactive kiosks are devoted to climate change and the Native Peoples of Maine, inviting hands-on learning. By the time you read this, visitors should be able to borrow Apple iPads at the visitor desk, adding new dimensions to the experience. One example: In front of an exhibit of shadow puppets, use the iPad to watch them in a performance. In a more traditional direction, plans also called for building a wigwam in the gallery; it may be there by now.

"This is not like an art museum, where objects are bought for display," said director Gretchen Faulkner. "These are all things our former director cherished. There are some that are extraordinary. The range, including art and objects from the Pacific Northwest, Africa, and Native American cultures in a variety of areas, is not what you'd expect."

The museum was created around a core of more than 280 pieces of ethnographic material gathered by founder and former director Dr. Richard G. Emerick during his fieldwork among the Havasupai of the southwest United States (1949–1953), the Iglulingmiut of the Canadian Arctic (1953–1954), and the Kapingamarangi and Kusai of Micronesia and Western Polynesia (1956–1957). To this, Emerick added 22 objects explorer Vilhjamur Stefansson collected from the Arctic (1906–1912), including weaponry and domestic items, and 28 objects from the North American Plains and Pacific Northwest.

An internationally known collection of 2,828 pre-Columbian ceramics, lithics, and gold objects dates back 2,000 years to the Spanish conquest. Contemporary objects come from Mexico, Guatemala, and Panama. From Papua New Guinea, there are objects from the Tari culture, 1880–1890, prior to contact with the West. Traditional musical objects came from Cambodia, Thailand, and Laos.

A large gallery devoted to Maine Native Americans focuses on traditional culture of the Micmac, Maliseet, Penobscot, and Passamaquoddy people. Three birch-bark canoes and examples of woodworking skills and decorative arts, including 180 baskets made between 1870 and the present, are among more than 400 objects, including the largest institutional collection of Penobscot basket-making tools in the region.

Additional standouts include clothing: a parka and mukluks made from caribou hide; a Cheyenne or Sioux girl's dress of tanned hide with beaded moccasins worn in the late 19th or early 20th century; a richly embroidered woman's dance costume worn in religious and agricultural festivals in the Andes during the 1950s. Or perhaps you'll find yourself drawn to the Kwakiutl Tsonoqua mask (circa 1890) representing the wild woman of the forest. In northwest coast mythology, she is venerated as a bearer of wealth but feared by children because, according to legend, Tsonoqua steals young ones and carries them home in her basket to eat.

As part of the University of Maine, the Hudson Museum offers numerous educational and cultural programs for all ages, kindergarten through the Maine Senior College Network. Guided tours led by volunteers can be arranged with advance notice.

USEFUL INFORMATION:

• An annual holiday event is the Maine Indian Basketmakers sale and demonstration in December. Basket makers sell their handmade, traditional, and unique fancy and work baskets made of ash splints and sweetgrass. Other traditional crafts, foods, and dancing are part of the day held in partnership with the Maine Indian Basketmakers Alliance, www.maineindianbaskets.org.

• Gallery programs for groups of 10 to 25 can be arranged by calling 207-581-1906.

• For accommodation of persons with disabilities, call the museum office at 207-581-1901.

• Go online to see photographs and learn about many of the current and past exhibits at the Hudson Museum: www.umaine.edu/hudsonmuseum/ExhibOnline.html#World.

• The Page Farm & Home Museum of agricultural history is a short walk from Collins Center on the UMaine campus.

Time to allow: 30 minutes
Admission: Free
Fee is a charge for guided group tours.
When it's open: Mon.–Fri., 9 am–4 pm
Sat., 11 am–4 pm
Closed Sun., holidays, and when the University of Maine at Orono is closed for inclement weather.
Directions: In the Collins Center for the Arts at the University of Maine in Orono.
From I-95/Maine Turnpike, Exit 191, to Kelley Road. Turn right (east) and stay on Kelley Road to its end at an intersection. Turn left (north) and go through Orono. After crossing the Stillwater River, bear right at the top of the hill and go 1 mile to the University of Maine entrance on the left. Enter the university campus and bear left at the fork. The Collins Center for the Arts is straight ahead. The Hudson Museum is on the second floor.

Page Farm & Home Museum
University of Maine
5787 Museum Barn, Orono
www.umaine.edu/pagefarm
207-581-4100

WHAT YOU'LL FIND HERE: Agricultural history and rural life in Maine, 1865–1940. Barn (circa 1833) with two floors devoted to farming and community in late 19th, early 20th century. Animal husbandry and other trades. Reproduction farmhouse rooms and country store. Vintage farm implements. Historical photographs. Authentic one-room schoolhouse. Replica carriage house and blacksmith shop. Heritage gardens. Special events, workshops, children's programs, and monthly lecture series. Gift shop.

WHY GO: A short walk on campus from the new Hudson Museum of anthropology, Page Farm & Home Museum is a step back in time. While both UMaine museums focus on themes of work and community life, they approach their subjects very differently and it's interesting to compare. The Hudson is sophisticated and academic, with contemporary exhibits enhanced by interactive technology and artifacts behind glass; visitors feel removed from the objects but the scope is broad and the objects represent the best of their kind. Page Farm & Home Museum is narrower but deeper, and feels more human-scaled, as if you've walked into a century-old farming community. You're more likely to be enveloped by the sights and sensory experience of earlier times in rural Maine. As you browse, you get a sense of how farmers and their families lived in an earlier era, what it meant to work on the family farm and in related trades and how schooling was valued in Maine, which is still a heavily agricultural state.

Most of this is inside White Barn, the last original agricultural building on the Orono campus. It's filled with stories from the past: newspapers and photographs

Janet Mendelsohn

A reproduction of a farmhouse kitchen at Page Farm & Home Museum.

chronicle the role of county agents and 4-H Club activities in the 1930s; assorted patent medicine bottles and a pharmaceutical log book reveal the range of medical concerns treated by doctors from Caribou to Portland who ordered the prescriptions between 1902 and 1906; and fading posters describe Gilbert Gowell's poultry product experiments when he was the first employee of the agricultural college to conduct research in the field. Gowell taught poultry husbandry here in the late 1890s. Inside the barn, too, are furnished rooms replicating those of a late 19th-century farmhouse. A bedroom looks comfortably homey with its rope bed, crib, well-used desk, leather chest, leather-bound books, and chamber pot. A parlor seems ready for guests expected for tea; a carte de visite photography album rests on a table near the tea set in case visiting friends want to view their hostess's trading cards, a popular entertainment during the Victorian era. In a large country kitchen, there's a fire going in the cook stove, implements are set out on the table, a basket of shirts is ready for the wringer washing machine, and, in the corner, there's a spinning wheel. Only the people are missing. It's as if they've stepped outside for a break from their chores.

Near an animal husbandry display of tools and harnesses are black-and-white photographs in a series, "Hard Times in Acadia." Captured for the national Farm Security Administration in 1940–1941, these selections come from a national archive of 164,000 images documenting rural and small-town life in this country and the adverse effects of the Great Depression and increasing farm mechanization. The series gave many Americans their enduring image of hard times during that era.

Upstairs in the barn you can learn about maple sugaring and woodcarving, and see examples of locally made goods: stenciled and painted tinware, chairs, and serving pieces; textiles and weavings. There's a children's puppet stage for school programs, and space for public programs. At the rear is a replica of a Grange hall, the rural community centers that since 1867 provided places for American farmers and their families to meet and socialize.

Outdoors, there's a fully furnished one-room schoolhouse relocated from Holden, Maine, where it was used from about 1855–1955. Students at all grade levels were taught by one teacher who rarely had time to cover more than the basic "Three Rs"—reading, 'riting and 'rithmatic—as well as good penmanship, which was considered the sign of a cultured person. Since most farm families were religious people, they wanted their children to be able to read the bible, but they also needed the other basic skills to farm or become shopkeepers, millers, or craftsmen. There are also reproductions of a traditional blacksmith shop and carriage house. Heritage gardens have rows of vegetables, herbs, and flowers that were grown here in the late 19th and early 20th centuries.

Janet Mendelsohn

Page Farm & Home Museum on the campus of UMaine Orono.

USEFUL INFORMATION:

• The old-fashioned country store and post office in the barn also serves as a gift shop where Maine-made or -grown gifts such as pottery, beans, local art, and iron hardware are sold.

• Annual events include a plant sale, History Fun Day, traditional community picnic, Open Farm Day, wreath-making workshops, and an old-fashioned holiday party.

• Tours for school groups can be arranged in advance around a variety of program options.

Time to allow: 45 minutes
Admission: Free
When it's open: Tues.–Sat., 9 am–4 pm
Closed Sun., Mon., holidays, and when UMaine is closed for inclement weather.
Directions: From I-95/Maine Turnpike, Exit 191, to Kelley Road, turning right (east) to stay on Kelley Road to its end at an intersection. Turn left (north) and travel through Orono. After crossing the Stillwater River, bear right at the top of the hill and go 1 mile to the University of Maine entrance on the left. Enter the campus and bear left at the fork. Page Farm & Home Museum is in the center of campus.

Leonard's Mills—Maine Forest & Logging Museum
ME-178, Bradley
www.leonardsmills.com
207-974-6278

WHAT YOU'LL FIND HERE Authentic reenactments of work and family life in a 1790s logging and milling community. Water-powered sawmill, blacksmith shop, log cabin, and trapper's line camp. Restored steam-powered Lombard log hauler. Nature trails on 400 forested acres with a stream and covered bridge. Special event days. Outdoor amphitheater and large picnic area.

WHY GO It's best to visit the Maine Forest & Logging Museum at Leonard's Mills during one of numerous special event days when this early pioneer settlement springs back to life. On selected summer Saturdays and certain weekends from spring through fall, volunteers in period clothing recreate home life and work as it was during the 1700s in the milling community that was located here for about 150 years. You can see the old stone dam on Blackman Stream and the foundations of several original buildings.

"The special events are what people expect," says this living history museum's executive director, Cathy Goslin. On Children's Days, half the activities are the same things youngsters did a century or two ago, including tasks that involved taking care of animals. "Kids are surprised to find they can have fun in sack races, petting animals, or a tug of war, without using their thumbs at all!"

On Woodmen's Day, and again when it's the Lumbermen and their Machines event, the focus is on the tools and skills needed for logging. Often there's lively competition among modern woods teams. Encampments give everyone a chance to enjoy rides in bateaux and wagons and taste traditional bean-hole beans and reflector-oven biscuits. During the Blacksmith Round-up in September, professional blacksmiths teach forging techniques in the morning and visitors can try their new skills in the afternoon.

The biggest event is Living History Days, held during peak foliage season. Volunteers in period clothing press cider, play bagpipes and fiddles, and demonstrate traditional Maine crafts such as spinning, weaving, and blacksmithing. In January, February, and March, weather permitting, visitors can go on horse-drawn sled rides in the snowy woods.

Leonard's Mills operated from the late 1700s to around 1850, then sat dormant for about a hundred years before folks in the logging industry decided to re-create the buildings, said Goslin. Now the events draw about 7,000 visitors a year from all over New England, along with many Canadians and a few Europeans.

"Most have heard stories of loggers going into camp for the winter but we present the whole family situation," she said. "There are two houses here and several reenactors are mountain men who bring their tents and talk about trapping and hunting. Others are families living in period tents made of white canvas because they haven't built their houses yet. Children were probably home-schooled but they may have walked to school in Bradley [the nearest town]."

Plans call for five more mills to be relocated to the museum from other parts of the state by 2012. Donated equipment awaiting reassembly at the time of this writing included a clapboard mill from Sedgwick, a rotary-powered saw mill from Cornville, a planer mill, and a shingle mill. However, the biggest project involves the complete restoration of a 100-year-old Lombard log hauler. One of the first successfully tracked vehicles, the steam-powered Lombard was capable of towing multiple sleds bearing up to 125 cords of logs. It replaced the labor of 50 horses. Four men were required to operate it: an engineer, fireman, pilot or steersman, and a conductor. Museum volunteers and the University of Maine's Mechanical Engineering Department repaired damage to the log hauler done by work and weather during decades when the sidelined machine was stored in the woods. At last report, only restoration of the boiler was needed to finish the project.

"Because lumbering and logging are such important parts of Maine heritage, we show lots of aspects of what that work was like," said Goslin. "Many visitors have family members who worked in the industry. We can show them what Grandpa did."

USEFUL INFORMATION:

• Dates vary year to year for events that range from horse-drawn sleigh rides in winter to woodworking, a blacksmith roundup, preserving the harvest, and an inter-tribal powwow.

• Pre-registration is required for Children's Days.

• Self-guided tours involve a leisurely walk around the Leonard's Mills site for the quiet of the North Woods, keeping an eye open for wildlife. Look for interpretive signs at points of interest. But there is no planned activity and no one to describe what took place in the buildings—unless you arrive on selected Saturdays or special event days. Check their calendar.

Time to allow: Half-day for special events plus picnic.
Admission: $5 Adults
$3 Children
On Living History Days: $8 Adults; $3 Children
When it's open: Open daily, April–Oct., for self-guided tours.
Nature trails open year-round.
Summer Saturdays, 10 am–3 pm, offer a varied schedule of craft and woodworking demonstrations, cooking and canning activities, music programs, and talks on topics of historical interest.

Directions: The museum is located between Milford and Brewer, about 15 minutes from Old Town and not far from Orono. From ME-9 North, turn left onto ME-178 and look for a sign for the U.S. Forest Service and Penobscot Experimental Forest, and a smaller sign for Leonard's Mills. Turn onto the unpaved road that serves as the entrance for the experimental forest and the museum. Follow the bumpy, dirt and gravel logging road 1 mile to the Leonard's Mills site.

Courtesy of Leonard's Mills

A college team saws a log at a Woodsman Day competition at Leonard's Mills.

Penobscot Nation Museum
12 Down Street, Indian Island
www.penobscotculture.com
207-827-4153

WHAT YOU'LL FIND HERE: The imprint of time on tribal history and America, past and present. Cultural heritage of the Penobscot Nation and the Wabanaki people, which includes the Passamaquoddy, Micmac, and Maliseet tribes. Art, traditional crafts, historical photos and documents, birch-bark canoes, garments and ceremonial wear, baskets and artifacts, including stone-age tools, spanning 1,000 years of Maine history. Outreach programs. Videos, including *The People and Their River*. Small reference library. Gift shop.

WHY GO: Unlike more polished exhibits of Native American life in university collections and other, better-funded museums, this interesting collection is human-scaled and heartfelt. Rather than a studiously documented anthropological record, it is a more personal introduction to the Penobscot people.

Housed in a former Bureau of Indian Affairs office on Indian Island, reservation land on the Penobscot River near Old Town, the collections at first appear dry and stodgy. But as you look more closely, stories of human experience emerge. Although you are welcome to browse on your own, allow Penobscot elder James Neptune, museum coordinator, to guide you through the three rooms. Neptune seems adept at sensing his visitors' interests. He will explain where traditions came from and how his people have dealt with great challenges. Theirs is not always an easy history to hear but, if you are interested, he will describe the Great Dying that began in the late 15th century, when the Europeans arrived in the Americas, bringing with them infectious disease that nearly eliminated native peoples throughout the Americas. Neptune will also answer sometimes difficult questions about current affairs. But this is not a dour place. Much of what you see here is an impressive selection of traditional arts. As a tour guide, Neptune knows when to step away, allowing the stories and craftsmanship to sink in. History speaks for itself.

The exhibits are neither judgmental nor political. Nor are they all about the past. Neptune said the Penobscots have the oldest government in the United States, with chiefs going back to the 1600s. Today nearly 450 people live on Indian Island, one of the smallest islands on what is left of the reservation. Approximately 2,260 Penobscots currently own 4,866 acres of reservation land, with many more acres in trust and fee lands. "During World War II," said Neptune, "when a lot of our people served in the

Janet Mendelsohn

A 200-year-old Penobscot canoe.

armed services, they found someone, fell in love, married, and lived out there, but they always come back to visit family and to work."

The Penobscots traditionally were hunters and gatherers who lived in eight–10 villages along the river. In spring, some went to the coast for essentials, such as shellfish that they dried in birch-bark containers, seaweed, and grasses. A clan wheel is painted with nine animals representing nine of the original 23 family clans (22 remain). Each family has its own clan symbol to denote what and where they trapped.

Near the museum entrance, Neptune points out a corner cabinet. It is a fine example of the rustic-style furniture, crafted of twigs and birch bark, for which the Penobscots are famous. Nearby are basket-making tools—sweetgrass, knives, and basket forms—and an array of traditional Penobscot baskets, tightly woven and practical. A Penobscot headdress rests on another case. Its upright eagle feathers rise from a beaded headband with side tassels in a simple yet powerful design.

Even if you're not familiar with Molly Spotted Elk (1903–1977), the stage name of actress and dancer Mary Alice Nelson, look for her hand-sewn and beaded dresses, shoulder bags, dolls, moccasins, and books. They were donated by her daughter. Several books have been published chronicling Molly Spotted Elk's stage career in New York nightclubs, her move to Paris in the 1920s, where she met and married a French journalist, and the years when she and her daughter were forced to flee France at the start of World War II. She returned to the reservation, torn apart by her love of performing and the prejudice of European and white American society that forced her to fulfill their stereotyped expectations.

About a dozen carved ceremonial root clubs hang on one wall. "They were used by our people for a long time, at first to put animals out of their misery," says Neptune of the intricately etched birch roots, each about the size and length of a baseball bat. "In the late 1800s, when tourism increased and anthropologists came to buy material for their exhibits, we saw a way to carve the clubs for the tourist trade. We made simple carvings that sold cheaply. Then, to satisfy customers who wanted something 'Indian,' we began carving more elaborate designs." Some look like totem poles. Others have war bonnets on the end. Both designs are typical of the Plains Indians, not the Penobscots, said Neptune, but that's what people wanted to buy because that's what they saw on TV and in movies.

Neptune is not a trained curator. He is an artist with deep pride in his heritage. He almost fell into the job more than 15 years ago, when the previous coordinator asked him to check on the museum during his absence. Finding boxes and dusty cases of donated items, Neptune began to clean the place up. He opened the garage doors to air the place out and people started coming in. He spent days adding to the collections, and they turned into years. Some of his family photos hang among others on the walls. He added art and more crafts to the diverse collection that ranges from arrowheads and stone implements found on the island to a 19-foot-long, Penobscot-made, birch-bark canoe that is 200 years old. Ask him how it was made.

"I try to keep the spirit of my people alive, who we are and strive to be," he said.

Time to allow: 45 minutes

Admission: Free

Groups of 10 or more should give at least 72 hours notice; a small fee is charged.

When it's open: Mon.–Thurs., 9 am–2 pm
Saturday by appointment made in advance.
Closed when James Neptune is away. Call ahead to check.
Directions: From I-95/Maine Turnpike, Exit 197, turn right onto ME-2 toward Old Town. Follow ME-2 for 3.1 miles, passing the dam. Turn left at Indian Island Bridge. The museum is the fifth building on the right.

Moosehead Marine Museum
Lily Bay Road at the south end of Moosehead Lake, Greenville
www.katahdincruises.com
207-695-2716

WHAT YOU'LL FIND HERE: The *Katahdin,* a fully restored historic steamboat for scenic cruises on Moosehead Lake. Small maritime museum with photos and regional memorabilia from the age of steamboats and log drives on Maine's rivers.

WHY GO: There's no better way to experience the steamboat era than on a cruise aboard the *Katahdin,* a National Historic Landmark owned and operated by the nonprofit Moosehead Marine Museum. Summer day cruises of varying lengths recall life here from the mid-1800s to early 1900s, when steamboats were a major means of transportation beginning in 1836. At one point, about 50 of the sturdy vessels carried mail, livestock, passengers, and supplies to resorts on Mount Kineo in the middle of Moosehead Lake, as well as to small villages and hunting camps on the shore. The last of them was the *Katahdin,* built in 1914 at Bath Iron Works and later converted to diesel. When roads were built around the lake, she was refitted as a towboat for hauling logs. That ended in 1975 when the *Katahdin* was used in the nation's last log drive.

The following year, Moosehead Marine Museum was founded with the steamboat as its centerpiece. Since 1994, more than $750,000 has been invested in restoring the vessel. She now has capacity for 225 passengers as well as a snack bar and speaker system for narrated tours of Maine's largest lake—one of the state's last great unspoiled wilderness areas. Whether or not you have time for a cruise, the small museum at the steamboat dock in Greenville is a pleasant brief stop where you can learn about the early development of the Moosehead region. Old photos, tools, and artifacts from the age of steamboats share space with exhibits on various themes, like logging, steamboat captains, and Mount Kineo in its heyday, when the hotel on that island in Moosehead made this an especially popular vacation destination.

USEFUL INFORMATION: Children ages 10 and under are required to wear life jackets on the *Katahdin*. You may prefer to bring your own.

Courtesy of the Moosehead Marine Museum

Cruises on Moosehead Lake are the way to enjoy the historic steamboat Katahdin *(1914).*

When it's open:
Late June–early Oct.
Museum
Mon.–Sat., 10 am–4 pm
Katahdin cruises
Tues.–Sat., most departures at 12:30 pm for 3-hour or 4½-hour cruises. See website for details, special events and fall sailing dates.
Admission: Museum—Free
3-hour *Katahdin* cruise:
$32 Adults
$28 Seniors (older than 62)
$17 Ages 11–16
Free Under 11, accompanied by an adult
Directions: From I-95/Maine Turnpike North to the Newport/Moosehead Trail exit. Take ME-7 North to Dexter, then ME-23 to Sangerville. Turn left onto ME-15 to Greenville. The museum and dock are in the center of town behind Camden National Bank and across from Shaw Public Library.
From Bangor, take ME-15 North to Greenville.

BANG(AREA)R

Maine Discovery Museum
74 Main Street, Bangor
www.mainediscoverymuseum.org
207-262-7200

WHAT YOU'LL FIND HERE: The largest children's museum in Maine. Three floors of interactive exhibits for infants to age 10. Vacation camp programs (ages 5–12).

WHY GO: Two puzzled 7-year-olds from the local YMCA had their noses close to a turtle tank. One whispered, "What is that?" Without figuring it out, suddenly they raced off to climb a spiral staircase "tree," rejoining their group on the floor above. Meanwhile, two volunteers in a room nearby spread out sheets of handmade paper to dry so the junior artists who made them could take their paper home. And in a replica lobster boat, two serious young brothers methodically worked out the logistics of using a tall, hand-cranked crane to load cargo boxes onto a conveyor belt.

"Our exhibits, by and large, are unique to Maine Discovery Museum and designed with an emphasis on Maine," said executive director Andrea Stark. "Very few activities here are 'off the shelf.' A lot of museums take advantage of technology, but we're still focused on giving our visitors the real experience of hands-on activities."

Janet Mendelsohn

A Frog Clock above the Maine Discovery Museum in Bangor.

In the "Sounds Abound" recording studio, kids can sing karaoke-style and take home their recorded voices on disk, or they can listen to a familiar tune in different musical styles. "Booktown" puts youngsters inside the settings of literary classics, like *Goodnight Moon* and *Charlotte's Web,* or pretending to pump gas at Condon's Garage of *One Morning in Maine.* They can see how animated movies are made by arranging toy critters in front of a camera, then playing back the scenes. "Body Journey" has an esophagus tunnel to climb through and a cycling heart pump to ride in place, with veins and arteries that light up red and blue.

Dress-up is popular. A girl with long black hair and a stethoscope draped over an oversized lab coat wanted to test the vision of her friend, who was more determined to try using a walker, then crutches. The "doctor," with patience and a smile, seemed ready for medical school. Two would-be astronauts in "Mission Discovery" sat before a spaceship console, moving a robotic arm to raise and grab objects. Their competitive aggression was attracting a small crowd.

2011 marks the 10th anniversary of the museum. Look for new activities emphasizing health and wellness.

USEFUL INFORMATION

• The Association of Children's Museums offers an ACM Reciprocal Membership at more than 165 participating children's museums in the United States and Canada. Benefits vary from place to place but generally include free admission for a minimum of four members of the same household. Ask about the ACM Reciprocal Membership at this or any participating museum, or see www.childrensmuseums.org/visit/reciprocal.htm.

• Free parking for two hours at the public garage, one block away.

Time to allow: 2 hours

When it's open: Summer hours

  June–Aug.

  Tues.–Sat., 9:30 am–5 pm

  Sun., noon–5 pm

  Regular Hours

  Tues.–Sat., 9:30 am–5 pm

  Sun., noon–5 pm

  Closed Mon. except some school holidays.

Admission: $7.50 per person (subject to change)

  Free 12 months and under

  Free First Friday of the month

  Children age 12 and younger must be accompanied by an adult.

UMaine Museum of Art
The University of Maine
40 Harlow Street, Bangor
www.umma.umaine.edu
207-561-3350

WHAT YOU'LL FIND HERE: Four galleries exhibiting modern and contemporary art. Works by regional, national and international artists working in photography, sculpture, installation, prints, and painting. Year-round programs for children. School tour programs. Art@Noon gallery talks for adults, a lecture series, special events, and studio workshops. Outdoor garden.

WHY GO: When the University of Maine Museum of Art moved from the main campus in Orono to downtown Bangor in 2002, the idea was to make its collections more accessible to the citizens of Maine and serve as a regional fine arts center. Unlike most other fine art museums in the state, its permanent collection neither focuses on Maine nor strives to be encyclopedic. Instead, the emphasis is on modern and contemporary art, emphasizing 1920 to the present, mid-career artists, and those of national scope. Exhibitions change every three months.

The UMaine art collection was established in 1946 by art professor Vincent Hartgen to expand art appreciation and learning opportunities for the people of Maine. Today it is the only institution owned by the citizens of Maine to house a permanent fine arts collection. With more than 7,000 works, and particular strength in mid-20th century artists, you'll always find selections from the permanent collection by such artists as Eugene Atget, Georges Braque, Childe Hassam, David Hockney, Edward Hopper, Yvonne Jacquette, Käthe Kollwitz, Roy Lichtenstein, Robert Motherwell, Pablo Picasso, Diego Rivera, Frank Stella, and Andy Warhol. Artists with significant ties to Maine are also represented, including Berenice Abbott, Sam Cady, Richard Estes, Winslow Homer, Alex Katz, John Marin, Emily Muir, Neil Welliver, and Andrew Wyeth.

"We exhibit the best of Maine artists but also bring in artists from all over New England and the country," said George Kinghorn, director. "We want to contribute to the intellectual community here and, as part of the university, bring new ideas to the forefront by presenting works by a diverse roster of contemporary artists." In 2010, the inaugural exhibition, "I-95 Triennial: A Survey from Four New England States," launched a series of juried shows to be held every three years featuring artists from Maine, Massachusetts, New Hampshire, and Rhode Island. Eighty-two works by 44 artists showcased a wide range of media and styles, from fine-art documentary to abstract to humorous.

"Conserving the Collection" features selections from the permanent collection on a rotating basis to show how that one work of art benefits from the process of conservation and reframing.

Winslow Homer (American, 1836-1910), Eight Bells, 1887, etching, 18¾ x 24¼ inches. Collection of the University of Maine Museum of Art. Gift of Adeline F. and Caroline R. Wing.

Time to allow: 45 minutes
Admission: Free
When it's open: Mon.–Sat., 10 am–5 pm
Closed national holidays and for installation of new exhibitions. Also closed when the University of Maine is closed for inclement weather.

Directions: Located in downtown Bangor. Take I-95 to Exit 185, Broadway (Bangor, Brewer). Turn left at the light onto Broadway, ME-15. Go just over 1 mile and turn right onto State Street (ME-2). At the light at the bottom of the hill, turn right onto Harlow Street (a one-way street). Merge left. The parking lot will be on your left and the museum is behind that.

Cole Land Transportation Museum
405 Perry Road, Bangor
www.colemuseum.org
207-990-3600

The Vietnam Veterans Memorial at the Cole Land Transportation Museum.

WHAT YOU'LL FIND HERE: More than 200 vehicles, from horse-drawn carriages to a diesel locomotive and freight haulers. Vintage automobiles, trucks, firefighting equipment, military vehicles, and railroad memorabilia, all with historic connections to Maine. Antique snowmobiles, baby carriages, and sleds. Construction, farming, logging and delivery trucks dating back decades. War memorials and displays of U.S. military uniforms and memorabilia. Covered bridge (circa 1840). Programs for school groups, veterans' groups, and others. Gift shop.

WHY GO: Don't only think antique cars—although there are a few gems. And don't be confused by the outdoor World War II and Vietnam Veterans memorials that flank the building, although the museum honors the men and women from Maine who have served in the military. Think transportation and think broadly: milk trucks, farm tractors, fire engines, railroad cars, snow plows, carriages, motorcycles, snowmobiles, sleighs, and military vehicles. If it moves on wheels or rail transporting passengers or freight, or was pulled by a horse, or used to clear land, build roads, plant or harvest crops, or deliver goods, especially during the early 20th century, you're likely to find it here.

Bright orange Coles Express 18-wheelers once were a familiar sight throughout the northeast. For decades, they carried freight from Maryland to the Maritimes and especially throughout Maine. The company was founded in 1917 by Allie Cole, who later brought his sons into the business. During the 1930s, Coles was the largest trucking company in New England. Gradually rebounding from hard times during the Great Depression, the company expanded. Its workers packed and hauled potatoes across Maine and transported food and construction materials for the Air Force during World War II. By the time the Cole family businesses were sold in 1993, they included warehouses, a large tire and truck repair service, computerized transportation systems, as well as the Coles Express motor freight carrier company. Galen Cole eventually succeeded his father as president but he never forgot a promise he made during World War II, when, as a 19-year-old infantryman, he was the only survivor after a German tank attacked his squad. Cole promised that if he made it through the war, he would leave his community better than he found it. The Cole family subsequently purchased a farm and established a home for orphans and troubled youths, where they could learn farming. It also was among the first companies in Maine to participate on a corporate level in literacy volunteering.

After 50 years in the trucking business, Galen Cole founded this nonprofit museum, announcing he would pay for the building if Mainers would donate their families' antique vehicles. By the time it opened in 1990, 77 vehicles had been donated to the collection which now includes more than 200 donated by people throughout the state. The museum reflects the full scope of this personal and business history.

Inside a large, spotless warehouse, vehicles of all shapes and sizes are packed tight in rows organized by category and era. Among 10 trucks on Fire Engine Lane are a 1923 American LaFrance hook and ladder truck from Augusta, a 1931 ladder truck from Old Orchard Beach, a 1907–08 steam pumper, a 1944 military fire truck, and a manually operated hose cart built in 1910. Across the "street" from them is a parade of Maine snow plows over the ages—reportedly the largest collection in the United States—and a snow roller that prior to the advent of motorized plows was used to pack snow on rural streets in the early 1900s. Among "Early Birds" are a Prairie Schooner (1843), a 300-year-old Brazilian ox cart, and a dump cart used for clearing farm land in the 1850s. You'll find the first Ski-Doo sold in Maine (1960), a boxy mustard-colored thing resembling an arcade bumper car. Pre-1920s wicker baby carriages have wooden wheels or tires made of iron, or hard or soft rubber. There are children's sleds from the 1900s.

For the legions of car nuts, Nostalgia Circle has a 1923 Packard Roadster that was a Harvard graduation gift for Hollis Wyman from his father. You may know the Wyman name from the family's blueberry canning factory, the largest in the world at that time, or from their sardine cannery, or because Hollis Wyman was a state senator.

Nearby are a 1928 Buick Coupe Model 58 and a 1938 Lincoln V-12 that's an exception to the museum's focus on vehicles for the working man. The Lincoln was chauffeur-driven, especially while serving as the hotel car at a Mount Kineo resort on Moosehead Lake in 1950–51. There's an REO light delivery truck (1912) and a Stanley Steamer (1913), a racing sulky and a Chenango Camper tent trailer made in 1925. Potato diggers and delivery trucks, a "timber tosser" Ford F600 for logging, and . . . well, you get the idea.

At one end of the warehouse is a line of huge Coles trucks from the company's first, a fully restored 1927 Reo, to a tank-van that hauled heating oil in one direction and potatoes or paper on its return trip. You'll find a collection of railroad cars and the Maine Central Railroad's Enfield Station, complete with authentic equipment predating 1960. Exhibits line the hall with vintage automotive and truck advertisements and more than 2,000 photos that chronicle early life in Maine communities and the Coles companies' history.

Galen Cole's promise also honors those who serve in the military. A room devoted to the Fifth Armored Division focuses on the unit that saw service in North Africa during WWII: The unit's command car and a Willys Jeep are surrounded by maps of the various troop movements, a display of shoulder patches, arms, and flags. On Maine Street, there are displays of uniforms worn by women in several branches of military service, primarily as nurses; and men's uniforms and artifacts from the Civil War, WWI, WWII, Korean War, Vietnam, and the Persian Gulf War. A 1943 U.S. Army White Half-Track propelled by tank-like tracks in the rear is exactly like the one Cole was in when his fellow soldiers died.

Outside the museum are the State of Maine World War II Veterans Memorial, the Purple Heart and Korean War veterans memorials, a Huey Helicopter UH-1D and M-60 tank, and a Vietnam War Memorial that lists 339 Mainers killed or missing in action.

Time to allow: 1 hour
Admission: $6 Adults
   $4 Seniors
   Free Ages 18 and under
When it's open: May 1–Nov. 11
   Daily, 9 am–5 pm
Directions: I-95/Maine Turnpike to Exit 182A and follow the signs to War Memorials.

FUN FACT A taped chorus singing "America the Beautiful," followed by the playing of "Taps," washes over the museum grounds and outdoor war memorials daily when the museum closes at 5 pm.

SPOTLIGHT

Ways of the Woods—a Museum on Wheels

At the Fryeburg Fair, near a popular taxidermy display of two moose with locked horns,* we walked up to a 53-foot tractor-trailer covered with larger-than-life photographs of forest life. Tree-blanketed landscapes are overlaid with close-up images of loggers at work, canoeists on a secluded lake, a white steeple, and a hiker spellbound by a green valley. The truck is a mobile museum called Ways of the Woods: People and the Land in the Northern Forest, and during this one week at the fair, nearly 9,000 visitors will take a break from fried dough, farm animals, and carnival games to learn about the history of people like themselves and the changing nature of their connection to the Northern Forest. The vast region covers 30 million acres that stretch from northern Maine into New Hampshire, Vermont, and New York, southern Quebec, and the Maritime Provinces of Canada. The Fryeburg Fair was the year's last stop on a warm-weather tour that brought the museum-on-wheels to schools, festivals, and community events in four states.

"We tour around areas that have been having very hard times during the past 20 years," said Mike Wilson, who founded Ways of the Woods with a former colleague at the Northern Forest Center. "Employment is down, partly because paper mills have closed and the need for forest products has decreased, but mostly because the industries have changed. Take Millinocket, where in 1990 about 2,000 people worked in a mill that is now shut down. Plus land ownership has changed.

"When a paper mill closes, the culture that grew up around it goes into decline, leaving an uncertain future," said Wilson. "People want to get out, to find jobs elsewhere. In those small and often isolated towns, the Ways of the Woods make them feel good about where they live. This is the story of their communities. They see, first, that someone cares enough to build something like this exhibit and, second, that we want to bring it to them."

Ways of the Woods reaches out to one person at a time with a dual message: Our region has a proud heritage we all share and job opportunities are on the horizon. The mobile museum was created by the Northern Forest Center, a nonprofit organization founded in 1997 to help rebuild communities, ecosystems, and local economies across the region.

"When we began working on this 10 years ago, our goal was to help people in the Northern Forest feel that what they and their neighbors did was not worthless," said Wilson. "If people realize real creativity and energy in these communities made them special places, they start to think about creative ways to make them successful again."

The project evolved from Wilson's love of the region and concern for protecting the land. Raised in Falmouth on the coast, he spent a lot of time visiting his grandparents who lived inland along the Kennebec River, where he remembers seeing the last log drive in 1976. For many years, his family had a camp on Moosehead Lake, where he and his dad had to go through lumber camp gates to reach favorite fishing spots. On both sides of the company's roads were logs stacked way over their heads. As an adult, those experiences led him to advocate for forest land protection.

Ways of the Woods helps people explore the history of the region, share their personal connections to the land, and think about the future of their communities.

In the course of that work, he met people who opposed forest protection but still cared deeply about the forest, and it surprised him. "They had other priorities," he said, "like the guy who asked, 'Who are you going to protect it from? Me?' Getting Ways of the Woods on the road has been important to me. It has demonstrated that what drives passion about the forest debate is that people really love the woods. Although it's subtle, this museum helps a broad range of people bond around this issue."

Indoors and out, it's interactive, a hybrid of museum and trade show display. Inside, flat-screen videos show profiles of people who live, work, and play in the Northern Forest and explain research underway. A must-see is the *Rings of Time*, where nature drawings are projected in rings radiating outward on the huge cross-section of a 130-year-old white pine tree. Place your hand above the image of a bear, leaf, fish, or wolf, slowly moving your hand outward. Chimes tinkle, then traditional folk or Acadian music plays, accompanied by spoken word, then vintage film clips appear of ice skaters, snowmobilers, and logrolling on river drives. The closer to the center of the ring, the earlier the era.

Outdoors, an awning shelters contemporary wooden kiosks where photographs, artifacts, and activities blend science with history in attractive, informative displays. "Be a Forest Explorer" involves you in hands-on challenges such as matching fishing flies with the species they attract, and testing your nose by lifting trap doors to identify scents that are not always sweet. Avoid the beaver!

Old logging photographs, specialized tools, and spiked boots worn by log rollers help tell the story of longtime forest industries. At "Hopes for the Future," visitors anonymously write thoughts inspired by the forest on magnetic leaves, then post them on a wall for others to read. "I enjoy hunting with my Dad and his friends. I use a bow," wrote a fifth-grader. "I want to be a poet that bases my poems on the woods," scribbled a third-grade student. Wilson said, "Especially in Maine, dialogues begin to take place about the forest. Some mention Plum Creek's plans for development or property taxes and how expensive it is to keep their family's land. In Vermont, messages written are more about farming and the dairy industry."

Ways of the Woods was made possible by a National Endowment for the Humanities grant of $300,000, which paid for the truck and initial development of professionally designed and built exhibits. During the August 2006 inaugural tour, its exhibits attracted close to 8,000 people in 16 communities. By October 2009, it had reached more than 100,000 people in 95 Northern Forest locations. The nonprofit now exists thanks to smaller grants from state humanities councils in Maine, Vermont, and New York, several foundations, and support from TransCanada Corp. Schools and event hosts from Aroostook County to upstate New York pay modest fees to cover expenses when the museum travels to them for local fairs and education programs. "It has been a real challenge to cover operating costs because they are significant," admitted Wilson. And there is another reality.

"After four years, about 125 venues, and 130,000 visitors, we are a bit exhausted from the road," said Wilson in 2010. "As an alternative, we are exploring opportunities to work with existing institutions, such as colleges and other museums, to install Ways of the Woods as a longer-term exhibit. The idea is to set up for four to eight weeks at a time and train venue staff to operate the exhibit rather than moving it from event to event every three to four days and keeping staff literally on the road 24/7 for six to eight months at a time." When those partnerships are established, the schedule will be posted on Ways of the Woods' website.

Increasingly, there's also a shift in focus toward emerging forest-based economic opportunities that could create jobs and help families stay in the region they love. The Northern Forest Center is collaborating with academic researchers investigating forest-based renewable energy generation and global climate change. One example is how the forest's significant capacity to store carbon may mean income potential for landowners, said Wilson. "If we can present people with new ideas, we can help some of them reconsider forest industries as a viable career path." But the team is still loyal to its original goals.

Do visitors ever suspect there's an ulterior motive? "Occasionally," he said. "Some people just want to pick a fight. You can see them coming, the look in their eye, but you can't tell if it's because they think you're a front for the paper industry or a tree-hugging environmentalist takeover. After all, this is an expensive-looking truck. But when they actually come in and read what's here, they get all excited and want to sit down and talk about it."

At the Northern Maine Fair in Presque Isle, a man arrived alone and began reading intently. "I tried to catch his eye but he wasn't looking to chat," recalled Wilson. "He spent a long time here, reading everything and looking at all the pictures. When he was done, he wrote something in our log book. Then he walked away. Once he was out of sight, I looked at the book. He had written, 'Great exhibit. I'm welling with pride.'"

Ways of the Woods: People and the Land in the Northern Forest

Northern Forest Center
P.O. Box 671
Bethel, Maine 04217
www.northernforest.org
207-824-8263

*"Final Charge," a display created by taxidermist Mark Dufresne of Gray, Maine, for L. L. Bean and the State of Maine, is usually exhibited at L. L. Bean in Freeport.

The following are intended to help you zero in on museums that are particularly strong in certain areas. Keep in mind that these lists are starting points and are not all inclusive.

Another good way to begin is with the online statewide collaborative **Maine Memory Network**, www.mainememory.net, where you'll find searchable selections from some 200 organizations.

Maine Civil War Trail 2013

An assault on Fort Sumpter in Charleston, South Carolina, marked the beginning of the Civil War on April 11, 1861, and it continued for four long years. From 2011–2015, the sesquicentennial of the Civil War will be commemorated nationwide. Maine will recognize the 150th anniversary with reenactments, lectures, workshops, programs, and exhibits at dozens of museums and historical sites statewide. Programs began in 2010 and all participating organizations will hold events during the summer of 2013. A website for the Maine Civil War Trail 2013 is planned; until it goes live, news of related sesquicentennial events are posted in a calendar on the Fifth Maine Regiment Museum's website: www.fifthmainemuseum.org.

State government information on Maine's observance is online at http://maine.gov/civilwar/.

Maine's Civil War Monuments, a list with photographs of more than 148 "silent sentinels" statewide, compiled by Maine's state historian, is at http://maine.gov/civilwar/sentinels.html.

The Maine Art Museum Trail

 There are seven collaborating fine art museums. See www .maineartmuseums.org for more information.

Bates College Museum of Art (Lewiston)...........148
Bowdoin College Museum of Art (Brunswick)...........75
Colby College Museum of Art (Waterville) 192
Farnsworth Art Museum (Rockland) 104
Ogunquit Museum of American Art (Ogunquit)...........32
Portland Museum of Art (Portland)...........55
University of Maine Museum of Art (Bangor)...........222

Other fine collections of art and photography

Abbe Museum (Bar Harbor)...........124
Brick Store Museum (Kennebunk) 20
Center for Maine Contemporary Art (Rockland) 114
Museum of African Culture (Portland)...........53
Saco Museum (Saco)...........34
Stanley Museum (Kingfield)...........169
Tides Institute & Museum of Art (Eastport)...........144
University of New England Art Gallery (Portland) 62

The Maine Folk Art Trail

These art and history museums held concurrent exhibits in 2008 highlighting their folk art collections. Each is also likely to offer folk art exhibits on an ongoing basis.
Bates College Museum of Art (Lewiston)...........148
Colby College Museum of Art (Waterville)...........192
Farnsworth Art Museum (Rockland) 104
Maine Historical Society Museum (Portland) 49
Maine Maritime Museum (Bath)........... 82
Maine State Museum (Augusta)...........179

Museums of Old York (York)...........24
Penobscot Marine Museum (Searsport)...........115
Rufus Porter Museum (Bridgton) 159
Sabbathday Lake Shaker Museum (New Gloucester)...........152
Saco Museum (Saco)...........34

Children's Museums

Coastal Children's Museum (Rockland) 113
Children's Discovery Museum (Augusta)...........175
Children's Museum & Theatre of Maine (Portland)...........43
Maine Discovery Museum (Bangor)...........220

Global Exploration

Osher Map Library (Portland)...........64
Peary-MacMillan Arctic Museum (Brunswick)...........77

Maritime Heritage

Numerous local historical society museums and libraries, as well as several light-
houses, tell stories of Maine's maritime connections. Among them are:
Bar Harbor Whale Museum (Bar Harbor)...........127
Fishermen's Museum (Bristol)...........80
Kittery Historical & Naval Museum (Kittery)...........22
Maine Coast Sardine History Museum (Jonesport)...........140
Maine Historical Society Museum (Portland)...........49
Maine Lighthouse Museum (Rockland)...........110
Maine Maritime Museum (Bath)...........82
Maine State Museum (Augusta)...........179
Marshall Point Lighthouse Museum (Port Clyde)...........87
Moosehead Marine Museum (Greenville)...........218
Peary-MacMillan Arctic Museum (Brunswick)...........77
Penobscot Marine Museum (Searsport)...........115
Portland Observatory (Portland)...........61
Sail, Power & Steam Museum (Rockland) 113

Automobiles, airplanes, trolleys, and trucks

Native American history and arts

Trades and industry

Historic homes and buildings

Weird science

Bygone ways of life

Natural History

Music and mania

NOTES

NOTES

NOTES

NOTES